SO-BJB-270

"This deeply moving story of a lesbian Christian's journey to self-acceptance is a rare celebration of life. I found myself alternately weeping and then laughing out loud at Jacqueline Taylor's memoir of her staunch Southern Baptist father and clever but sometimes manic mother, of her missteps on the road to a long-lasting, committed relationship, and of the wit and wisdom of her adoptive daughters."

—Reverend Mel White
author of *Religion Gone Bad: The Hidden Dangers of the Christian Right* and cofounder of Soulforce

"Especially compelling is the way in which the author never completely abandons religion, either for herself or for her children, and shows that fundamentalists and evangelicals cannot be painted with one brush. With a fascinating and gripping narrative, *Waiting for the Call* engages with current debates not only about homosexuality but about definitions of family, of mother and father, of child rearing, of education, of community."

—Linda Kintz
author of *Between Jesus and the Market: The Emotions That Matter in Right-Wing America*

"We have deeply needed a book that shows an intelligent LGBT person as a Christian—this is that book."

—Louise A. Blum
author of *You're Not from Around Here, Are You? A Lesbian in Small-Town America*

WAITING FOR THE CALL

WAITING FOR THE CALL

*From Preacher's Daughter
to Lesbian Mom*

JACQUELINE TAYLOR

The University of Michigan Press   *Ann Arbor*

Copyright © by the University of Michigan 2007
All rights reserved
Published in the United States of America by
The University of Michigan Press
Manufactured in the United States of America
⊚ Printed on acid-free paper

2010   2009   2008   2007   4   3   2   1

No part of this publication may be reproduced, stored
in a retrieval system, or transmitted in any form
or by any means, electronic, mechanical, or otherwise,
without the written permission of the publisher.

A CIP catalog record for this book is available from the British Library.

Library of Congress Cataloging-in-Publication Data

Taylor, Jacqueline, 1951–
     Waiting for the call : from preacher's daughter to lesbian mom /
Jacqueline Taylor.
          p.   cm.
     ISBN-13: 978-0-472-11594-5 (cloth : alk. paper)
     ISBN-10: 0-472-11594-4 (cloth : alk. paper)
     ISBN-13: 978-0-472-03238-9 (pbk. : alk. paper)
     ISBN-10: 0-472-03238-0 (pbk. : alk. paper)
        1. Taylor, Jacqueline, 1951–.   2. Christian lesbians—United
States—Biography.   I. Title.
     BR1725.T29A3   2007
     277.3′082092—dc22
        [B]   2006039823

CONTENTS

Prologue:
Tongues of Fire

It's Pentecost, June 8, 2003. The front of our sanctuary, in commemoration of this particular day in the life of the Christian church, is swathed in red. A rich red cloth drapes the altar, puddling onto the floor. Red ribbons wind in and out of the bricks that form a rough-hewn cross over the altar. Extravagant bouquets of red flowers bedeck the altar and the podium. Much of the congregation wears red, too. Red shirts, red shoes, red dresses, red scarves, every possible shade of red flashes from each corner of the sanctuary.

Pentecost, in the Christian calendar, falls fifty days after Easter. Told in the book of Acts, the story of Pentecost is in some ways the story of the birth of the Christian church. Seven weeks had passed since Jesus' resurrection. On Pentecost, we are told, the early Christians were "all with one accord in one place." Suddenly, there was the sound of a "rushing mighty wind" and tongues of fire descended on the heads of the apostles in an outrageous outpouring of the Holy Spirit. Thus filled with the spirit, these early believers began to speak "with other tongues, as the Spirit gave them utterance." Amazingly, the crowd that gathered in Jerusalem on that day heard the apostles speaking as if in the native language of the listeners.

There are several improbable features to this story. Who can believe in literal tongues of fire resting atop the heads of those early Christians anyway? Or in the capacity to hear a language other than the one being spoken? But notice, our pastor tells us, how extravagantly God arrives in our lives and how willing this God is to celebrate diversity, to meet the listener in his or her home language. The red that flashes through our sanctuary is a reminder of those red tongues of fire descending, of God arriving in a manner both lavish and unexpected. Whatever one might make of this, there is no denying that red is a wonderful color for fire, for life, for celebration.

For Carol and me, it is a momentous day, not because of Pentecost but because our older daughter, Lucy, after three years of study and preparation, is about to be baptized and confirmed. Dressed in a bright red, short-sleeved sweater, a short black skirt, and black heels, she holds in her palm the outline of the speech she has prepared, the one that will tell us why she has decided to join Broadway United Methodist Church. We have no idea what the speech says, because she wants to surprise us, but she insists that she is ready.

Our two pastors, Greg and Vernice, call Lucy, and us—her two moms—and her sister Gracie to the front for the ritual of baptism. When the liturgy (the words of the ritual exchanged between pastors, members of the congregation, and our daughter) is completed and Greg has placed a handful of water on Lucy's head, it is time for her speech. We return to our front-row seats, and I feel the familiar jolt of adrenaline that always pumps through me when either of the girls faces a special challenge.

Lucy, at fourteen, stands four feet ten inches in heels, just tall enough to peer over the lectern as she addresses the congregation. A Peruvian adoptee, she has the shiny black hair and bronze skin of the Quechua people who are her biological kin. She faces the room and pauses, collecting herself, a small, but commanding, presence.

"Some of you know that my Grandaddy is a Baptist preacher," she begins. "When I was little, I thought he knew everything there was to know about God and the Bible. He was always giving us presents to help us learn more about the Bible. Bible storybooks and games. Bible puzzles. He even gave us a video of the entire book of Matthew."

I'm moved that she would begin her description of her developing faith by mentioning my father. And yes, a four-hour video containing the

2

entire text of the first gospel was his idea of a great gift for the grandkids. The fellow who played Jesus in the video was pale, with light brown hair and a relentless, almost silly, cheerfulness. The first hour of the video graphically depicted the slaughter of the innocents, after which Lucy and Gracie never had the stomach to watch the remaining three hours.

"One year he gave us a game called Bible Trivia," Lucy continues. "Whoever got the most right answers could advance to Heavenly Knowledge. He knew so much about the Bible, I figured we didn't have a chance. I was so surprised when he got a couple of answers wrong and Gracie made a couple of lucky guesses and jumped all the way up to Heavenly Knowledge before him."

Everyone laughs. The audience is right with her. Carol and I exchange a look of immense pleasure and pride. That's our girl. That's our Lucy.

"Since I've been in confirmation class and studied with Greg, I've learned so much more about God and the Bible than I ever knew before."

Members of our church can fill in the unstated connection here. They know Greg's approach to Bible study is less literal and more interpretive than what would likely come from a Baptist preacher.

"I used to wonder what God was like. When I was little I thought, what is God, a big blob up in the sky? Then, in sixth grade, I learned about the Holocaust, and I wondered how God could let such a thing happen. Was God there? Now, studying with Greg, I've come to understand that God is there, but it is up to all of us to do God's work in the world."

In the next section of the speech, Lucy begins to explain why she has decided to join our church. Her eyes shine with feeling as she speaks about the tremendous amount of work people do on various committees, the gorgeous decorations the environment team produces for each Sunday's worship. She knows those committees well, having participated in several of them during her three years of confirmation preparation. She mentions the preaching, the beautiful music, the diversity of our congregation. "I love you guys," she says, "you guys are great."

"Most of all," she says, "I want to be a part of this church because it is a place where," she fights back hard on her tears, "both of my moms are welcome." The emotion in her voice spills over and now she is openly weeping. I want to leap from my seat right then and wrap her in my arms.

Our church, located in the heart of what Chicagoans know as Boys Town and with a membership that is between 30 and 40 percent gay, has spent the last several years openly engaged in a struggle with the national United Methodist denomination for a more inclusive church. In the pews each Sunday sit a couple of hundred folks who have fought hard to create a welcoming space for gay Christians and dozens who have experienced rejection from the churches in which they grew up. For such a congregation, it is intensely powerful to witness a teenager pouring her heart out about how deeply she appreciates the welcome they extend each Sunday.

She is crying hard now, her shoulders shaking. Everyone in the congregation seems to be sobbing with her as Vernice, our beautiful assistant pastor with the big gospel voice, envelops Lucy in a hug. I'm simultaneously crying, smiling, and passing tissues up and down the pew.

She pulls herself together and concludes with a thank-you to her pastors, her confirmation mentor (the woman who met with her each month during her confirmation study), her moms, and her sister. A bit later in the ritual of confirmation, she will share with the church, as each person does when they join Broadway, what she sees as her ministry. "My ministry," she says with firm assurance, "is making music and supporting my family and friends."

I hug her tight as she returns to her seat. The congregation thunders its applause. Someone reaches over the pew to pat Lucy on the back. Someone else gives my arm a squeeze. "That didn't sound like any fourteen year old I ever heard," another member whispers to me. Even Gracie, no emotional pushover, needs a Kleenex.

Speaking with an openness that few adults could muster, Lucy has summoned the language that brings together so much that I hold dear: my loving, lovable, proselytizing father; the tensions between an evangelical and a progressive theology; our motley church congregation of gay and straight, old and young, black, white, brown, and Asian church members; and our two-mom, two-daughter, interracial family.

In this moment, I am thinking, church lives out its promise. Lucy, at fourteen, describes church as a radically welcoming place and each of us as the hands and face of God in the world. It really could be that simple.

1

The Call

My Baptist preacher father, Eldred Taylor, surrendered to the call when he was thirteen years old. That's how you say it. The call. And surrendered. You get the idea from such language that God has mounted a long and fierce assault on a person and met with a sustained and stubborn resistance. But, in the end (against God, what choice do you have?), the person surrenders. The Bible is full of stories in which God calls out to one person or another. He tells them what he wants. Sometimes they do it right away, sometimes they resist, but sooner or later they all surrender.

We were Southern Baptists. This is the largest Protestant denomination in the United States, with a current membership that tops 16 million. A worldwide church, the highest concentration of Southern Baptists occurs in the Bible Belt. Sometimes when people hear the words "Baptist preacher" they picture tiny churches in the middle of nowhere and uneducated country preachers. That was not us. Both my parents were college and seminary graduates. My father pastored a large church (nearly two thousand members) in a small town (about ten thousand people), which means we were highly visible members of this community. When I say that I grew up as a Baptist preacher's daughter in a small town in Kentucky, I always believe I've said something fundamental about my identity.

When I was about ten years old, I desperately wanted a call. I wanted to be chosen. I felt certain I had special work to do here on earth, and I wanted God to let me in on what it was. God, I believed, had a plan for my life. When he got good and ready, he was going to reveal it to me. In our Southern Baptist world, God didn't call girls to be preachers, so I wasn't listening for that. Still I was pretty sure he wanted me for something nobody else could do, something that involved plenty of action. I was chock full of pep and big ideas. He would surely send me to do something remarkable.

I persuaded myself that God was calling me to be a missionary. This girls could do. After all, the special end of year donation for foreign missions was called the Lottie Moon Christmas Offering. Lottie Moon was a famous unmarried lady who had gone to China in 1873 and pretty much single-handedly launched Southern Baptist foreign mission work. She stood only four foot three inches tall, but she was full of stamina and spunk. She turned down a marriage proposal and left behind home and family to head off to China to spread the word. She had lots of adventures and endured all kinds of hardships in order to do God's work. Maybe it should have worried me to learn that she died of starvation because she would not eat while the people she served endured famine, but it did not. We all looked up to Lottie Moon. Each December we put a big drawing of a thermometer up on the wall of the church and watched the temperature rise as the gifts poured in toward our Lottie Moon Christmas Offering goal. Sometimes instead of a thermometer we had a map of the world with lights scattered over it that were gradually illuminated, one by one, as our gifts lit up the world. Lottie Moon proved that God was just as willing to call women as men.

When I was about eleven, I wrote to the Southern Baptist Foreign Mission Board in Richmond, Virginia, and told them about my call. They were happy and sent me a welcoming letter and lots of materials describing the work Baptists were doing in various locations on the globe.

In my bedroom, I devoted one of my three desk drawers to Foreign Mission Board materials and correspondence. There were slick brochures and shiny maps dotted with Southern Baptist Foreign Mission sites. They confirmed that in fact women worked all over the world as teachers, nurses, and doctors. Some had husbands and children, but others, like Lottie, just launched off on their own. They unpacked bags full of Bibles and soap and bandages and got busy making more light in the world. One brochure I received explained how much education and preparation missionaries had to have. I could see that this work was not for the faint of heart.

Oh, how I wanted to be called. If you've got a call, everything you do takes on a certain weight. My mother and sister Jeannie and I believed in this and waited for God's instructions, but our calls seemed only for supporting parts. Daddy was Diana Ross, and we were the Supremes. Not when the three were really singing out full throttle, more like when Diana was letting it rip and Flo and Mary were standing behind her smiling, snapping their fingers, and humming along, like they couldn't quite believe how good she sounded.

We worked hard at making Daddy look good. We politely answered the phone and took messages. We discussed his sermons and the work of the church at nearly every meal. Sometimes Mother helped him refine his analysis of a particular passage of scripture. Our entire family served as examples for the community, and we never lost sight of the fact that they were watching us. This wasn't hard to remember, even for a kid, because the parsonage where we lived was situated right smack next door to the church and had three enormous picture windows. "We live in a goldfish bowl," my mother snapped nearly every evening as she turned on the lamps and drew the heavy drapes shut with a magnificent swoosh.

Metaphor and concrete fact kept close company. We lived on Main Street, in the literal and figurative shadow of the church.

I had been only seven years old when Daddy's call swooped the family up from Louisville and delivered us to the little town of Somerset, nestled in the foothills of the Appalachians. Surrounded by farms, Somerset was the county seat and, despite its small size, the largest town in five counties. Although only 130 miles from Louisville, it was, in many respects, a whole world away, with a dialect and culture all its own.

When we pulled up in front of the parsonage, we thought it was even better than they had told us. The red brick house was huge. It had eleven rooms. Inside lots of people bustled around fixing it up for the new preacher and his family. Carpenters, electricians, and painters were scattered throughout, but the real power seemed to be in the hands of a committee of churchwomen.

Mother looked at paint chips and fabric swatches and made decisions with a brisk dispatch and an air of authority I had never seen in her before. The walls in the four enormous front rooms, she told the churchwomen, would be painted mauve beige. It was a beautiful color with a beautiful name.

Mother selected a heavy mauve fabric for the thick drapes. Mrs. Tandy, the church member who would make the drapes, marched about like a tiny stout general, nodding briskly and measuring the windows. Her snapping dark eyes could take your measure and know exactly how many yards of fabric she would need to make you a nice Sunday dress.

Once we moved into the parsonage, it turned out to be harder to manage than it had looked and almost impossible to keep clean. The church, the parsonage, and a lot of other buildings in town were heated with black Kentucky coal, which, as it burned, produced a fine layer of soot that settled over every piece of furniture. This coal dust was joined by the exhaust blasts of hundreds of the cars and trucks that regularly downshifted in front of our house on the way up Harvey Hill. Main Street was also Highway 27, a major thoroughfare that brought plenty of roaring traffic. Our elegant crystal chandeliers, soot coated as they usually were and laborious to clean, came to be the bane of Mother's existence. The half bath in the front hall had a commode that seemed to overflow every time company was coming or we were in a hurry to get out the door. The contents would drip through the floor and run down into the basement while Mother mopped furiously and spewed Baptist swear words such as "Dad-blamed," and "Confounded," and "Plague tak-ed commode!" To say the house was heated seems an exaggeration. During cold spells we would wear coats in the house and cut the fingertips out of old pairs of gloves so we could do our homework or practice piano.

Daddy's previous job, Director of Missions and Evangelism for Kentucky Baptists, had kept him on the road a lot, traveling all over the state. Now he was home all the time but also working all the time. He wore a suit and tie seven days a week, and his "weekend" seemed to last only

8

from the end of Sunday evening service until early Monday morning, when he began working on the next week's sermons (one for Sunday morning service, another for Sunday night). The family had to pack a weekend's worth of relaxation into the hour and a half between the close of the evening service and bedtime. After church, Mother, Jeannie, and I raced home while Daddy finished shaking hands with the church members. Mother made popcorn or whipped up a pan of fudge. We opened the mahogany cabinet doors that encased our black and white television set (and which we had learned as children to slam shut whenever one of those nasty beer commercials came on). By the time Daddy walked in the door at nine o'clock, we were seated with our snacks, ready to watch *Bonanza*. We all loved that show. Those pesky Cartwright brothers, Adam, Hoss, and Little Joe, always getting into one scrape after another, Pa always there with a firm but gentle hand to make sure everything came out all right. The boys' mothers (all three of them) were dead, and most any woman who fell for any of the Cartwright men soon met an untimely end, but this lack of females wasn't really a problem. The male housekeeper, Hop Sing, cooked and did household chores. Pa, with loving authority, took care of everything else. This, Mother and Daddy said approvingly, was good wholesome entertainment, the kind the whole family could enjoy.

It never troubled any of us in those days that the boys who seemed in such desperate weekly need of Pa's firm guidance were grown men, some decidedly middle aged, or that this admirably wholesome family represented, despite the occasional fleeting girlfriend, a curiously homosocial world. In the world of the sixties, a firm but loving patriarch was, I suppose, the sine qua non of a wholesome family life.

Mother and Jeannie and I were public figures in Somerset in ways we never had been back in Louisville. Once school began, I quickly figured out that being the preacher's daughter made me different from other children in my class. My second-grade teacher, Miss Guffy, was a church member. I was a quick student and often finished my work early. I'd then look around to see who wanted to talk. "Jackie Taylor!" Miss Guffy barked. "Quit talking. What would your father think? You're supposed to set an example."

Not too crazy about small-town life, I soon began to beseech God to

9

call my father back to Louisville on the theory that if God had called him once God could call him twice. But God's plans and mine never coincided on this point.

I asked my father how it was that he knew he was being called to preach. Did he hear a voice? Did he have a vision? When God called the boy Samuel, Samuel heard a voice call his name so distinctly that he thought his rabbi and master, Eli, was calling for help. Samuel ran to Eli three times before Eli, finally realizing that it was God calling, sent Samuel back to bed with instructions about what to say when God called once more. "Speak, Lord, for thy servant heareth," Samuel was told to reply.

Eldred Taylor had heard no voice. He just knew. He was filled with a conviction. God called him, loud and clear, voice or no, and then he just kept on calling, so my father never needed to question his call.

Daddy's call was foreordained. An older brother had died at two years of age. His mother prayed to God that if he would give her another son she would give him back to God. Maybe she had been reading about Samuel's mother, Hannah. Hannah was the one who had no children, the favorite wife of a man who had two wives. Hannah was downcast about her barren state. As a last resort, she prayed to God for a son, one she would give back. Evidently God liked this prayer because Hannah conceived. When Samuel came along, she kept him just long enough to get him weaned and then took him over to Eli to be raised in the service of God.

Like Hannah, Grandmother prayed and not long after became pregnant and had a son. Grandmother was a taciturn woman and didn't tell my father about her pact with God. Maybe she figured it wasn't her place to tell her son God's and her business. Maybe she figured if God wanted him God would come and get him. She evidently held a mighty faith in God's ability to manage God's own affairs.

Her plan worked. My father publicly responded to his call at age thirteen at a special Thanksgiving service at Third Baptist in Owensboro, Kentucky. The church had a visiting preacher that day, and he gave a special invitation to anyone who felt the call. Baptist services almost always involve an invitation or what some Christian churches refer to as an altar call. The congregation sings a hymn, while the preacher stands at the front of the sanctuary awaiting anyone who wants to come forward and acknowledge a decision to join the church or make what Baptists call a profession of faith. That day the invitation was especially addressed to young people who felt called by God to special service (preaching, mission work). Four or five young people stood up. Even when young Eldred made his call public, Grandmother kept her silence. She let many years go by before she divulged her role in Eldred's call, and when she finally told, she didn't tell my father; she told my mother. And then only after Eldred had grown up, gone to college, gotten married, graduated from the seminary, and been ordained as a preacher.

Jeannie and I were true believers at an early age. What other path could we have imagined? Jeannie, two years older than me, made "a profession of faith" and joined the church when she was six years old. Daddy baptized her, wearing a big white robe and dunking her (clad in a smaller white robe) all the way under the water in the baptismal font behind the choir loft. Later she came back out and sat on the pew with us, dressed again in her Sunday clothes, shivering slightly, her neatly parted hair dripping.

Watching all this, I was fascinated. At four years old, I knew I loved Jesus, but I hadn't known children that young could join up. Baptists speak of "the age of accountability," the age when a person realizes she is a sinner and makes a decision to become a believer. While this moment occurs at different ages for different individuals, Baptists often expect that young people will begin making professions of faith at the age of eight or nine. If a child reaches thirteen or fourteen years of age without such a decision, everyone starts to worry.

Once my sister joined the church, I waited to see what would happen next. When was Daddy going to talk to me about this important business? Weeks went by. He carried on with his work, often traveling around the state. I bided my time, expecting any moment we would have our talk. Finally, I took matters into my own hands. One afternoon I found him in his study, working on a sermon. "Daddy," I asked him, "when are you going to talk to me about trusting Jesus?" He looked a little surprised, because he probably wasn't quite sure that the age of accountability might extend down to four, but he laid aside the sermon he was writing and told me we could do it right then. He pulled out his

Bible, I sat in his lap, and he went through the New Testament verses that he had so often used to explain that Jesus loved us and had died for us, that we were all sinners, and that by trusting Jesus we could have him in our lives forever and be saved. It seemed really simple to me, an easy decision. He questioned me, trying to discern whether I understood what he was telling me. When he was satisfied that I did, he told me I could say the prayer that would invite Jesus into my life and make me a Christian. We knelt in his study, leaning on his desk chair, and I invited Jesus into my life. I was happy. I wanted to join the church at once, but Mother and Daddy thought me too young. They stalled. I waited as long as I could bear and then asked them again when I could join. Finally, when I had nosed past my fifth birthday, they made an appointment for me to talk to our Louisville pastor, Brother Hubbard. He, too, questioned me about my decision, but in the end, like Daddy, he agreed that I seemed to understand what this was about. And so, at age five, I became a member of St. Matthews Baptist Church and was baptized.

I wonder, now, what a decision like that means when taken by a five year old. How did I interpret the notion that I was a sinner in need of redemption? Surely my worst transgressions were on the order of coming to blows with my sister, refusing to eat my peas, and talking in church. As near as I can recall, I thought less about the sin than about God as a source of love and Jesus as my ever-present friend, yet I did fervently believe in a God who held us all to a mighty high standard, and I regularly asked forgiveness for not following him as closely as I believed I should.

Growing up in such a world, amid such stories, Jeannie and I felt pretty confident that we didn't need to make any of our own big plans. God had it worked out already, our life's work, our future husbands, how he was going to make use of us and the particular gifts he had bestowed on us so we could be helpful. All we had to do was study hard and stay faithful so when the call came we would be ready.

Jeannie has described the nine years she spent in Somerset as the time when her family kidnapped her and forced her to live as a hostage in a small town. By the eighth grade, nearly six feet tall and rail thin, she spent her spare time paging through fashion magazines and fantasizing about her eventual fame and fortune as a runway model. I'm not sure whether this life in the glamorous world of high fashion fit with her belief in her still-to-be-revealed call or whether, as seems to me more likely, the two dream worlds traveled parallel tracks, never really bumping into one another.

As much as I hated the pressures of being a preacher's kid, I loved the church and really did want to be helpful. I sang every hymn with gusto, proudly casting the hymnal aside and singing from memory. I stuck my hand up each time the Sunday School teacher asked a Bible question, eager with answers, glad to be right. I wanted to be a witness, helping to win folks to the Lord. I would pick up tracts from the rack at the back of the church that helpfully laid out the plan of salvation, intending to give them to my friends at school.

But the moment never seemed right, and most of them already went to our church. I worried that my peers might not know I was saved, since it had all happened before we moved to Somerset. How was I going to win my classmates to the Lord, if they didn't even know I was a believer? I hated the idea of going around talking about it. I resolved to lead by example. Every couple of years I would come forward during the invitation hymn at a revival service to rededicate my life to Christ. I didn't have much opportunity for any very significant sins, but this was one way I could show my friends I was saved and wanted them to be too, without having to sit them down and pepper them with Bible verses.

It seemed easier by far to imagine myself bearing witness in a far-off land in another language. The career paths for women in Somerset were few: schoolteacher, nurse, secretary. I wanted no part of any of these. As a missionary, I could have a leadership role and travel about the globe. God could use me and my big strong speaking voice.

I tried to divine just what country God was calling me to, poring over the maps of Africa, China, and the Middle East. But I never got any clarity on that point and gradually, as junior high gave way to high school, my correspondence with the Southern Baptist Foreign Mission Board faltered and then collapsed altogether. They were tactful. If you didn't write them, they didn't write you. Which was smart. They didn't want to take a chance on recruiting someone who didn't really have the call.

2

Mother's Daughter

My mother, Marjorie Kerrick Taylor, grew up in western Kentucky during the Depression. She had come to believe, by the time she graduated from high school in 1939, that she was going to live and die on the backside of nowhere. She was the baby of six children and the only one left at home. Home was a small farm and tiny house that one of Marjorie's grown brothers had bought so his parents would have a place to live. The farm was located in a section of Daviess County so remote that they could hear a car go by a mile away.

Marjorie's life careened between great highs and terrible lows. She was born in March. "You're just like March weather," her mama used to say, "cloudy one minute, sunny the next." When she felt good, she felt better than anybody (in fact, she just plain sparkled), and when she was low the depths were blacker than a moonless night. She spent a lot of her time that first year after high school reading poetry, walking in the woods, and praying. The record provided in letters reveals that she busied herself doing household work, washing clothes in washtubs, cooking on the wood-burning stove, and helping her mama raise chickens.

No doubt she spent some of that year in pure despair. Two years earlier she had had to drop out of high school because she had begun having seizures. Epilepsy was poorly understood then and highly stigmatized. Her treatment included surgery to remove cysts from her ovaries on the peculiar theory that they caused the seizures. Eventually, the seizures abated, probably more from sheer luck than anything the doctors tried, and she returned to school.

That senior year had been a time of possibility and intellectual awakening, but with graduation the possibilities seemed to dwindle and then disappear. By the time summer had given way to fall, she believed her life was pretty well over. If she married at all, and there were no great prospects in sight, she would marry some farm boy and go on much as she was going. She loved to draw and paint and was more than commonly good at it. She dreamed of studying art. Her almost but not quite possible dream was to attend a school of interior design—art with a purpose.

Mother loved literature, music, and art and had a romantic streak as wide as a barn. In the stories she spun about their courtship, my father was the one man who quickened her pulse from the first day she saw him in her high school senior English class. They fell in love through a series of achingly sweet and earnest letters exchanged between January and May of 1941, after he had left the farm to attend a small Baptist college in Missouri. By Valentine's Day, Mother was shipping a box of homemade candies to my father, and he was sending his new love the college catalogue and his assurances that he was praying that it might be God's will that she join him at college in the coming year.

My parents married in June of 1942. In their early years, they were college students with barely enough money to get by themselves let alone support a family. Mother dreamed of devoting herself full time to homemaking and children, but first she had to get through school. By 1946, Daddy was enrolled full time as a graduate student at the Southern Baptist Theological Seminary in Louisville, and he was also pastoring a little church over in Richmond, Kentucky. Mother was finishing up her bachelor's degree through a series of correspondence courses and working the switchboard at a hospital downtown.

In a diary from that time, she marked each entry B, M, or H, tracking her mood: Blue, Medium, or Happy. Sometimes she added a plus or minus to these letters. During the winter, there were many Blue days. She hated her hospital job. To her mind, the workplace was a vicious pit, full of crude, malicious, spiteful colleagues. Her squeamishness about vulgar language and coarse talk became a source of merriment for several of her coworkers. The more she objected, the more they took pleasure in trying to shock her.

They pounced eagerly on her mistakes. Frequently she reported that her boss had bawled her out or that a coworker observed that all preachers and their wives were cranks. It was not unusual for her to come home in tears. "The work was terrible today," one entry reported. "I came home and cried from rebellion and despair. What a comfort sweet little old Eldred is to me."

While work rankled, she delighted in her young husband. Yet he sometimes grew impatient with her moodiness and complaints. When a string of Happy days followed a stretch of Blue ones, she grew philosophical and wrote as if from the vantage point of a decades-long relationship. "All in all this has been another grand day for us. Always after the deep valleys are behind, the sunlight seems richer and mellower than it has ever been before. I guess that explains why a true companionship grows richer with the years."

When she was Blue, she tried to cheer herself up and berated herself for not being a better wife. "Came home from work and I was blue about our little apartment, my having to work, and our low finances. But I tried not to let Eldred know about the latter. Poor little old boy! He has a coward for a wife!"

She exhorted herself to better behavior. "I threw a tantrum at lunch today because I have to work. From here on I'm going to see how little griping I can do and how cheerful I can be. If you can't do what you like, Marjorie, how about liking what you have to do? Remember that, whiner!" But her resolutions were impossible to keep. That night she scrawled the following addendum: "[A coworker] made fun of me tonight. The detestable bag!"

The weather wove through her narrative as both a metaphor and a source of her moods: "Today was a typical rainy, dark, gloomy Louisville day. The weather was quite warm but the dampness made it unpleasant. Eldred and I were both blue as Indigo this morning. We felt we should sell the car, quit the church and Seminary and go to the farm. However, about noon the clouds all lifted and we are happy once more."

Marjorie wanted to leave the job that plagued her and devote herself to what she saw as her real work: taking care of the house and Eldred and starting a family. Many of the seminary wives were pushing strollers around campus, others were announcing pregnancies, and that spring her best friend adopted a two-year-old boy. She confided in her journal, "Eldred and I made a pretty definite decision." A few days later, "We decided we had better take out hospital insurance."

When Marjorie quit her hospital job, B and M disappeared from her journal, replaced with H and H+ and sometimes even H++++++. She loved being at home taking care of the house. She also exulted in the return of spring, which brought with it a lift in her spirits. "This place out here is just like Paradise," she wrote of her once too small seminary apartment. "It seems that since quitting work I have awakened from a terrible nightmare to find everything beautiful and safe once more."

It is interesting to see how explicitly she linked home and safety versus work and danger. "It has been wonderful," she wrote, "to be here at home and not have to go anywhere! We went to the grocery, poultry house (for necks and backs for soup) and to the fruit market. We had fried chicken and fruit salad and then laid down and talked awhile after lunch. Eldred studied and went to Greek and Theology. I worked off a hard history lesson this afternoon and Eldred is finishing up his Hebrew exegesis to hand in in the morning." She was happy fixing my father's meals, sharing life by his side, and enjoying the natural beauty of the seminary campus. Like many other women in those post–World War II years, she looked forward to the baby that she hoped would come before too much longer.

At last, she got pregnant. By now she had finished college and a master's degree at the seminary, and Eldred had graduated from the seminary as well. She was so happy. They had a small house. This was married life at last, as she believed it was supposed to be lived. They held a party for some close friends and announced that a baby was due May 17, 1948. She and my father fixed up the baby's room. Her mother crocheted a baby blanket.

But the story ended in sorrow. The baby girl was stillborn after four grueling days of labor. Our boxes of family photos contained multiple copies of a glossy 8 × 10 of the dead baby, lying in silent perfection in her tiny satin-lined casket. Marilyn. The name, Mother explained to us, meant "bitter."

How strange to have a perfectly formed baby sister who had had to die so that my sister and I could be born, I used to think. Mother had explained how one among thousands of eggs and millions of sperm joined to make the unique person that I was. What an amazing stroke of good fortune, I marveled when I was in the third grade, that the sperm and egg that made me had found one another, that I was an I. It was like winning the lottery, only even more unlikely. Or else it was the work of a directive God, calling my sister and me into being in the shadow of that loss. If Marilyn had lived, the timing of Jeannie's and my conceptions would have changed, and Marilyn (who would have had a different name, one that was a blessing instead of a curse) would have had a different sister, maybe named Jackie but not me.

Marjorie, still weak from the long ordeal, believed only another baby could assuage her sorrow. Ignoring the doctor's advice, she planned another pregnancy.

Eleven months later she gave birth to her second daughter, my sister Jeannie. The baby of her family, Mother had had no younger siblings to help care for. But she loved children dearly and had been teaching four and five year olds in Sunday School since before college. Her new baby, conceived one night after Prayer Meeting, had long, beautiful fingers and toes. In fact, she was long all over. She was a beautiful baby.

But when Mother held her in her arms to cuddle her Jeannie stiffened and pushed away. To Mother's profound disappointment, her baby was not a cuddler. She was a pretty baby, a smart baby, a good baby, but she was a baby that often as not, when her mother picked her up, pushed against her mama's chest like she wanted to be put down again. She had a weak, almost polite, little cry. She sucked so lackadaisically that Mother began to worry that Jeannie might starve to death. She supplemented breast-feedings with bottles just to be on the safe side. She hoped there was nothing wrong with this baby, who had kicked so gently in her womb and now moved her long, long legs and arms almost dreamily, like a long-necked ballerina doing stretches and warm-ups for a ballet.

She felt deliriously happy and yet anxious and uneasy at the same time. She wasn't certain she really knew how to take care of a baby; they looked so awfully fragile. She checked little Jeannie again and again as she lay sleeping in her bassinet to make sure she was really breathing.

Jeannie was a quiet little baby, with an alert look in her big bright eyes, but she often looked faintly worried. She walked and talked early. Her first sentence was an expression of sorrow at her Daddy's absence. By the time she was born, my parents had moved their little family back to Owensboro, where Daddy served as the associational missionary. His work sometimes took him on the road, and Jeannie missed him terribly when he was gone. There was no doubt about it. She was Daddy's girl.

By the time I was born, in 1951, Mother was bound and determined to have a baby she could cuddle with. Fortunately, she got one. From the first time she picked me up, she could see that I loved to snuggle, that I wanted to be as close to her as she wanted to be to me. At last she had the one who loved her back, the one who really understood her, the one she hoped would be just like her, only braver and better.

One afternoon, when I was about five, I stood in the doorway of Mother's bedroom and watched as she got ready for my father's return. She was wearing a Sunday dress and pumps with two-and-a-half-inch heels. She clipped a pair of gold-plated earrings to her ears and dabbed Tabu behind each ear and on each wrist. How beautiful she is, I thought, as I admired the ample curve of her breast and the way the two-inch-wide patent leather belt cinched her pretty waist. My own cheerful five-year-old chest swelled with love for her. My father had been on the road two weeks. Even at home, he worked such long hours that he was a near stranger. I knew I was supposed to love both of my parents, but my father, though fascinating, was remote. I felt a stab of guilt at how desperately I loved my mother and how much more of a stranger my father seemed. "I love you and Daddy both the same," I said bravely as I stood there at the threshold of their bedroom, because I believed I really ought to love them equally and, in the moment of doubting that I did, I felt I really must assert it. "But I just know you a lot better." "I know you do, honey," Mother said absently, as she blotted her bright red lipstick and checked her makeup in the big cherry-framed mirror. She wasn't thinking too much about whether my filial love was measured out in equal quantities. She was thinking about the big love of her life coming home to transform her from married mom into cherished sweetheart. When he was home and not working, she made sure we all knew it was a celebration.

Mother loved language, and she resolved that we would, too. She read to us all through childhood. When she read me stories, I grew impatient. I wanted to read them back to her, I wanted to be the one with the speaking part, and I would bang on the book and holler and try to pull it away from her. But when she read verses from Mother Goose, and later poems from *101 Famous Poems,* I was all hers. I loved those magic rhymes and sure-footed rhythms. "The highwayman came riding, riding, riding / The highwayman came riding / Up to the old inn door." You could hear the horse gallop.

She had a fine sense of the absurd and a quick wit. I remember a lot of laughter at the dinner table, usually instigated by Mother or Jeannie or me and often erupting just as Daddy was trying to get us to bow our heads so he could ask the blessing. We shared her love of wordplay and smart-mouthed remarks.

I was a tomboy growing up, just as she had been. We both thought Jo was the only character in *Little Women* worth emulating. Like her, we liked to climb trees and act out dramas, we whistled and strode about, we couldn't hide our true feelings, and we scribbled poems and plays.

When I was seven, Mother bought us the game Anagrams. Mother and I played every chance we got. When Daddy was late for supper, we would run into the living room and grab the anagrams. No one else in (or out of) the family liked this game as we did. We loved to touch the cool wooden tiles and study the letters, thinking about how we might recombine them. "That old bird is going to fly over here to me and become a bride," we might say as we gleefully captured the other's word.

Until she died, Mother found it hard to imagine that I wasn't, in almost every respect, a carbon copy of her. When I turned out to be different, she never failed to be surprised. Food was a case in point. She was always certain that anyone she loved would want to eat exactly what she wanted to eat exactly when she wanted to eat it. She expressed love for all of us by dropping uninvited morsels onto our plates that she herself was enjoying. She did this with a little pleased smile because it made her happy to be sharing something so delicious. She liked her fried eggs hard and peppered within an inch of their lives. I liked mine soft and with no pepper. This over-easy, unpeppered egg seemed so wrong to her that she continued sliding eggs with rock-hard yolks, crusty whites, and heavy layers of black pepper onto my plate for as long as she could stand and flip a spatula. She laced her vegetables with as much bacon grease as possible. After my gallbladder was removed and I had to limit fats, she responded to my protests about bacon grease as if I had insulted both her cooking and her character.

One of Jeannie's last memories of Mother centers on a Chinese dinner they shared. Weak and shaky, Mother could not hold the fork without her hand trembling, but with her shaking fork she still managed to transfer most of the little miniature corn from the stir-fry onto Jeannie's plate. Jeannie doesn't especially like baby corn, but for Mother this was a special treat, a food so exotic as to be almost unimaginable. Each time she found one, she quiveringly transported it over to Jeannie's plate and deposited it there with a little happy smile, like a mama bird triumphantly dropping a choice worm into her baby's gaping beak. By that time, Jeannie knew better than to send that baby corn back. She just said thank you and ate it.

Mother never thought I uttered an uninteresting word. She listened to me so attentively that sometimes she would interrupt a conversation she was having with someone else in order to answer me over in the next room. But if I came out with something that was wildly different from what she thought or felt, she would calmly contradict me. If she said I was happy or sad or worried, there was no use saying I wasn't because she figured she knew me better than I knew myself. After all, didn't I come right out of her body? She knew me even before I was an I.

Indeed, we were alike in many ways. But there was in her an insecurity and a tempestuousness that were not present in me. Something in her made me feel, even as a small child, protective. "I know you'll miss me," I told her as I climbed out of the car on my first day of school, "but don't worry about a thing. And don't cry. I'll be fine."

3

Cutting Loose

Growing up in Eldred Taylor's household, I vacillated between adulation and resentment. It's not easy to live with someone who knows he is right and knows it because God told him. I liked being so closely affiliated with the power center. When he walked into the church service on Sunday morning wearing his dark blue suit, a red rosebud pinned on his lapel, his well-worn Bible tucked under his arm, he was a handsome and powerful sight. Often after he sat down, while the organist continued to play, he would look out over the congregation. When his eyes came to rest on me, he would wink, claiming me. After church, he would stand at the back of the sanctuary and shake the hand of everyone who came out his door. He would stand and talk until everyone was gone but the janitor. When the crowd was pretty well thinned out, I would walk up beside him. Without pausing in his conversation, he would reach out and put his arm around me, pulling me close. Claimed again.

But the constraints of that preacher's daughter role were real and wearying. By the time I got to high school, I knew I had some substantive differences of opinion with him on the right and wrong of a number of things. The first big theological difference came when I was about eleven. Jeannie and I were getting ready for bed. Daddy stopped in to tell us good night, and I chose that moment to question him about salvation. We had been taught that if you were going to be saved from eternal damnation you had to accept Jesus Christ as your personal savior. The absolute nature of this requirement had begun to worry me. "But what about," I asked, "people in some part of the world where no one has ever heard of Jesus? What about them?"

"They would go to hell," my father explained. "That's why we have to work so hard to make sure everyone has a chance to hear."

"But that's not fair," I argued, bursting into tears. "If God doesn't send someone to tell them, how can God send them to hell? I can't believe that's right."

My father reminded me again of how important it was for us to tell the good news to everyone we could so this wouldn't happen. But I knew in my heart that Daddy and I had parted ways. I dried my tears. God could not possibly be that rigid, that dead set on a Jesus-only route to heaven.

Of course, just as Daddy feared, once you admit one chink in the theological armor, the whole outfit threatens to fall to pieces. Baptists attract a fair amount of ridicule for their long list of don'ts. We weren't allowed to dance, drink, smoke, bring playing cards into the house, say "gosh" or "gee," or go to a picture show on Sunday. All of these restrictions are based on the notion that Baptists are by and large an intemperate lot and once they get started with something they just can't hold back. We weren't allowed to dance because when a man holds a woman close in his arms he gets all worked up and inflamed, and the next thing you know she's pregnant. We weren't allowed to drink because after one sip you might not stop, and the next thing you know you're an alcoholic. We couldn't smoke because it was an addiction and one that didn't look very Christian. We couldn't have playing cards in the house because playing cards are used for gambling. First poker and then, before you can say "I'll see you and raise you two," you're down at the racetrack betting on the Kentucky Derby and drinking mint juleps in the middle of the afternoon. Saying "gosh" or "gee" is just a step away from saying "God" or "Jesus," which is taking the Lord's name in vain (as specifically prohibited in the Ten Commandments). Going to a movie (what we called "the show") on Sunday gets in the way of remembering the Sabbath to keep it holy, which you cannot do while watching a picture show. We couldn't work

ner, though somehow pastoring the church didn't count.
ng the Sunday dishes. You could even sew a button on if
hing you needed to wear to church. Even the Old Testa-
ɔ, anted a few special exceptions for that "no breaking the Sabbath"
rule. After all, sometimes the ox was in the ditch, and the poor old thing
had to be hauled out so it would stop bellowing.

By the time I got to high school, I didn't buy most of this. The idea
behind all these prohibitions, I suppose, is the one contained in I Thes-
salonians 5:22: "Abstain from all appearance of evil." That directive cuts
a mighty wide swath.

Not dancing was the hardest. Jeannie and I wanted to dance so bad.
We watched *American Bandstand* and worked on our dance floor technique in the living room with the television on. We practiced as best we
could and dreamed of the day when we could get out there and cut the
rug with the best of them. We were about as adept at this as most white
Southern Baptists who have been discouraged all their lives from contacting any body parts that might wiggle or sway.

The high school regularly organized sock hops. These informal
dances were the major form of social life available outside of football and
basketball games. You didn't even have to have a date to go. Girls could
go in groups with their friends. I believed that if I could go to the sock
hops my social isolation would end. Friends urged me on. Even the girls
whose daddies were deacons were allowed to dance. When I was a
sophomore, I became convinced that there was a way out of this dilemma.
I thought long and hard about it, planning what I would say, and then one
morning I marched into my father's study to present my proposal.

"Daddy, can I talk to you?" I asked as I knocked on his door.

"Sure, honey, come in." He laid aside the exegetical text he was
studying in preparation for next Sunday's sermon and the notes he was
taking.

"Daddy, I know you and Mother think dancing is wrong." I swallowed hard and took a deep breath. "But I've been thinking a lot about
this, and I don't agree with you. I realize that if I were to go to the dance
as your daughter people in this town would be critical of you. But here's
what I'm thinking. I'm not you, and we don't agree. So what I thought
was this. I can go to the sock hop as myself."

He fixed me with a baffled look. I barreled on recklessly.

"I'd just go as myself. If anyone asked what you thought, I'd tell them you didn't agree with me but that I was there as myself. Not as your daughter."

He gave me a kindly smile, with just a pinch of long-suffering indulgence thrown in. "Jackie, honey, I don't think there's any point in our talking about this. You know your mother's and my position on dancing. We don't believe it is right. If you go to a dance in this town, it reflects badly on you and it reflects badly on our family. I'm sorry you don't agree with us on this, but I have to say no."

A wave of helplessness and humiliation washed over me. A hot blush crept up my neck and spread over my face. I felt like my circuits were seconds away from meltdown. "OK, then," I muttered quickly as I hurriedly backed out of his study. I was dizzy, and my head was growing lighter. I rushed to my bedroom just as my vision, in slow motion, began to dim, as if someone were dialing down the lights on a rheostat. Everything faded to black. A few minutes later I found myself on the floor of my bedroom regaining consciousness from the second grand mal epileptic seizure of my life.

The first had occurred during Sunday morning service when I was eight. My mother had frowned at me because she had caught me whispering in church. I wasn't really being disruptive, and I thought Mother's stern censure unfair. A mixture of shame and indignation washed through me. When I stiffened and fell, one of the men of the church carried me out. My father, who didn't see who had fallen, prayed for the family of the sick child who had left the service. Mother followed me out and took me home. She had seen my jaw working during the seizure and diagnosed the problem before they hooked me up to the first EEG. She knew from experience the metallic taste I had in my mouth when I came to, and she knew that a sip of Coca-Cola would chase it away.

Like my mother, I seemed to have some pretty sensitive wiring. For years during my childhood I took medication to control the epilepsy that was diagnosed after that first seizure, and for years I was cautioned to lie down ("Hit the deck!" my doctor would bark) whenever the lights started to dim. I was warned not to reveal to any of my friends that I suffered from this highly stigmatized condition. It was, I felt then, just one more way I was different. By my sophomore year, the epilepsy was almost outgrown, and I had eased off the medication, but the sense of helplessness and injustice I felt when my father vetoed my plan to show up as myself swamped my system.

In that moment, when I stood in my father's study, seeking a path out of the clearly demarcated world of right and wrong he had constructed, it felt as if everything was at stake: my parents' love, my independence, my chance for love and romance, any hope of ever having meaningful connections beyond my family. I grew increasingly impatient with my parents' simple rules, yet I loved them fiercely and wanted to do what was in my power to help them look good.

By the end of my senior year, I had managed to make one good friend who was not a Baptist. Sally was Presbyterian. She was magnificently unimpressed by my father. She seemed, somehow, to like me for myself, and she regarded my preacher's daughter condition as an unfortunate circumstance that I could not help and for which I should be pitied but not ostracized.

Bonnie and Clyde, the Faye Dunaway and Warren Beatty film about two notorious bank robbers, had come out nearly two years earlier. At last it had made its way to Somerset. When I mentioned to my father that I wanted to see it, he told me that it was a film that glorified a life of violence and contained too much sex and that it would not be an appropriate film for me to see. End of subject.

Sally decided to throw a birthday party for one of her friends. The party would begin with a barbecue in her backyard, and then we would all go together to *Bonnie and Clyde.* I told her my father would never let me see that movie. Sally laughed at the very thought of such a ridiculous position. She was sure he could not object to my going with a bunch of girls. I was equally certain that he could. But, fortified by Sally's gentle prodding, I resolved to take him on.

I told my father that we needed to talk. We sat down together in the living room with the two big picture windows and the window seat, he in the upholstered rocking chair with the gooseneck arms and I on the couch with the new slipcover Mrs. Tandy had made. This slipcover had roses that matched the mauve beige carpet and walls. It was a sunny weekday afternoon in May. I don't know how I managed to catch him at home on a weekday afternoon, a time when he was usually out visiting church members who were in the hospital. But there we sat across from each other, he in his suit and tie and I in the poly-cotton skirt I had made myself and hemmed a good two inches shorter than he and Mother thought looked decent.

"Sally's having a birthday party for Debbie that I really want to attend," I began.

"That sounds like fun."

"She's going to have a barbecue in her backyard, and then we are all going to go down to the movie theater to see *Bonnie and Clyde*."

My father frowned impatiently. "Jackie, we've already covered this. That movie is not appropriate. I can't permit you to go. *Bonnie and Clyde* is a trashy, vulgar film that glorifies a life of violence and glamorizes sex outside of marriage."

I was anxious, of course, and yet, in some way, strangely calm. I was enough my father's daughter to be fearless when I believed I held the moral high ground. Words filled my mouth. "That's possible," I said. "But I'm going anyway. This is my rebellion. For eleven years, ever since we got to Somerset, I've followed every one of your rules and done everything in my power to make you look good. I understood that everyone was watching us and our every action reflected on you. Preachers' kids are supposed to be rebels and troublemakers but not us. Jeannie and I have been veritable Baptist nuns. I haven't always agreed with you, but I've always tried to make you look good. Now I'm three months away from leaving home for college. Once I get there, it will be up to me to make decisions about where I go and what movies I see. So far, I've made all these decisions based on your beliefs. Once I get to college that's over. At college, what I do reflects on me and me alone. I can tell you right now, once I get there, I'm going to go where I decide to go and do what I decide to do. I'm cutting loose."

My father had the good sense not to interrupt me as I barreled on. "If you've done such a poor job of raising me that ninety minutes in a movie theater is going to cause me to take up a life of crime, then there's no hope anyway. I'm not convinced that *Bonnie and Clyde* is the wicked film you think it is, but even if it is I don't think it's going to turn me into a bank robber. I'm going to go see that film, and you can't stop me. This is my rebellion. And here's the beauty of this rebellion. No one will even guess that I'm rebelling but you. Anyone who sees me there with a gang of girl-friends will just figure I'm celebrating my friend's birthday. So your rep-utation can remain untarnished. I'm going to that movie, and you can't stop me. But I wanted you to know."

At last I paused and Daddy got a chance to speak. "Jackie," he said gravely, "I know you've worked hard to follow the rules that your mother and I set forth and that it hasn't always been easy for you. We really appreciate how hard you and Jeannie have tried to follow the teachings and principles we have provided. I also respect what you have said to me this afternoon, and of course I don't believe that watching *Bonnie and Clyde* will make a criminal of you." He stood up and walked to the middle of the room.

"Come over here to your Daddy," he said. When I approached, he reached out his arm and pulled me close to his side. "I'm so proud of you. I still don't think you ought to see this film, and I'm not going to give you my permission. In fact, if I did give you my permission it would ruin your rebellion. But I understand and respect what you have said to me this afternoon. So, if you do decide to go to this movie against my will, I will accept, even if I do not condone, your decision."

When you stop to think about it, it was a puny rebellion indeed. Like I said, just between us. No one else even knew about it except, perhaps, Mother. Still, standing up to him even this much had felt to me like an act of raw courage. And I had given him fair warning. I was fixing to kick over the traces. My days as an overachieving, Goody Two-shoes, Baptist nun were drawing to a close.

4

Six-Track Mind

I pulled the 1958 two-toned Chevrolet into the Ramseys' driveway on Friday night, turned off the ignition, stepped out, and pocketed the key with something approaching a swagger. I had been driving for only a year and couldn't quite get over the stroke of good fortune that had placed in my possession, if only for two weeks, this ten-year-old, green and white beauty in mint condition.

I was staying with Bill and Eula Ramsey because my father was in Owensboro preaching a revival, Jeannie was away at college, and my mother, recovering from a hysterectomy and still too weak to manage on her own, was in the care of Opal Gay, another church member and friend. The two had sealed their friendship with a multitude of blackberry-picking sessions, sessions that gave them a chance to discover their shared love of the natural world and their similarly irreverent senses of humor. Mother seemed to be doing better than anyone could have expected. She was amazingly optimistic and energetic for someone so recently out of surgery. In a burst of relief and creativity, she had written a poem, "Joy at Dawn." Her poem described her laughing, crying, talking to the birds and to God. "No! I was not drunk / Only filled with God's Spirit," the poem explained.

Mother clearly felt lucky to be alive. She looked out from her hospital bed at the sunrise with a surge of emotion that was almost overwhelming. If we had seen this poem then, we would have thought that anyone who could write verse only a week or so after surgery that rose to such a crescendo of exclamation points and rhymed and scanned so well must surely be on the road to recovery. Daddy undoubtedly believed that her powerful faith was sufficient to sustain her through anything life could offer.

For me, the past five days had bestowed a giddy freedom. Our family had only one car, an Oldsmobile Ninety-Eight. I drove it seldom, generally when my parents needed me to run an errand. I walked to school and every other place I needed to go. So I was thrilled to have the keys to the Ramseys' old Chevy. Brother Ramsey was one of our deacons. But here we were blessedly spared weekday morning Bible readings and devotions. They didn't even have a blessing at breakfast, a surprisingly relaxed affair. We just wandered in and helped ourselves to cereal or toast or whatever.

Like my mother, Mrs. Ramsey was a great cook and an exuberant cutup. She was glad to see me when I came home, but I felt none of the tension and conflict that had come to characterize my relationship with my own mother. She had, for instance, no interest at all in how short my skirts were. She didn't seem to mind if I was sleepy or preoccupied rather than animated and cheerful at breakfast. She didn't even have an opinion on my posture.

Brother Ramsey, probably in his fifties by then and bald, was a tall, kind, handsome, blue-eyed man. They were fun, they weren't my parents, and they had given me a shiny vintage car to drive.

I was on the committee busily planning the senior prom, one I would never attend. Eldred Taylor's prominence in the community and implacable opposition to dancing had made me virtually date-proof. A tall, bony, bookish girl, I carried around a list of novels our English teacher told us we should read before college and carefully checked off each one as I completed it. I loved them all. When I finished the list, I searched out other books by the same authors. I raised my hand before anyone else in my trigonometry class and helped the boys with their homework. I shared my ideas freely and was profligate with unsolicited advice and opinions. All told, I was a walking compendium of behaviors designed to guarantee social oblivion.

But, during that week Daddy was away at the revival, as I worked on the prom committee, selecting the theme, planning the decorations, and then driving myself home in "my" two-toned '58 Chevy, I felt, in my borrowed life, almost like an ordinary teenager. That night I lay in bed reading *Jane Eyre* until well past eleven. No one told me to turn off my light. I was free. But not for long.

On Saturday morning at 6:15, Eula Ramsey called me out of a sound sleep. It took me a minute to figure out where I was. Mrs. Ramsey was telling me something about my mother, but it didn't make any sense. My mother was having problems (what kind of problems?), and someone (Opal Gay? The doctor? Mrs. Ramsey?) wanted me to go help her. My mother, ten days postsurgery, was having some kind of mental breakdown. She was talking nonstop, and much of what she said made no sense. The family doctor had been by, but he couldn't seem to get her calmed down. Mrs. Gay had called in church friends from down the road, Allen and Dixie Davis (another deacon and his wife), but no one could figure out how to help Mother. The adults had run out of ideas, and someone had decided that if Mother could see me she might settle down and come to herself.

I was out the door within five minutes. I remember asking questions, trying to get clear on what was happening. I remember feeling hyperalert. Mother was in trouble. I could help her.

Looking back on that day, I wonder what the adults thought a seventeen year old with exactly zero experience dealing with psychotic breakdowns would have to offer. I've always been a can-do, take-charge kind of person. I don't seem to inspire protective impulses. But still I can't imagine that my scrawny, stoop-shouldered, teenage self looked equal to the job of facing a mother who had gone wildly, ravingly, extravagantly mad. Only overwhelming panic and a powerful belief that this was family business could have led them to pin their hopes on me.

When I walked into the little bedroom right off Opal's tiny kitchen, Mother was sitting up in bed shouting, "Damn! Damn! Damn!" At the conclusion of this string of the only curses I had ever heard pass my mother's lips, she flopped back on the bed shrieking with laughter. She caught sight of me, and a look of zany delight spread over her face. "Oh, here's Jackie. Now don't worry, honey. You probably don't know what to think seeing your mother like this." I didn't. I felt raw terror. Up until this point, my family, and especially my mother, had seemed a safe harbor in the midst of a public life in which I often felt like an odd bird and an outsider. Now my mother, certainly a bit prone to mood swings but always, before, my mother, looked and sounded like a crazy person. I was horrified. But my conviction that I had to find a way to take care of her was far stronger than even my terror. "Damn! Damn! Damn!" she shouted again, with the exuberance of someone who had been biting back curses for forty-seven years. She once again fell back laughing.

I went into the room and gave her a hug. She looked like herself and yet not. She was my big, beautiful, familiar, wonderful mother. And she wasn't. She wore one of her pretty pastel nylon gowns. It had a row of buttons down the front of the scooped neck, a neckline that showed several inches of her ample cleavage. But a large safety pin firmly fastened the top of the gown. What's more, a plain cotton print robe, surely borrowed from Opal, was pinned around her shoulders.

Mother weighed about 150 pounds by this time, a good 20 pounds more than her ideal weight. She always prided herself on the fact that no matter what her weight she maintained her beautiful proportions (defined by her as a matching measurement of bust and hips and a waist that was ten inches smaller). Her long, shapely legs remained, at any weight or age, one of her finest points. But 150 pounds was more weight than she wanted, and she had been dieting in the weeks before the surgery. The doctor had given her a prescription for amphetamines, a common practice at the time. Women all over America were prescribed these drugs as a diet aid.

By the time I saw her, she must have been a chemical and hormonal stew. The amphetamines and the stress would have revved her up. She was still recovering from the anesthesia. She was also given painkillers after the hysterectomy, Demerol in the hospital and later some other prescription drugs. She had been plunged abruptly into menopause with the hysterectomy, a plunge uncushioned by hormone replacement therapy. We now know that these circumstances can send any woman into an emotional and physical tailspin, even one who does not suffer from mental illness. But we didn't know any of that then.

Her brown, softly permed hair showed the wear and tear of ten days in bed. She moved with that special caution anyone tender and sore from abdominal surgery takes. But it was her face that showed the greatest strain. She looked wild around her eyes and terribly anxious. At the same time, she looked electrically charged—superalert. I sat on her bed, and we held hands as she talked and talked and talked about everything that had ever bothered her in her life. Her mind leaped from one topic to the next in a bizarre sort of stream of consciousness.

As for me, I was both deeply frightened and strangely calm. I felt catapulted into adulthood, not into the fun parts, like driving your own car and reading as late into the night as you liked, but the scary, hard parts, where you're in charge but no one has shown you what it is you are supposed to do next. Where maybe no one really knows.

She stroked my hand. "Your hand is so warm. Poor little Jeannie has such cold, sweaty hands. They have an operation they can do now where they cut the nerve, so your hands don't sweat so much. I wonder if Jeannie should have that operation. She has such clammy little hands." My sister was nearly six feet tall, and there was nothing little about her hands, but Mother always used *little* as a term of endearment. "I don't know how much it would cost to get an operation like that or whether they even do it in Somerset."

"Poor little Eldred, he works so hard. People think we live on Easy Street because he drives a great big Oldsmobile Ninety-Eight and we live in a great big house. We don't live on Easy Street, we live on Main Street, and the traffic goes by night and day."

She plucked at the opening of her gown. "They pinned this up," she told me mischievously. "They're afraid I won't keep it buttoned." And she laughed with glee and fidgeted with the pin. "Just leave that alone. You're fine," Dixie Davis instructed from beside the bed. Opal and Dixie were hovering in and out of the bedroom, making another pot of coffee on Opal's little stove, opening or closing the windows, conferring quietly in the adjacent living room. Allen Davis had gone back down the road to tend to his livestock. The doctor had come and gone before I arrived.

Mother had awakened at three in the morning. She often had trouble sleeping, and it was not unusual for her to get up as much as two hours before her usual 6:00 am, but this was different. She had begun pacing anxiously around the house, asking for my dad, begging to go home, and becoming more and more upset and incoherent. As she grew wilder, she talked more and more rapidly and disjointedly. Soon, the cursing started, and then, after Dr. Spraddlin and Allen and Dixie Davis arrived, she began ripping open the front of her nightgown and flashing her big, beautiful breasts at the family doctor, the startled deacon, and her two good friends. Mother was an extremely modest woman. She had probably never flashed so much as a petticoat up until that day. Dr. Spraddlin, who had cared for her for years, and Allen, Dixie, and Opal, who thought they knew her well, must have been astonished.

She was wild with anxiety and didn't want to stay in bed. She became belligerent. She refused the capsules the doctor offered. She paced and ranted. Finally, forcibly, Dr. Spraddlin injected her with what he described as enough tranquilizer to knock out a horse, but she was unfazed. By the time I arrived, just before seven, Dr. Spraddlin had run out of ideas and headed off to see his other patients. Opal and Dixie had persuaded Marjorie to get back in bed and pinned her gown securely shut. But her mind was still racing.

Now she was talking about her parents, how hard they always worked, how little they had, how short they were, how tall she was, how she towered over them, her sister, and two of her four brothers. She talked about how the older brothers and sister had teased her. "Stick your chest out, Marjorie," she said with a laugh and reached again for the top of the gown, but it was pinned tight. "Stick your chest out, Marjorie."

Now I got it. Mother had told me this story many times before. Whenever she slumped, her mama would say, "Stick your chest out, Marjorie." One day, when she was about nine or ten, her mama said this in front of Marjorie's older brother. He roared with laughter. "Mama," he said, "don't be telling her to stick her chest out. She doesn't have any chest to stick out."

At that moment, Mother realized that her flat little-girl chest was going to grow breasts. She was embarrassed by her older brother's laughter but secretly delighted at the discovery that she would someday have a woman's chest. This idea had never occurred to her in a family so gripped with Victorianism that they called the chicken breasts white meat and the legs dark meat rather than speak the words *breast* and *leg* at the dinner table.

Because I knew all this, I knew Mother was not irrationally flashing the hapless church members. She was acting out her mama's instructions as she had understood them. But now, relieved of inhibition by the wild spell that had her in its grip, she was acting those instructions out with a certain gleeful celebration of the fact that, all these years later, she unequivocally and emphatically had a chest to stick out. When I asked Opal and Dixie, I learned that she had indeed shouted "Stick your chest out, Marjorie!" as she flashed her breasts again and again at her horrified friends.

That same eerie juxtaposition of madness and truth characterized most (maybe all, if I'd known every referent) of what she said through that long day. I held her hand. I listened to her stories or fragments of stories or rantings that pointed toward stories. It almost made sense, but it was too much, too fast, too out of control. The inhibitions and conventions that ruled Mother's life had fallen away. She was speeding wildly down a winding mountain road without brakes. I felt like I was watching some sort of race car that was headed toward the inevitable four-car pileup.

Someone called Daddy that morning. Since the doctors didn't understand what was going on, he understood even less. As near as they could tell, the combination of the hysterectomy and the drugs had sent Mother over the edge. The doctor told Daddy his wife was having some sort of nervous breakdown.

The revival was scheduled to end the next day, but Daddy came home that afternoon. One of the men from the church flew across the state in his small plane to pick my father up. Two of the deacons drove down to preach the remaining three messages. On Sunday night, after the final service, they would drive his car back from Owensboro. All this took time to arrange, and through it all Mother raved and ranted on.

At about 2:00 pm, Mother began to complain that her mouth was dry. We gave her water, but it didn't seem to help. "Jackie, feel my tongue," she instructed me. "It's like a big old thick piece of cotton." She stuck out her tongue in my direction and gave me a no-nonsense look. In the upside-down world she inhabited, examining your mother's saliva production by taking hold of her tongue was the most ordinary thing in the world. I reached up and touched her tongue. There wasn't a speck of spit on it. She had a most amazing case of cotton mouth. "It's as dry as a bone," I agreed. "You have no spit whatsoever. Not a speck."

"I want a cup of coffee. Would you go in there and fix me one?" "Coffee?" I thought. Mother was still as speedy as a rocket. But she had been racing for nearly twelve hours, and the doctor's medicines had dried up nothing but her spit.

"What can it hurt?" I said. "I don't think her motors could race any faster. If she wants coffee, let's give her coffee. Her mouth is bone dry."

I fixed a cup of instant coffee with one saccharin pill, measuring the coffee with a slightly rounded teaspoon, as I had been taught to do. I brought the steaming cup back to Marjorie, and she drank it with relish. "Oh, that tastes good." She smiled her approval at me. "You know just how I like my coffee." She turned to her friends. "Jackie makes my coffee just the way I like it," she said proudly. "She always knows just how to make my coffee." You would have thought making a cup of instant coffee was some rare skill, the mastery of which was proof positive of my amazing talents.

Almost immediately, as if the coffee contained some magic potion that could quiet troubled minds, she began to calm down. The speeding slowed and then stopped. Her agitated face began to resume its normal expression. "Whoowee, I'm feeling better now. That must have worried you, honey," she said to me with a squeeze of my hand and a pat. "I was on a roller coaster. My mind was flying down six tracks at once." My heart swelled. I could have wept for joy to see her coming back, delivered back into herself by the cup of coffee that she had somehow known to ask for and I had somehow known to give her. The relief I felt at helping in even a small way, after hours of helplessly watching her race and rant, was vast.

It had been an exhausting ordeal, and within a half hour of drinking the coffee Mother was fast asleep. Opal and Dixie and I sat in the living room. We could see Mother through the bedroom door. We repeated what she had said and went back over the events of the day, but we really didn't know what to make of it. We were just so glad to see her quiet at last.

She slept for three hours. By the time she woke, Daddy was home. He must have been wild with worry. Nothing short of a full-blown emergency could have pried him away from the final meetings of a revival, but he projected his usual calm, capable demeanor. He walked into Opal's small farmhouse and enfolded his wife in a big, warm hug. He spoke to her in a soft, gentle voice. She beamed with pleasure at the sight of him. She apologized for all the fuss and for interrupting his revival. Looking at her now, Daddy could not possibly imagine what we had lived through over the past twelve hours.

Daddy gathered us up, and we headed for the parsonage. Someone must have driven us, since we had no car in town, but I remember nothing of the ride or who was at the wheel. We were used to the support of a dedicated core of church members who would step up to help in any crisis. Even a privately piloted plane didn't seem that unusual. Mother was weak and tired, a little confused, and very embarrassed, but she seemed like herself. It had been a horrific journey, but it was over. It was a bizarre aberration, an anomaly, a reaction to the trauma of surgery and the drugs.

Except that it wasn't.

At Bill and Eula's, I had enjoyed a delicious taste of what I thought of as normal teenage life. I desperately wanted to prolong it. I redoubled my efforts on the prom planning committee as the meetings gave me a reason to stay out of the house. I put in extra hours working on the yearbook. I invented excuses for visiting the library.

Meanwhile, Mother fought for balance. The newest incision gradually healed into one more wide, pink, abdominal scar crisscrossing her craggy belly. Soon she returned to running the household. But her mind would not stop racing.

She became convinced that some of the folks from out in the country who drove into town on Saturdays to shop, parked in front of our house, and sometimes picnicked in our front yard, were spies. Urgently she pointed out anyone who appeared in front of our house more than once and then anyone who lingered at all. She advised us to call the police. The house, she believed, was bugged. She suspected that any time Daddy and I stepped out of earshot to speak to each other we were talking about her. (In fact, because of our concern, this was often true.)

She objected to my busy schedule, convinced that I was working too hard. She urged me to rest when I could plainly see it was she who was exhausted. Gently, firmly, sometimes angrily, I would insist that I was needed elsewhere, then feel guilty at the relief that flooded me when I escaped the house.

It was a bit more than a year before I could leave for college. I studied the slick college brochures that arrived in the mail as I had once studied the materials from the Foreign Mission Board. I couldn't wait to begin my own life, one that I was certain would include less church and more books.

In moments of clarity, Mother would count the number of preacher's wives in our county who had suffered nervous breakdowns. She knew it was not coincidental that the number was in the double digits. Someone, she thought, and I thought with her, might want to look at how the pressures of her life contributed to her illness.

That same summer, about three months after her hysterectomy, Mother was hospitalized with what the doctors diagnosed as a mild heart attack. I was away from home when it happened, working on the kitchen staff at Cedarmore, a Kentucky Baptist summer camp. As before, I was in a state of near bliss, living in a dorm underneath the dining room with the other female staffers, mooning around with my first boyfriend, another staffer, and lounging by the pool between meal shifts. Once more I was called to Mother's side. Jeannie and I were catapulted into a seemingly endless round of laundry, meals, and dishes as we struggled to take care of the house. Daddy's schedule was, as it had always been, unaccommodating.

Our family had planned for over two years to travel to Europe and Israel in July and early August. Some twenty people, many of them church members, had signed up to take this twenty-one-day tour under Daddy's direction. Yet two weeks before we were to leave, Mother was still in the hospital.

Daddy was reluctant to go, worried that Mother would need him, but she insisted that she was fine and he should leave. The psychological symptoms that had plagued her throughout the spring seemed to have abated. Mentally and emotionally, she appeared to be her old comforting, comfortable self. The doctor assured Daddy that he could travel if he needed to, and he needed to. I hated to leave her there. Much as I had looked forward to my first international trip, it did not seem right to go with her lying in the hospital, just barely back on her feet after the health trials of the spring. I offered to stay behind, but in the end my parents said go, and so we left.

On the trip, Daddy assumed his customary role of leader. He wore an odd little hat to protect his bald head from the sun and would lead our group of twenty or so by striding before us, his hat held high so we could follow him in a crowd. With our group, he was cheerful and confident, but when the bus stopped rolling at the end of the day he was often lonesome and worried about his wife.

Mother and Daddy wrote to each other throughout the trip. The letters provide a record of care and connection. From La Guardia International Airport in New York, Daddy sent a postcard of the Statue of Liberty.

> It was hard to leave you this A.M., but everything is all right here and I am sure it will be with you too. You were so pretty and sweet and your wonderful faith is an inspiration and testimony for God. . . . We love you dearly.

Mother's first letter described the many church members who had visited her in the hospital and the various gifts they had brought. She wrote that she was feeling better and had slept well: "Maybe I will become a useful citizen, church-member, and wife and mother again some day. I still HOPE!"

"You are all of that now," Daddy replied. In the fifteen letters Daddy wrote to Mother and the eight she wrote to him, there are many references to her health but not a hint of the dark cloud of mental confusion and paranoia that had shadowed the previous months.

We still had no name for what had happened to Mother that spring and no real notion of how to treat it. By the time she was hospitalized with heart trouble, she had seemed normal mentally, yet she felt as if the ground was crumbling beneath her feet. She would come to characterize "that year I was so sick" as one in which first her femininity and sexuality, then her mind, and finally her body gave way. Behind the sunny bits of news, liberal sprinkling of exclamation points, and plucky expressions of hope that she would again become a "productive citizen, church member, wife, and mother" lay a deep fear that she would not. Each time she climbed out of what we began to describe as one of her "episodes" we hoped we were free of them.

But Daddy began making notes. This was a man who budgeted the family finances and tracked expenses down to the last cent, who carefully catalogued each typed and dated sermon in three-ring binders, who labeled and catalogued the books in his home library according to the Dewey decimal system. Now he began recording the onset and duration of each of Mother's episodes. They recurred three to four times a year, often coincident with the change of the seasons. She was not, as he would remark from time to time, out of the woods yet.

Mother was forty-seven in 1968, when all that I have described happened. Her mother had died in 1962 after two agonizing years in which her circulation became so poor that she had to have first one and then the other leg amputated. Mother was her baby and, I believe, her favorite. That same year, although I knew nothing of it then, Mother experienced such a profound depression that she sought counseling. That seems unremarkable now, but it was unusual in that time and place.

By 1968, Mother feared her world was coming apart. She had built her life on making a home for her family and being a good Christian wife and mother. She had brought to this work her considerable intelligence and enormous creativity. But the world she found herself in was not the world she was raised to expect. She felt her looks fading. She noticed that shopkeepers no longer raced to wait on her. She had grown up with clear notions of what being a lady involved, but she couldn't seem to interest Jeannie and me in the lessons she had struggled to acquire and now wished to impart. The world was growing increasingly angry and unpredictable. She was disturbed by the protests over the war in Vietnam, the growing militance of the civil rights movement, and the assassinations of John F. Kennedy and Martin Luther King.

In the midst of all this, I imagined her longing for me to live a life full of the freedoms and opportunities she had been denied. She had wanted to be a writer, a painter, a country dweller, and a mother of four sturdy children. Her intelligence, I believed, was greater than my father's, her creativity far beyond his. I wondered what her life might have been like without the illnesses, the Great Depression, the lost firstborn child, and the demands of caring for the physical and emotional needs of her busy, important husband.

As I departed for college the following year, I was filled with my own longings for a rich and creative life, but it was not always easy for me, at eighteen, to figure out which of my dreams were my own and which were the ones she was dreaming through me. There was no doubt in my mind, however, that I would refuse to live my life in the shadow of any man.

5

~~❦~~

Why Don't You Just
Meditate on Jesus?

I arrived at Georgetown College in 1969, just as the institution was seized by the rapid currents of social change sweeping the country. Woodstock, the three-day music festival in upstate New York that served as a cultural marker for my generation, occurred just a few days before new freshmen arrived at Georgetown for orientation. Later that same fall, several of my classmates would join 250,000 protestors in Washington, DC, for the largest antiwar demonstration to occur during the Vietnam War.

Georgetown College is a tiny Baptist liberal arts school located in the heart of Kentucky's Bluegrass region. When my classmates and I arrived on campus that August, the college was still dedicated to producing gracious Southern ladies. Rules prescribed when and where women could wear slacks (never before 4:00 pm and not to dinner). Women could smoke only in certain rooms, mostly out of sight of the men. Tight curfews governed our comings and goings. Dancing and drinking were strictly forbidden on campus. Soon, however, the slacks ban fell, unenforceable as numbers of us arrived in class not just in slacks but in frayed and patched jeans. The women who smoked refused to do so in confinement, and the smoking ban also withered away. While the administrators struggled to keep alcohol off campus, they failed to notice (and probably still wouldn't have recognized) the marijuana spilling from car windows as local boys transported personal harvests from dad's back forty into the dorms.

I quit going to church. God, if there was a God, surely wasn't confined to church services. I had had enough of church. Now it was time to seek a life outside of what had become, for me, a stifling place. I was impatient with the relentless Baptist focus on dancing, drinking, and sex and its apparent obliviousness to or outright support of the immoral war being waged in Vietnam.

I reveled in my studies. Beginning with an English major, I soon added a major in communication and a minor in philosophy. I delighted in the hours spent reading literature or delving into English history. I joined the debate team, where I honed my research and reasoning skills.

As my world expanded, questions accumulated. Why would Jesus, the great liberator, want to keep women out of the pulpit? How could a moment in front of a preacher and a piece of paper from the state suddenly make sex between two people who loved each other acceptable in God's eyes when the same act had been abhorrent to God a few moments earlier? Who or what was God? Did God exist? If so, where was my call? Why did my prayers echo inside my head but bring no clear answers?

In my philosophy of religion class, I was assigned to write a paper arguing either for or against the existence of God. Convinced that the existence of God could not be proven, I gamely launched into a paper arguing against. In the middle of the night, three-quarters of the way through my paper, I recognized its fundamental flaw. Just as God's existence could not be logically proven, neither could God's nonexistence. At that moment, it came to me, the uneasy position I would have to occupy either way. If no proof is possible in either case, then both God's existence and nonexistence require a leap. Given those alternatives, my wavering faith seemed more sustainable to me than a belief in only that which we can see and touch. From doubt in God's existence, I always found myself wandering back into belief; praying at moments of joy, sorrow, or uncertainty; singing hymns without having consciously thought to sing; and sensing a spirit much greater than my own at large in the universe. I read in the Apostle Paul's first letter to the Corinthians that faith, like gifts of healing or the ability to prophesy, was a gift of the spirit, one of many that Christians might receive. OK, then, I thought. When the spiritual gifts were being bestowed, faith was not one of which I was given an abundant portion, but in my own tentative, struggling way I continued to believe. "Lord I believe," I prayed in the words of the anguished father in the gospel of Mark who asked Jesus to heal his son. "Help thou my unbelief."

In the midst of all this intellectual growth and the active search for my own beliefs and values, I found myself living parallel lives—the one I was drawn to and the one I imagined my mother wanting for me. In Kentucky in 1969, a young woman's adventures were expected to end early and at the altar. Like most girls growing up in that time and place, I was raised with the hope and expectation that at an early age I would find a good man, marry him, and raise a family.

Mother spun for us a fairy-tale version of her courtship and marriage. It took us years to figure out that Daddy wasn't the next nearest thing to God, not only because he looked like the main attraction each Sunday at church, nor even because the whole town deferred to him, but because Mother's eyes brightened whenever she talked about him.

She all but promised Jeannie and me a future with a similar pattern. Once we entered our gawky early adolescence, we began to grasp the full import of our family's dancing prohibition and our location as the preacher's daughters for our social life. The deadly effect of Brother Taylor's job on our prospects became increasingly clear as we moved through high school. Jeannie and I often grew discouraged about our lack of boyfriends.

Mother's optimism was unflagging. "Someday your prince will come," she chirped. "Someday you'll find the one." We weren't so sure. The song, and her confidence about our ultimate ability to attract Mr. Right, grew increasingly irritating as the years passed. We doubted that her experience, based as it was on a pioneer past, related to our lives in any way. But we had plenty of encouragement to fantasize about just such a turn of events. Marriage, happily-ever-after marriage, was pretty nearly the only path available for a woman who wanted to experience heaven on earth.

Within weeks of starting college, I began dating Mike. Soon I was wearing his fraternity pin, and then we became engaged. The young man I chose was the first one who showed any serious interest in me, a kind and gentle artist. He had played football in high school because his father's love of the game and his own powerful build left him little choice. After games, he retreated to his attic bedroom, where he made art out of found and recycled objects. He could do one hundred push-ups without breaking a sweat. My parents were bound to approve, because he was a Baptist boy, the son of a deacon.

The first time Mike took me to a dance, he was on crutches and could only prop himself up and sway. This, for me, was the perfect gentle introduction for a girl who at eighteen had never danced, except with my sister in the living room. I liked Mike, not only because he was a tall, nice-looking young man with the most amazingly thick head of curly brown hair I had ever seen but also, and more important, because he made me laugh. He was sweet and low key, even passive. He would never push me around. When he told me he loved me and asked me to marry him, it seemed reason enough to do so. I suspect he seemed like a reasonable blend of those two tracks of my life. He shared my politics, helped develop my interest in rock music, and encouraged me in my studies, yet he never pressured me about my reluctance to have sex before marriage. He was a Baptist but only went to church when we visited his parents or mine. I convinced myself that he was the prince my mother had promised.

My fellow debaters were shocked when I told them I was engaged. They cautioned that I was too young and should date others. I got a sick feeling they might be right and returned from a debate trip ready to break it off. But I couldn't do it. I thought he'd be too upset, and I didn't want to disappoint everyone who was already busily helping us plan the wedding. In the end, I let myself be carried along by the current of his interest, the momentum of the wedding plans, my enjoyment of his company, and my own insecurity.

I was nineteen. Mother thought I was too young for marriage, but she didn't say so. Her youngest brother had married a woman her parents had harshly disapproved of. The more they warned against her, the more determined he became to marry. The woman made his life a living misery. Mother, eager not to replay this painful script, resolved to say nothing, and so I married with my parents' blessing.

Neither my husband nor I had real jobs or any clear notion of where we were headed. Like many of the men of our generation, Mike quit shaving and grew a great curly auburn beard. His hair curled to his shoulders. On the rare occasions when he wanted a trim, I cut his hair with sewing scissors. We lived in a tiny wooden box in married student housing. We drove an aged green VW Beetle. We talked vaguely about what we would do when college was over. Sometimes we drove around the countryside and imagined ourselves "going back to nature," living on the land, since at the time that seemed to be the thing one did. I wrote poems and short stories and wondered whether I was a fledgling writer or just another English major who loved language. How was I to make use of myself in the world? What might be the contours of a meaningful life? In my heart, I still expected to be called, somehow, to something, somewhere, I knew not what.

My sister had left Georgetown College just as I arrived to live in New York City and study at the Fashion Institute of Technology. By the middle of my sophomore year, she was back at Georgetown, where she completed another semester before dropping out of school to set up housekeeping with one of the few campus hippies. During this time, she signed all her letters to our parents "Love and peace." Mother wrote back, signing hers "Love and grief."

In early 1972, my husband and I traveled to Mexico with a winter-term study group and came back with suitcases full of embroidered shirts and handwoven blankets. Along with the other students enrolled in this course, we took a Transcendental Meditation class. On visits to Somerset, we would postpone a midafternoon helping of homemade pie (because our stomachs needed to be empty) and retreat to a back bedroom to meditate for twenty minutes. "Why don't you just meditate on Jesus?" Mother asked. Where, she no doubt wondered, was the daughter she had assumed was so much like her? I felt angry and embarrassed, impatient at the way our simple relaxation technique scared her. She suspected we were just one step away from joining a cult, perhaps a band of Hare Krishnas. Soon, she imagined, we would be standing at airports, our heads shaved, wearing tie-dyed shirts and shaking cups in the faces of strangers. Behind my impatience, my heart ached at seeing the fear and sorrow and confusion welling up in her.

In February, Mother and Daddy led a group of travelers on a tour of foreign mission sites in Asia. The three-week trip took them to eighteen cities in twenty-one days and required them to cross the international dateline twice. Many of the mission sites brought them face-to-face with a disturbing level of poverty and need. The minority status of Christianity in these cultures and the prominence of Hinduism and Buddhism also troubled my parents, especially Mother. The pace of the trip was grueling.

When the two weary travelers disembarked in Louisville, Jeannie and her boyfriend and my young husband and I were at the airport to meet them. With the innocence of dearly beloved children, we arrived with utter confidence in ourselves as the best of all possible welcoming committees. We stood there at the gate in our bell-bottom jeans and T-shirts. I'm sure we were all quite clean, but our hair hung long and lank and the young men were a furry lot. Jeannie and I wore no bras and no makeup, but there was probably a dab of musk or patchouli behind each ear, causing each of us to smell faintly of incense or perhaps worse. Handmade earrings dangled from our pierced ears. Our jeans were faded and patched, the patches brightly colored and unapologetic.

In any outfit and with or without makeup, Jeannie was beautiful. She had a way of putting clothes together, and an elegance and grace in the way she wore them, that made even the most ordinary clothes look better. A fraction of an inch less than six feet tall in her bare feet, she had wavy light brown hair that reached nearly to her elbows. She had the strong chin and jaw and prominent cheekbones that show up across generations in the Taylor family, and she had great big, almost blue eyes. She waited at the gate with her arm draped casually over the shoulder of John, her shorter, potbellied, balding boyfriend, the one for whom she had dropped out of college to "live in sin." Slightly more respectable on account of being married, Mike and I in no way conformed to what my parents would have considered proper attire for a young married couple. Seen everywhere now, in 1972 jeans and T-shirts were a generational and political marker.

Mother and Daddy stepped off the plane dressed in clothes they might have worn to church except for Mother's walking shoes. Her polyester suit traveled well. She clutched her large leather purse tightly under her arm. A travel bag hung over one shoulder. Daddy carried another bag, the camera, and the luggage claim checks. They greeted us through a blur of exhaustion. The smell of patchouli tangled with a faint scent of Tabu and the stale odors of the smoky, cramped airplane. Mother looked slightly disoriented and a shade wary. There was an awkwardness. "You must be tired," I said, trying to find a safe name for the distance between us. She frowned.

"We're worn out," she said. "We just ran and ran the whole trip."

"Did you have a good time?"

"It was a good trip," Daddy said.

"But not one that gave us any rest," Mother added. They both looked bone weary, but who wouldn't be after such a long journey? Still, Daddy strode through the airport with his usual commanding style, organizing the other travelers and making sure all the right bags got into all the right hands.

Over the next five days, Mother never slept. At the end of that time, she was beside herself—exhausted, agitated, suspicious, and delusional. The psychiatrist Daddy contacted made arrangements to admit her to Our Lady of Peace, a Louisville hospital for the mentally ill.

At the time she was admitted, Mother knew something was dreadfully wrong. She told the examining doctor, "My motor is racing away inside of me and I cannot slow it down. I may look calm on the outside, but I'm feeling very, very uncomfortable inside myself." She explained to the doctor that she was being tested by God, her husband, and the doctor. Her troubles had started, she believed, on the trip to Southeast Asia, where she got so tired she did not know what to do and became quite aggravated by the fact that she was not permitted to rest but was pressed and pushed to go all the time. Her husband's work, she explained, was an added source of stress. The case history recorded by Dr. Hayes describes the shock she felt when she returned to Kentucky and our cheerful welcome. The report states that her daughters had adopted a "quasi-hippie way of life" with men who are "unkempt, unclean and not very appetizing to look at." The shock of seeing us, she told the doctor, was more than she could emotionally bear.

When I read the doctor's report, twenty-eight years after it was written, I felt as if I held in my hands at last tangible evidence of the fear shared by nearly all children of emotionally disturbed or mentally ill parents. I had made my mother crazy. I had done it. After all, wasn't I always on hand just at the moment she cracked? Now here it was at last, written in the doctor's own notes. She had taken one look at my sister and me in all our heedless glory and plunged off the deep end.

I know, of course, that I did not make my mother crazy. But deep in my heart I also know that I did. That we all did. That the whole family was a part of the web of need and demand that was sometimes more than her fragile self could bear. For years of my adult life, I had a recurrent dream about my mother. I dreamed that I had called her on the phone to tell her something about myself. But when she got on the line she was not the loving, welcoming mother I had expected. Instead, she would scream at me in fury until I finally managed to awaken, shaken, from the nightmare mother of my dreams. For me, her manic bouts were always, on a terrifying primal level, abandonments.

Although Mother was able to give the doctor accurate information about person, place and time, her state of mind was obviously precarious. The doctor noted "evidence of suspiciousness and some delusional material and the lack of clearly interpreting the data that is being discussed. There is a suspicion of some hallucinations." The passive voice conceals the source of the suspicions, but I imagine they were shared by anyone who talked to her for long.

Mother was indeed delusional. One nurse was so kind and loving to her that Mother became convinced that this middle-aged black woman was actually me in disguise. She invited the nurse to sit in her lap, and, God bless her, that nurse sat right down and put her arms around Mother's neck. The room, Mother knew, was bugged. She knew she was being tested by God, the hospital, the doctors. But at least some of the nurses were her buddies.

Mother remained in the hospital for thirty-five days. She turned fifty-one there. She celebrated her birthday without me, and I celebrated mine without her. I was sick with worry and fear. If mothers could fall through the air into insanity, then the world was a much more dangerous place than I had imagined. Somehow I had reached the age of twenty-one with a largely unexamined but profoundly American belief in progress. Life

49

was always, I had thought until that spring, unfolding into something more wonderful than what had gone before. Getting older and going to college had gotten me out of Somerset and so offered some limited support for this naive hypothesis. Mother had been noticeably sick for four years. But somehow, perhaps largely because of my adolescent self-absorption, I had thought she was gradually getting better. We were all, all of us, always getting better, smarter, stronger, growing up, moving forward, achieving goals. But now, my faith in a line of progress was shattered. There was no way I could believe that Mother was improving when she was locked in a hospital unable to tell the difference between me and a middle-aged black nurse. I plunged into a conviction that life not only didn't get better and better every day but that it got worse.

We learned that Mother's illness had a name: manic depression. Moving in the closest rhythm to hers that I could manage, I became depressed myself. I hummed hymns to myself, but they had lost the power to comfort. I prayed but doubted anyone was listening. If God wasn't going to make my mother whole again, what good was God?

My mild-mannered and amiably passive husband became a source of irritation. Why didn't he know anything? Why couldn't he do anything? Why did I have to decide everything? As I lost the ability to make decisions myself, I came to feel as if I were adrift in a leaking boat. The kind, gentle, good-humored man in question had seemed to me a perfectly fine husband when I was feeling strong and in control and when my mother, not incidentally, was watching my back. Now I could no longer decide what I wanted to eat, where I wanted to eat it, or even, at times, why I should bother to eat at all. I could scarcely admit to myself that I was also beginning to have real doubts about my marriage, about my life, about God. Wouldn't this be a good time for God to show up and start talking to me? I both longed for and didn't expect such an event.

Vernon Mallow, my beloved world religion teacher at Georgetown College, understood my dilemma. In his survey of world religions he manifested a respect for the many faces and forms of the sacred that differed starkly from the bright, cold lines separating the saved from the damned in Southern Baptist theology. His kind eyes crinkled with a gentle smile as we talked, over endless cups of coffee, about what we did or didn't, could or couldn't, believe. He had the kind, warm countenance I associated with people of deep faith, and yet he refused to tie that faith to a particular church's creed. He and his wife had moved to the country and built the house they lived in with their own four hands. Lifelong Baptists, they quit going to church. Asked why, Dr. Mallow smilingly explained, "We've outgrown it."

I thought I had, too. Organized religion had been and often remained on the wrong side of too many conflicts and issues. I decided God was bigger than any single church, or even any single religion, and couldn't really be contained by these all too human institutions.

I both yearned for and could no longer bring myself to believe in a God who was the magic fix-it man in the sky. When my mother plunged into mental illness, I had to ask myself where God was, how God's will could possibly be manifested through such heartbreak and pain, and why my prayers didn't seem to change anything. These were aspects of an age-old question, of course: Why does God allow bad things to happen to good people? I thought perhaps it would be easier to give up altogether on the notion of God. Except, of course, I couldn't. Jesus was not so easy to shake. He had often been critical of organized religion. He kept showing up on the side of the folks at the margin, the ones the church and society deemed unworthy. I kept talking to him, all the while wondering if he was listening.

Mother gradually calmed down. As the racing slowed, she went through a period of incredible lucidity and said things to us that she would never have said without the falling away of boundaries that can characterize this illness. "Eldred needs to slow down and quit working so hard and spend more time with me," she announced during one of my visits. "He needs to realize that Jesus Christ, not Eldred Taylor, came to save Somerset, Kentucky." Astonished as I was to hear her say such a thing, I had to agree.

After more than a month, Mother came home. She spent the next ninety days on a powerful mix of antipsychotic medications.

Mother continued to cycle in and out of manic phases for the rest of her life. But the diagnosis and medications gradually liberated her from the most devastating results of these cycles. Anyone who knew her well could learn to recognize the speeding up into mania in its earliest stages. What felt at first like a fabulous burst of energy and creativity deteriorated within a few days into anxiety, paranoia, and delusion. Daddy would implore her to start her medication as soon as the cycle began. For a decade, she stubbornly refused until the manic phase reached its disastrous height. In those first heady days, she was convinced she didn't need or want the medicine, whose side effects included a thick-tongued sluggishness and slowness of thought that was the unpleasant opposite of the creative zest with which the manic phase announced itself. But gradually she accepted the fact that starting the medication could drastically shorten the duration of the mania.

Once she began to comply with her treatment, the illness ceased to incapacitate her. Over a twenty-five-year period, Daddy continued to chart each manic cycle. He had the records to prove that you could manage this illness if you paid careful attention and followed the rules.

"Deo fisus labora" was the motto of William Jewell, the college where my parents did most of their undergraduate work. "Trust in God and work." It was a motto he lived by.

6

What'll I Do with All My Dreams of You?

My mother's illness affected me deeply and in ways I scarcely understood. I blamed her difficulties on the demands and constraints of her marriage. She was a splendidly creative and brilliant woman trapped in a high-pressure and isolating role. Her brilliance, it seemed to me, was mostly spent shoring up my father and helping him advance his work. I resolved that I must find a way to work that was my own. I did not want to emulate her role of helpmeet.

The second wave of feminism was flowering. I remember holding in my hands the first issue of *Ms. Magazine* and the first newsprint copy of *Our Bodies/Ourselves.* Women's liberation we called it then. Women's roles, the possibilities for women, rigidly narrow throughout my 1950s era childhood, were now in a period of exciting transition and expansion. Not surprisingly, I viewed Mother's difficulties through the lens of some of these ideas.

Life was harder than I had expected and more filled with loss and disappointment than I had imagined. As Mike and I entered our last year of college, we began to worry about what to do after graduation. Neither of us had anything approaching a plan. We talked for a time of becoming Montessori teachers, of living in the country, perhaps in some sort of commune. Each plan was more impractical than the one that preceded it. None had any relationship to our interests or abilities.

God, I had once thought, was going to open a path for me, show me what the next step should be. Now we stared into the dark with no idea of which way to go. I wished, irrationally, that the husband I had chosen for his amiable passivity would sprout a new personality, one that could blaze a path for us. He, too, began to feel frustrated. Abruptly that autumn he moved out of our apartment, explaining to me that he needed a trial separation while he tried to find himself.

The night he moved out, we drove together to a party in Lexington. When I was ready to go home, I found that he had left without me. I hitched a ride with a friend and felt the weight of my new solitary location in the world.

The next morning I awakened early and traveled back to Lexington to take the GRE (a standardized test required for graduate admission). Urged on by some of my professors, I was preparing applications to graduate school, plans I was determined to pursue despite the unraveling of my marriage.

Even in the midst of my early feelings of loneliness and abandonment, I felt an immense relief. It was as if the marriage had been a force pulling me off center, away from a knowledge of who I was and what I wanted. It was as if I had been living someone else's life. I knew, within days of Mike's departure, that this was no trial separation.

I worried about how my parents would react when they learned that my marriage had failed. Nervously, I told them just before Thanksgiving and felt their shock and hurt crackle over the telephone. I waited for them to invite me home for Thanksgiving, and when they did not my feelings of abandonment redoubled. I moped around and made plans to eat turkey with a friend until she told me I was being a goose and encouraged me to let Mother and Daddy know I wanted to be with them for the holiday. They immediately urged me to come, of course, despite their sadness and inability to imagine what might have gone so wrong with my marriage that it could have led to divorce.

I lived through a dark time. I invented explanations for what had gone wrong: We were too young, he was too passive, we weren't intellectually compatible, he wasn't a reader, I was too independent, there were no sexual fireworks.

I wondered, in my journal, if perhaps I wasn't the marrying kind. Wouldn't it be easier, I wrote, to live in a world of women? Wouldn't it be easier to be a lesbian? Even here I did not yet admit that I had begun having dreams of making love with women.

I still wanted to believe what my mother had told me. Someday my prince would come. The right man was out there somewhere. I just had to find him. Or better still, ask God to direct me to him. When I found him, I would know.

In 1975, I thought I knew, and I married again. Another kind, gentle man. Bill was quiet but stubborn, certainly not passive. A big reader, too. Raised Baptist, but he wore it lightly. He was a long, tall Texan, skinny as a beanpole. Six feet two inches tall, he didn't quite weigh 150 pounds. He wore cowboy boots for every occasion. I met him at the University Baptist Church, the most progressive Baptist church I could find in Austin, where I had moved to begin a doctoral program in performance studies at The University of Texas.

Bill hailed from West Texas, from Abilene. An only child, the son of the service manager at a Buick dealership and a schoolteacher, he enjoyed conversation but was not accustomed to the competitive conversational rules in my family, where you got the floor by interrupting or overlapping whenever the speaker seemed about to pause for breath. The first time I took him home, he couldn't figure out how to enter the conversation. "Bill has something he wants to say," I had to announce, in order to get everyone to slow down long enough to let him speak.

He loved his native state. Once I mentioned that a Greek friend of mine wrote a column for a newspaper published for Greek expatriates. "That's interesting," said Bill. "If I was living in another country, I wouldn't expect to find a newspaper published just for Texans."

"Bill," I replied, "I don't know how to break this to you, but Texas is your state. Your country is the United States of America." It turns out I was the one who needed to be set straight. Bill launched into a quick summary of the salient facts about Texas: its ten miles of offshore rights, its gross domestic product, which was larger than that of most countries, its land mass, its oil holdings. Those Texans are a breed apart and proud of it.

I knew I did not feel passionate about Bill, but he was a great friend to me. We rode bicycles together, jogged around Town Lake, ate Mexican food. Just finishing a master's degree in electrical engineering, he helped me find my way around the enormous university, introduced me to nachos at Scholz's Beer Garten, and taught me the Texas two-step. Romance wore off eventually, I told myself. Companionship was what mattered.

We planned a June wedding, a simple one with just close friends and family. We would marry under two big live-oak trees beside Onion Creek in the hill country outside Austin.

But in April Mother went into the hospital for emergency gallbladder surgery. The surgeon sewed her up without exploring the common duct that connects the gallbladder to the stomach and now connected the liver to the stomach. She had, in her words, sailed through the operation with flying colors, but she failed to get any better. As it turned out, the common duct was blocked by a large gallstone, and eight days after the first surgery she had to have another. The prospect of a second operation terrified her. In the hallway outside the operating room, she gripped Daddy's hand and muttered over and over through clenched teeth, "Pray. We have to pray." He hoped he was not seeing what he knew he was seeing: the onset of a manic episode.

After the second surgery, Mother began to improve physically, but her mental condition deteriorated. I flew up to lend a hand.

I didn't want to go. My wedding was only four weeks away. I had a lot to do to get ready, and I was just ending a semester of graduate study. I could not really afford the plane ticket and, most of all, I didn't want to be the one who always came to Mother's rescue. My sister lived only ninety minutes away. I wished it could be her this time. But she was working and had no vacation days available, plus she drove an old clunker that probably couldn't make the trip. And there was more. Jeannie simply didn't feel the need I felt to rush to Mother's side. My father, of course, was right there in the house with her. He would do his best. But I felt then, as I had felt over and over during those years, that if I didn't show up she would not get the care she needed.

She was walking around by the time I arrived, and her color looked good. But she was agitated and anxious. She spoke to me rapidly, excitedly, telling the story of what had happened and then telling it again, using almost the same words. She complained that she was having trouble sleeping. Within a few hours of my arrival, what limited hold she had on herself gave way.

Soon she was telling me in ominous and conspiratorial tones that the house was bugged and she was being spied on. She laughed strangely, and then her face grew dark. "Satanic," she spat out. "It's satanic." It was both terrifying and heartbreaking to see my mother in the midst of one of these psychotic breaks. I had no notion of how to comfort her. Yet I wanted with all my being to love her back to safety. I felt as if it was not only her mind but also her heart that was breaking. When the ground opened up beneath her feet and she entered free fall, the earth seemed to open beneath my feet as well. And yet, of course, it didn't. Since I was somehow miraculously still standing in the midst of this earthquake and, at least as it seemed to me, no one understood her pain as I did, I felt I ought to be able to pull her back from that abyss, to hold her tight so she would not fall. Yet I could not. I did what I could. I cooked meals. I sat with her. I waited while the medicine gradually brought her down from the delusional heights of her latest manic cycle.

When my parents arrived at my wedding three weeks later, Mother looked and acted very much like herself. But she was still heavily medicated, weak, and shaky. Daddy performed the ceremony, and the two lingered long enough to join us for our picnic lunch. Mother talked less than normal, but she was often shy in large groups. Daddy seemed a bit distracted. I was relieved and happy that they could be with us, although I tried not to notice the heroic effort their presence required of them. I needed to believe that my quest was finally over, that everything from now on would be a happily-ever-after epilogue.

Daddy signed the marriage license and prepared to leave. They wanted to get on the road before the day got away from them. He pulled me close to him as we said good-bye and whispered in my ear, "Now you're going to try real hard this time, aren't you?" What did I say in reply? I remember his words, and the way I flinched and recoiled when he said them, but I don't remember my own. Perhaps I smiled through gritted teeth and said yes, of course, I would. Inside I seethed at the reminder of the first failed marriage, at the implication that it was my lack of trying that had caused it to fail. That hug felt like poison, mixed, as it was, with advice, instruction, accusation.

They drove away, and I was not sorry to see them go. My friends and I changed into swimsuits and one by one swung out on a thick rope over Onion Creek and dropped into the water. We rinsed the sweat from the hot Texas sun right off. The freedom to turn a wedding ceremony into a raucous frolic in the creek exhilarated me.

With that swim, I felt as if I were somehow washing off the constraints of my tightly controlled childhood, the dully reiterative weddings I had watched again and again during those years, and the impossible expectations of my disappointed parents. I swung out over the creek and baptized myself into a newer, freer life. Or so I hoped. Of course, it never could have turned out to be as free or simple as it felt on that golden June afternoon as we whooped and shouted and celebrated by jumping out of the hot air into the icy creek.

That marriage lasted seven years.

Three years into it, as soon as I had finished writing my qualifying exams and begun work on my dissertation, we decided to start a family. I wanted a baby more than anything. From the moment we began trying to conceive, I gave myself over to elaborate fantasies of my life with this desperately wanted child. From one menstrual period to the next, I lived in a state of wild anticipation, thinking constantly about the new life that might begin, that perhaps had already begun, to grow inside me. When my period was late, as it was three times during the next few months, my excitement grew wilder and bolder with each passing day. Each time my hopes were dashed I plunged into a despair that was the negative image of my brilliant dreams.

I wondered if there were women who could try to get pregnant without thinking too much about it. There must be, but I could not imagine how such a state of indifference could be achieved. I figured if there was a polar opposite to the concept of detachment presented in Eastern religions such as Buddhism I was that opposite personified. Or perhaps Mother was the perfect embodiment of that opposite, and I was her daughter, the girl who had learned from her exhilarating example how to lean right into each emotional shift with all your might. It was an exhausting way to live but not nearly as exhausting as what was coming next.

After more than six months of this riot of emotions, I did become pregnant. The pregnancy ended almost as soon as it began at about seven weeks. Three months later I conceived again. Just past the two-month mark, the doctor heard the baby's heartbeat. The baby was due in December, a few days before my husband's Christmas Eve birthday. "The heartbeat is a really good sign that you're going to make it with this one," the doctor told me. "If you can get through the next three weeks, we can start to relax."

I left the doctor's office and drove immediately to the fabric store to stock up on material and patterns for maternity clothes. Living seemed to me to have a heightened purpose now that my body contained my life and one other. Eating and sleeping, even breathing, took on a much greater significance, an element of altruism. By caring for myself, I was caring for a precious new life. Taking a nap became virtuous. The imperative to amount to something, to contribute to the world, to make a difference seemed suddenly and simply answered just by being.

Nevertheless, it wasn't going to be long before I would need something else to wear. I pulled out a pattern and got busy. By the time my husband came home from work that day, I had the first dress cut out and ready to sew. By the next afternoon, I was hemming it.

Forty-eight hours after my doctor visit, I started to bleed. The miscarriage proceeded by fits and starts over a harrowing and painful four days. For three nights, I hemorrhaged. Each morning the cramping and bleeding would subside, and the doctor kept thinking the spontaneous abortion (as they call these events) was complete and I would not need further treatment. Each night the miscarriage would resume. If actual labor feels any more painful than that, I cannot imagine why anyone ever agrees to give birth to a second child. Eventually I landed in the operating room at Baptist Hospital and then back home again. The sorrow that took hold of me that Memorial Day weekend was again inversely proportional to my earlier joy.

Sorrow gripped me throughout the summer. My mother understood the enormous sense of loss that engulfed me. She sang to me the World War II era song that had run through her mind again and again the summer after her first daughter was stillborn.

> *What'll I do*
> *With all*
> *My dreams of you*
> *That won't come true?*
> *What'll I do?*

Mother couldn't take away my sorrow, but she plumbed its depths with her song. My sister and my friends tried to assure me that it was for the best, that miscarriages are nature's way of clearing up mistakes. But Mother understood that it was not a tragedy I was dreaming of but a beautiful and perfect baby.

If Bill had not ridden his bicycle no-hands down a steep hill and across a pothole one August morning, I don't know when my despair might have ended. But when he limped home dragging his bent bicycle, his body covered in bruises and scrapes, two ribs and a cheekbone broken, I could see I had work to do. At the hospital, they found the fractures on the X-rays and asked me to decide whether his left cheek looked noticeably flatter. It was flatter, I told them, and they operated. As I pureed meals for him to suck through his wired jaw, I abruptly recovered a sense of myself as an agent in the world.

Once he was back on his feet, I set about writing the first draft of my doctoral dissertation. My research compared narrative strategies in fiction and film. During the next nine months, I wrote, rewrote, and defended the dissertation. Bill, by this time, was working full time as an electrical engineer in Dallas. I commuted between Austin and Dallas for my last year of graduate classes and then more occasionally in the two years during which I researched and wrote my dissertation. Bill liked his job at Texas Utilities, and he loved his state. He was not interested in moving. I contacted every university in the area, shopping my new credentials around. Eagerly I sent my application to a college in the region with a tenure-track position that closely fit my qualifications. I received a letter informing me that the school had completed its search and made the "penultimate" decision. Good thing I don't have to teach there, I thought, they're too ignorant to know the meaning of the word *penulti-mate*. But I was worried. I had labored to earn this degree, even traveling between cities when my husband's job took us to Dallas. Now here I sat, weeks away from graduation, with no job prospects. I hated Dallas. There, it seemed to me, every woman wore her weight in jewelry and plastered herself with makeup. I was certain this could never be my world.

One day my dissertation director asked about my job search.

"I don't know. I can't find anything in the Dallas area. Bill won't let me apply for anything outside of Texas."

He arched an exceedingly skeptical eyebrow at me. "He won't LET you?" he asked, in his most disgusted baritone.

I traveled home that night prepared to tell Bill I was going on the job market and if I found a job he could come with me or not but I could not be dissuaded. As it happened, I caught him after a bad day at the office. "Just find a job someplace where there are opportunities for electrical engineers," he said, "and I'll come with you." Immediately, I expanded my job search.

I found out about a position at DePaul University in Chicago for which I was uniquely suited. I sent my credentials, was called almost immediately, and received the job offer the day after the interview. Bill, meanwhile, had reason to believe that his prospects for work in Chicago were bright. And so by the time I graduated it was settled that we would relocate.

But we still had no baby on the way. The world seemed to be filled to bursting with pregnant women. They were everywhere I looked. They waddled around with expressions of smug self-satisfaction. They patted and stroked their rounding bellies. They wore tacky maternity tops with the word "Baby" and an arrow pointing down. They filled the obstetrician/gynecologist's office nearly to bursting, crowding out the childless women seeking pap smears and delaying the doctors with their unscheduled deliveries. I wanted to smack them all. The ones who got pregnant the first time they tried could never restrain themselves from announcing it. "Who asked?" I wanted to snarl. "Don't tell me." Why did they think this made them special? I wondered. Couldn't they rise above this mindless celebration of gender roles? "So what does that make you?" I wanted to ask. "A fertility goddess? Superfeminine? A real woman?" The self-satisfied giggles were grating beyond words. I bit back the curses that popped into my mouth and offered congratulations. I smiled. I held the tiny babies who kept showing up in everyone's life but ours and sniffed their warm fuzzy heads. Their tiny fingers curled around my large one. I tried not to bridle at the oft-repeated suggestion that my husband and I needed to just relax and open a bottle of wine or maybe even plan to adopt and then we would find ourselves pregnant when we least expected it. It seemed that everybody who had ever had a baby was a fertility expert.

Once we were settled in our new home in Chicago, I consulted a physician who actually was a fertility expert. Under her care, after intrusive tests and with the help of a fertility drug, I became pregnant. Before I knew I was pregnant, I knew I was in enormous pain. The first thing I felt was something like a little pinch one afternoon. That evening, the pinch turned into something that roared through my abdomen with a fury. It was just a few days after my thirty-first birthday. We rushed to the emergency room at Northwestern University Hospital, where the first thing they did was administer a pregnancy test. When it came back positive, we wanted to celebrate, but I felt like hell and the young intern looked more worried than pleased. Because I was pregnant, the strongest painkiller he could prescribe was Tylenol. With the diagnosis of a bladder infection, he added an antibiotic. Four miserable days passed before the doctors realized that this pregnancy was ectopic (implanted in a fallopian tube instead of the uterus) and performed the surgery that ended the life-threatening condition and our latest hopes for a child.

After four years of trying, I had managed only three failed pregnancies, each more painful and traumatic than the last. I began to ask myself how much of my life I was willing to spend on expensive and emotionally draining fertility treatments. I ceased to believe they would ever work. I grew weary of planning my life around a pregnancy that never came. I became impatient with the temperature charts, the frequent doctor visits, the carefully timed sex life.

One night Bill and I sat in a circle in someone's living room, participating in a support group for couples with infertility sponsored by a group called RESOLVE (Resolve what? I wondered). I was growing impatient with the other couples, who had not yet wavered in their focus on a future in which baby made three. The social worker asked what we wanted to be if we were not going to be parents. My answer came to me in a rush. "I want to be a character," I said emphatically. In Kentucky, we had always pronounced eccentrics, self-directed individuals, and anyone with a big personality as "a character." "She's a character" was delivered with a mixture of approval and wonderment. As soon as I said it, I realized that I had always wanted, had always intended, to be a character. Perhaps I would not go to China and save the world like Lottie Moon, but surely I could be something more than the sleepwalking wife and would-be mother I felt I had become. "You already are a character," one of my fellows in disappointment assured me with a laugh, and the others agreed. But I looked around at these crestfallen couples and knew that they were wrong. They bored me. I didn't like talking about my sorrows with these bland, sad souls, the women all speaking a language of loss that mostly eluded their befuddled husbands. I was certain their notion of what constituted a character set the bar way too low. If I were really a character, I would not be sitting here. This ordinary, conventional life I found myself slipping into was not going to be nearly enough consolation without children to distract and comfort me. I had not even begun to be the character I wanted to be. I was sitting on myself, trying to fit myself into a life pattern that was not working because it was not mine.

I left that support group at the end of the evening never to return. The truth is, the character I was dead set on becoming had already begun to have her say. Over the next few weeks, she abruptly arrived, and just like that my marriage was over and I was a lesbian.

7

Crashing Out

In my family, homosexuality was utterly, unmentionably beyond the pale. Perhaps Daddy thought it a sin so uncommon in Somerset that he need not preach against it. Mother believed that with the destruction of Sodom and Gomorrah God eradicated such perversion once and for all. She was shocked, in the sixties, to find a reference to male homosexuals in *Newsweek,* an indication that Sodom and Gomorrah hadn't eliminated the problem after all. Still, she took comfort in the notion that women would never do anything like "that."

When I cast back for my earliest awareness of homosexuality, I find a sharp memory of blundering into this forbidden territory—in an encounter with our church secretary—when I was about eight. Lillian Vaughn was a "maiden lady" slightly older than my parents who lived with and cared for her widowed mother. She must have been in her forties at the time but seemed simultaneously girlish and ancient.

My father could not resist teasing her about her mortal terror of snakes. She parted her softly curled gray hair and pinned it off her forehead with a barrette. At the first drop of rain, she and her mother covered their hair with plastic rain hats, the fold-up type distributed by the funeral home that could be tucked in their purses in plastic envelopes smaller

64

than a credit card. Her thin, straight legs stuck out from the bottom of the shirtwaist dresses she favored. She often wore fine-gauge cardigans against the cold of the air conditioner fastened about the neck with pearled clips on a little chain. During services, she and her mom sat on the second row so when anyone came forward during the invitation she could whip to the front and collect data for the church files. Along with her clipboard and an ample supply of new members' cards, she carried her Bible, a clean handkerchief tucked inside. An air of perfect innocence and dedicated godliness enveloped her.

Because of the size of the congregation, we hired a second secretary, Edith Killip, from the Kentucky Baptist Building in Louisville. She, too, was unmarried and had years of secretarial experience. Much more the city girl than Miss Vaughn, Edith Killip was businesslike and assertive, with a ready laugh and buckteeth. She wore tweedy tailored clothes and sensible shoes. When she joined the staff at First Baptist, Lillian Vaughn was delighted. The two women took to each other, developing what looked to me like serious mutual admiration. I thought they had chemistry.

One day Mother and I were standing between the church and the parsonage talking to them. They were swapping compliments, each praising the work and fine points of the other, smiling and laughing. I slid along the rail next to the church basement steps, hanging upside down and clambering around in a series of gravity-defying maneuvers. Suddenly I chimed in: "You two are so crazy about each other, I think maybe you should just get married."

All three adults froze.

My mother threw me a sharp look. I felt acute embarrassment along with a sense of confusion about what had suddenly gone wrong. Mother briskly retorted that Lillian and Edith had no interest in marrying one another, then smoothly changed the subject and within a few moments brought our visit to a screeching halt.

During my senior year in high school, I found a play entitled *Tea and Sympathy,* in which a young man who fears he might be gay is helped by an older married woman to discover that he in fact is—big sigh of relief— safely heterosexual. That is the first literary reference to homosexuality I can remember.

I crashed out of the closet when I was thirty-one years old. I suppose

I should have seen it coming, but I didn't. The whole experience left me flabbergasted and so disoriented that for several months I even had trouble reading. I would hold books and stare at them, my eyes passing over each word, registering nothing. I would begin again only to find a few moments later that my eyes were absorbing words but my mind was blank. I felt in my new life this curious mixture of familiarity and estrangement, as if I had arrived home at last only to discover that I had never had a chance to learn my mother tongue.

Perhaps I shouldn't have been so utterly surprised. There were those dreams. I recognized that I was sometimes attracted to women. But I thought everybody was. I thought we were all really bisexual and I just had the guts to admit it.

In college, a lot of my friends were gay men, several so closeted that I did not realize they were gay until after we graduated. One of my dearest friends was bisexual. Ray had dated women at college, including one in particular whom he later married, but during his senior year a story began circulating on campus that he was involved with a man. The fellow who started the rumor was himself closeted. My friend didn't talk to me about what was going on, but I could see that he was heavyhearted. I decided to talk to him. As we walked across campus one day, I repeated to him what I had heard. "I'm not asking you to tell me whether this is true or not unless you want to talk about it," I said. "I just want you to know that you are my friend, and I trust you completely." He squeezed my hand, and his eyes held tears not quite spilling over. "Here's what I said to the person who told me this story," I told him. "Ray is my friend, and I don't care who he's fucking. I don't care if he's fucking chickens. I'm sure whatever he's doing he's thought it through very carefully." Ray roared with delight at this preposterous barnyard image. For a moment, the darkness lifted from his beautiful, sad face. My words of comfort sound crude to me now, but at the time they broke through my friend's despair and sense of betrayal, so they seemed to both of us exactly right.

I did not think same-sex love was a problem. I thought love was good. I thought people should be free to love whomever they choose. When I wondered in my journal whether my life wouldn't be a whole lot easier if I were a lesbian, I thought the question more a complaint about the sorry state of my encounters with men than a true expression of my own desires. Perhaps it's hard to imagine now, but in the fifties and sixties a girl could grow into adulthood without having a clear sense of who moved her most.

When I was thirty-one, I became friends with a lesbian at the university. In the same month in which I had surgery for my tubal pregnancy, she had an emergency appendectomy. We were acquaintances but did not know each other well. We started out commiserating about our operations. Everyone else had grown bored with the subject. As time passed, we found much more to talk about. Eventually, I realized that my heart was beating faster whenever she was in the room. I would walk out of my way in the hope that I would bump into her on campus and we could go to a nearby café for more talk.

She invited me to join her at a Meg Christian concert. I had never heard of this lesbian folksinger, but I went along. As we stood outside waiting for the house to open, I realized the line was made up almost entirely of women. I eagerly studied the crowd. My friend looked at the cars rolling slowly past us, their drivers craning their necks at the snaking line of concertgoers. She exhaled a big breath of cigarette smoke. "This is always my favorite part," she said with a cynical smile. "Dykes on parade." At the concert, Meg Christian sang songs that were specifically about and addressed to lesbians. In "Leaping Lesbians," she parodied the homophobic belief that lesbians were lying in wait to seduce any heterosexuals who crossed their paths. The crowd roared with laughter. I looked around the room and felt strangely comforted and simultaneously amazed at the presence of a world that had never been visible to me.

When I could no longer bear the level of sexual tension, I told this woman I was attracted to her. She drove me to a seedy little gay bar named His and Hers tucked under the el tracks near Wrigley Field. We sat in a dark corner on a Sunday afternoon. We ordered a couple of scotches. She lit a cigarette.

"So," she said, on a long exhale. "We're going to get in trouble together?"

"Yes," I replied, with absolutely no notion of how much trouble we might be talking about. She leaned over and kissed me, long and slow and deep, and I kissed her back, kissed her as if my life depended on it.

Until that moment, I thought the two of us were going to have an affair. I wanted to touch her more than I had ever wanted to touch anyone. And I somehow imagined that I could touch her and then go on with my marriage after what I suppose I believed was going to be a spicy little interlude.

My marriage had stalled in an endless cycle of fertility treatments. Bill coped with his own sense of loss by working more and more. As I had grown in confidence and independence with my new job, the balance of power in our relationship had shifted a bit, and we had drifted farther and farther apart. It was with such thoughts that I explained to myself the staleness of the marriage.

But after that kiss I knew my life had changed utterly, profoundly, and irrevocably. I had kissed, dated, and even married men who were considerate and capable lovers. I had had some truly enjoyable times. But I had never felt anything like this. That kiss went all over me. It made me want to shout hallelujah, and it made me want to cry from sheer joy at the enormity of what I was feeling and from utter sorrow at all the lies that had kept this moment from me for so long. I was utterly thrilled and absolutely horrified. For I now knew, without a shred of doubt, that I was a lesbian through and through, and this was a conversion experience just as sure as I was born.

Within three weeks, I left my husband. I bought a poster with a print of Georgia O'Keeffe's *Study in Grey*. I had wanted the print the first time I saw it, but my husband rejected it on the grounds that it looked too much like a woman's genitalia.

On those same grounds, I now hung it on my bedroom wall.

I thought my prince had really and truly come this time except that she was a tall, handsome, dark-haired, wickedly funny woman. She had been out since she was thirteen. That she was now only twenty-four, had not quite completed her BA, had no job, drank too much, chain-smoked cigarettes, gave conflicting accounts about both her past and most recent whereabouts, none of this mattered. I, who had never been able to abide the smell of cigarette smoke, now found it sexy when she lit up right after we made love. When we walked down the street together, carefully not holding hands, but with shoulders touching, I felt a current run between us. We were a pair of something wonderful and mighty. I felt we were unstoppable. I felt alive, electric, invincible.

I was in love, and in some ways I was like a teenager who had just discovered sex, passion, love, and all the rest. At last I understood what all the fuss was about, why people turn their whole lives upside down and inside out for the sake of desire.

Without such intense feelings, I never would have made that leap. I had married in good faith, but I could not stay married knowing what I now knew. I understood at last that my discontent in my marriages came not from choosing the wrong man but from choosing a man at all. Grief at the end of my marriage and sorrow for the pain I was putting my husband through were real, but they were mitigated by my certainty about the changes I was making. For the first time in my life, making love felt like coming home. It felt spiritual and healthy and natural—everything society told me it could not be. The contrast between my experience and the beliefs of my family and much of society was profound and profoundly disorienting. I had entered a world in which what I knew for certain to be true, right, and natural was seen by much of the rest of the world as false, abnormal, and deviant. I was scared about how my family would respond and uncertain about whether I would be able to keep my job (not yet tenured, I was working at a Catholic university where crashing out of the closet does not typically enhance your tenurability). But I was unwavering about who I had become and how I must live.

I told my parents about the separation and impending divorce right away, but I kept the news of my new love to myself. Or at least I tried to. My parents and I had always talked on the phone once a week and exchanged frequent letters. I'm sure I talked about my new friend frequently and with much too much enthusiasm. But I didn't name the relationship or share with them what I had discovered about myself.

I had thought my first divorce might kill my parents. Of course, they had surprised me by surviving, but that, I could easily see, had been nothing compared to this. I felt protective of them, especially my mother. I would have to tell them eventually, but I decided to take some time to get my bearings. I started therapy, where my major topic was how in heaven's name I was ever going to disclose what had happened in my life.

I hadn't counted on my mother's intuitive powers. She became increasingly worried about me and began having troublesome dreams. I believe it was in one of those dreams that she first learned that I was a lesbian.

Right after Christmas, seven months after I had left my husband, my parents came for a visit. We spent three days together. I was happy to see them but nervous about how it would go. I spent some time de-dyking my tiny one-bedroom apartment, removing any telltale book titles from the shelves and stripping revealing buttons or stickers from my bulletin board and refrigerator door. One evening my girlfriend joined us for dinner. I had told them that she would probably be moving in with me. I had presented this move as motivated by practical and economic considerations. This story I expected them to swallow despite the fact that the apartment had only one bedroom containing one double bed.

At my dinner party, no one felt comfortable. My father asked my "roommate" what church she had grown up in. In Kentucky, this is a common getting-acquainted question, like asking someone what sort of work they do. She almost choked on her iced tea as she sputtered out an answer: an answer that was altogether wrong. She was raised Catholic, she told them, but her family was not particularly religious. In my parents' eyes, it is hard to know what would have been worse, a Catholic who was religious (idol worshiper) or one who wasn't (infidel). After dinner, she lit a cigarette, carefully blowing the smoke out the side of her mouth and away from the table, as my parents watched in horror. When she bumped her elbow on the way into the kitchen and muttered "Jesus Christ," we all feigned obliviousness. For her part, the tablecloth, flowers, and precisely set table made her feel like an interloper. At her parents' house, everyone grabbed a paper plate and dished up their food buffet style. The men might settle down on the couch or in the La-Z-Boy recliner with their dinners and their beers to watch the ball game, while the women clustered around the picnic table in the backyard and watched the little ones run around and play. She was a first-generation college student from a working-class family, inexperienced with and disinterested in the middle-class dinner parties my family favored. Somehow we all muddled through.

The last morning of my parents' visit, my father announced that they wanted to talk to me. I felt a wave of apprehension. "Oh, let's don't do that," I said. But he persisted. "Jackie, we have always been a family that talks about our concerns with one another. Your mother has been terribly worried about you, and she has continued to have some apprehensions about you that we feel we ought to talk about together." My heart began to race. "Mother felt like we needed to ask you whether or not you are a lesbian."

I panicked. I didn't want to lie, but I didn't feel like I could take this one head-on just yet. "I wasn't expecting to talk about this today," I stammered. "I didn't expect this to come up." I barreled on, resorting to third-person generalities. "You know, women can be good friends without necessarily being lesbians."

My father looked relieved. "Yes, I know they can. Why, many of my closest friends are men. John Kruschwitz is a dear friend. He's like a brother to me."

This seemed promising. I forged ahead.

"All of my closest friends are women. I can't really foresee having an intimate relationship with a man at this point in my life. I'm really enjoying having a number of strong, wonderful women in my life. Certainly my friend and I are very close. There are no men around that I have any interest in dating, and I don't expect that there will be. I'm not sure what else to tell you. I really don't think I'm prepared to talk about this. I didn't expect it to come up today."

Daddy seemed to think he had heard an absolute denial. He looked relieved. "Well, I'm glad we talked. Marjorie just had these concerns, and we felt like we just needed to get them out in the open where we could address them. I feel a lot better now that we've had a chance to do that. Don't you feel a lot better, Marjorie?"

My mother was nobody's fool. She looked down at her hands, frowned, and began to slowly shake her head from side to side. Then she somehow managed to bring out a long, slow "Yeeeees" that ended on a rising inflection, as if it were more of a question. This qualified yes satisfied Daddy, who believed we had settled the matter to everyone's satisfaction. My mother, in contrast, knew perfectly well what had and hadn't been said. She understood that I had confirmed her fears, whether or not I was prepared to talk about it. Daddy brought our little heart-to-heart to a close, and we all said our good-byes. As they drove away, I breathed a huge sigh of relief and telephoned my therapist to schedule an extra session.

Even though I had not had the courage to talk to them about my lesbian life, I felt as if this stunted conversation had begun to dismantle the wall that had come between us.

Daddy had a conference near New York City in June, and my parents invited me to meet my mother in New York and spend five days seeing the sights.

Mother and I had a grand time. We visited the Museum of Modern Art and the Metropolitan Museum of Art, we took in the view from the top of the Empire State Building, we watched the Rockettes kick up their heels, we saw two Broadway plays, we ate well, we lived it up. I had thought that I might tell her the truth about my relationship. I even carried with me an article about parents who had learned their children were gay and had responded first with anger and grief and later with acceptance. But, although we talked and talked and talked, we somehow never managed to broach this subject.

To my letter of thanks, Mother responded with a long reply. The letter, dated July 21, 1983, contains a smudge that makes "July" almost illegible. Near the smudge, Mother added a marginal note: "This is a blot of water from my just washed hair (not a tear)." A tear? I must have thought. Whatever is coming next? She wrote of the good time we had had and of her expectation that we would have found time in New York to "really talk about the deeper experiences in our lives" but that it was for the best that we had "just plain had fun." I remember reading this and thinking, "She knows. She really knows." She hoped that soon I would "feel secure and comfortable enough to really talk openly and easily" with them about "whatever it is in your lifestyle which may be different from your past." Astonishingly, she assured me that no lectures, reprimands, or cheerful pep talks would be forthcoming. This I scarcely could believe, though I desperately wanted to. And then, most remarkably, she said this.

> Jackie, your Dad and I both want you to know we love you dearly, no matter what your way of life. . . .
>
> We know that you need companionship and friendship. We are human strugglers with you. We yearn for an adult to adult level of closeness with you. We depend on the same Grace from Jesus Christ that any struggler does. We will always be sure of his

love for you no matter what happens. He has said, "I will never leave you or forsake you."

We have freed you to be an adult long ago. We have nothing but comradeship and love for you.

I read this letter with amazement. My die-hard Southern Baptist mother had written the most loving invitation to come out I could imagine. Here I had spent a year and a half in a panic about how I would ever be able to tell them about myself only to find out that they already knew and were going to be OK with it. This was too good to be true. I spent several days writing and rewriting my reply.

I began with appreciation for the "loving invitation" to talk about my life. I had felt more myself and relaxed around them since our stilted talk at Christmas, knowing after that talk that Mother, at least, knew and loved me still. It was, of course, the fear that I might irrevocably lose my parents that had been the most terrifying. My further fear was that knowledge of my lesbian life would prove to be some sort of mortal wound. "Once I realized at Christmas that you did know, and that neither the world nor your love for me were going to cave in, I've been much more comfortable with myself and with you," I wrote.

I tried to imagine what some of their concerns might be and to address them, assuring them that I had not been coerced, that I did not hate men, that being a lesbian, while admittedly difficult, was not as hard as they might think. "Nothing," I assured them, "is as hard as trying to be someone else's idea of who you are."

I realized, of course, that the Bible and their understanding of it were at the root of the concern I was sure they felt. Naively, I thought I could reassure my seminary-educated parents with a few carefully chosen comments.

I know you . . . have always believed that homosexuality is against the teachings of the Bible. In fact, the Bible has very little to say about homosexuality and even less about lesbians. Some scholars believe that the sin for which God destroyed Sodom and Gomorrah was a lack of hospitality—whatever it was, their morality was substantially different from our own, since Lot was ready to give up his daughter to satisfy the men outside the gate.

I believe that what I am doing is natural and healthy and more right for me than anything I've done before, and so I cannot believe that God would count it as a sin. I'm living my life with integrity and love and respect for others and feel good about the spiritual dimension of my life. This may be hard for you to see right away, but I have hope that in time you'll recognize that I am happy and healthy and at peace.

I wanted to help them deal with this and somehow thought I could. I had found an article that described PFLAG (Parents, Families and Friends of Lesbians and Gays) and how affiliating with the organization had helped some parents work through their initial shock and grief. I had carried that article to Kentucky with me in the spring and again on the trip to New York but had never found the right time to share it. Now I enclosed it. We weren't a distant family. I was so happy that they wanted to let me in, that they wanted to know the real me.

I professed my love, of course, assuring them that "nothing in heaven or earth is going to change that or make either one of you less important or dear to me." I worried about them, but I hoped I could help them see that I was happy, hoped that in time they would be able to happy for me. "Please don't worry," I wrote, "I may be a stubborn cuss, but I'm more OK than you have imagined."

I mailed that letter off and nervously awaited their response. I told myself it would be OK because, after all, they had asked me to come out, they just wanted to be fellow travelers with me, and they didn't want to judge or control me. Yet I was uneasy. Nothing in our history led me to suspect coming out to them would go quite this smoothly. The days crawled by. We spoke on the phone in a stilted and off-key conversation. I worried. What were they thinking?

My parents' two replies arrived about two and a half weeks after they received my letter. My mother wrote:

> August 23, 1983
> Dear Jackie,
> . . . I don't know how or what to write. We are both deeply grieved over this choice you have made in your life. Daddy kept hoping against hope that you were leveling with us at Christmas-

time when we were there. He kept his spirits up that way. Now
he cannot speak of you or of your life without crying. We both
feel that the rest of our days are to be spent in grief and disappointment. It is incredible. It is almost unbearable.

I was flabbergasted. Where was the loving invitation to share as one fellow traveler to another? Where was the mother who just wanted to know
me? How could my letter have been incredible, unbearable, when in
truth she had known since Christmas? She continued:

We really don't want to debate with you about what code of con-
duct the Bible upholds or the moral standards found in there. In
fact, we feel this is a subject about which we prefer not to write or
talk over the phone but that it will be better to discuss it face to
face when time and opportunity affords. And even when we talk
face to face, we don't know what to say.

I saw the whiff of indignation in the initial sentence of that paragraph.
How dare I question their interpretation of the scriptures? I shuddered at
the suggestion that we needed to get together. Not yet, I thought. Not
right now. Her letter ended on a bleak note. "Right now we feel there is
no help or hope apart from God."

Tears stung my eyes. It was my mother I had counted on as my ally.
She probably had thought she could be. I swiped at my tears and looked
again at her first paragraph. It was dominated by Daddy's response. Perhaps the intensity of his shock and grief had overtaken the attitude of
acceptance she had mustered in her first letter. If this was Mother's letter,
Daddy's could only be worse.

He began almost formally, acknowledging that my letter had
confirmed what my Mother had been sure of since the previous fall and
that he had prayed was false. He thanked me for my honesty. "Your
Mother and I, with God's help, gave you life. Before you were born we
dedicated you to God." Me, too, I thought, they dedicated me to God
before I was ever born, too? The story of Samuel all over again except
now they think God delivered the wrong call. Or, rather, they're certain
the call I'm answering hasn't come from God. And how about that layer
of guilt? They (OK, God helped a little) gave me life. I'm not just a lesbian, I'm an ingrate. I read on. "You are a part of the very fiber of our lives

and we love you more than we love our own lives. That love for you is fixed in the center of our hearts and nothing can take it away." Too angry to find comfort in the assurance that his love was immutable, I fixed on his description of me as part of the very fiber of their lives. I am not, I thought defensively, one of your body parts. Next came a litany of all the pains and disappointments of my life, emphasizing how he had sorrowed with me each time (and rejoiced with me, too, but for some reason that was a shorter list). "However, with this turn in your lifestyle I do not know how I can ever understand what you have chosen to do." Now, I could see, I had moved beyond the pale of his previously long- suffering support.

He was "more deeply grieved than ever before" in his life. I wanted to scream. Both his parents were dead. His beloved older brother was dead. Marilyn, born dead. Mother, struggling back from a debilitating mental illness. Me? I was alive, more alive than ever before in my life. I was finally figuring out how to be happy and this was the greatest grief he had ever experienced?

There was more. He was "almost in a daze." He drove "the highways shedding tears," his concentration was "shattered," his mind and heart "overwhelmed." I felt angry and manipulated. I felt set up.

At the sound of my voice on the phone the previous Saturday, he "became limp," found he could hardly talk to me "without weeping." Buck up! I wanted to scream. Despite the devastating effects the very sound of my voice had produced, he wanted us to get together.

> We cannot successfully communicate in letters. We need to see each other's eyes and feel each other's warm presence as we discuss something so heavy. . . . I love you more than life.

Frankly, I could not imagine a less appealing prospect at that moment than to be in his warm presence. I was furious. How could they have written letters like these after inviting me to come out? I fired off my reply in the heat of that anger.

> You . . . claimed you simply wanted to be "fellow travelers" with me. Now I learn that you plan to spend the rest of your lives in grief and pain and that the very mention of my name brings tears.
> Well, I'll tell you something. I'm not dead yet. In fact, I'm

76

very much alive, as alive as I've ever been in my life, and I have no
intention of spending my life feeling anything but good about
who I am. I am not an extension of your bodies. I am a separate
person with my own integrity, who has had the courage and
strength and vision to discover something wonderful about
myself. I keep wondering whether someone else wrote that first
letter you sent, because it offers something so completely different from what you delivered in your double-barreled replies.

I suggested that their extreme grief and despair, especially Daddy's,
indicated a need for support. Perhaps counseling would help or talking to
parents who had been through similar experiences. If the phone calls
were so distressing, I suggested, why not discontinue them for a time? "I
can't get any pleasure or satisfaction out of the thought that talking to me
leaves you limp, tearful, and speechless," I wrote. I protested that it was
much too soon for a face-to-face visit.

I wondered to them if they could imagine how much courage it had
required for me to write what I had and assured them that it was not
something I had done to them. "I refuse to accept the load of guilt your
letters offer," I declared, and hoped I could live up to my bold declaration. Despite my anger, I wanted with all my heart to be close to them. I
closed on a conciliatory note.

> If I have to move on from here without your support, I can and
> will. But I hope that you will come in time to recognize that we
> can work through this and come to a fuller, more mature under-
> standing of each other if we want to. I am here ready to go that
> hard way with you, and I'll give you as much time as it takes.

The next Saturday Mother and Daddy did not call. The day crawled
by. Another Saturday passed. I wondered how long their silence would
persist. I wanted to talk to them, but even more I wanted them to want to
talk to me. On the third Saturday, they phoned. I was so glad to hear their
voices. And so nervous, as well. We chatted somewhat awkwardly about
the weather and what we had been doing. I could hear that they were nervous, too. With that conversation, they resumed their weekly Saturday
calls, but it was November before I got an answer to my letter, penned in
my father's distinctive left-handed scrawl. He explained the long delay by

saying that they had done a lot of "reflecting, praying," and rereading of our letters as they tried to figure out how to formulate a more helpful response. He affirmed my individuality, my adulthood, and my right to separate from them.

> However, while we grant you the right and privilege of your own individuality and integrity we believe we must be allowed to have our own individuality and integrity to disagree with you.
> It is true that you are not an extension of our bodies and it is not the plan of God that we have authority over you as an adult. However, you do have a heritage of which we are a part.

While expressing appreciation for my honesty, he reiterated his disapproval.

> It was necessary to say that we do not approve of the lifestyle you have chosen. We say that knowing that we cannot and will not attempt to impose our lives on you. However, we hope you can separate our disapproval of a lifestyle from our love for you. The two are not the same.

My suggestion that they consider therapy had apparently stung. And the PFLAG article was no help.

> We must be frank and honest to tell you that the article you sent represents a point of view with which we do not agree. We believe we have better sources for interpreting the facts regarding this matter. We are receiving therapy and have a fairly strong support group of our own. We appreciate your thinking of this need of ours and are glad to report that it is being met.

I translated what I read. Their support group was the church, their sources for interpreting the scriptures were the same ones they had always used, and their therapy was either with a seminary professor who taught pastoral counseling or their own pastor.

Once again, they reiterated the steadfastness of their convictions. Nevertheless,

> you are our daughter and our love will always be supportive of you even when we disagree with you and even when we disagree

with what you do. We must separate supporting a particular action and supporting you as a person.

The close of the letter urged me to visit. Subsequent letters contained the sort of news and reports on the weather that we had always exchanged in the past. Convinced that we were all treading around the topic, attempting to pretend it wasn't there, I sent a letter that used the word *lesbian* at least ten times. "Quit writing Mother and Daddy those awful letters," my sister helpfully advised. Mother still had not written. Everyone was tired from trying to communicate across this great divide. I decided I was not yet ready to visit them that Christmas. I wrote:

> I love you very much, and I'd like to see you, but I feel like our first visit since I came out to you is going to be emotionally charged for all of us, and I need to give myself a little more time. Mother, I haven't gotten a letter from you in a long time and I sure do miss it. I hope I'm going to get back on your list soon. I'll miss you this Christmas, but you'll be in my heart. And we'll see each other before too long.

Not long after I sent that letter, she began writing again. On New Year's Eve, my girlfriend dumped me. I was devastated at the time, but in fact she had done me a favor. When my parents called the next Saturday, I was in tears. They asked immediately what was wrong.

"My girlfriend broke up with me, and I'm heartbroken." I told them. "I don't want you to be happy because you think 'Oh, good, we never liked her anyway,' and I don't want you to be happy because you think, 'Oh, good, now Jackie won't be a lesbian anymore.' I just want you to be sad that I feel so miserable."

My mother answered without hesitation: "Oh, Jackie, honey, we would never be happy that you are feeling sad."

I knew then that we were going to make it through this somehow.

8

Hand to Hand

My lesbian relationship had started coming apart almost immediately. Witty, charming, and smart, my girlfriend trained on me the kind of rapt attention Mother had bestowed, which had elsewhere proved, to my abiding disappointment, exceedingly rare. Perhaps most seductive of all, she revealed, underneath an aura of certitude, vulnerability and despair, feelings it seemed I alone could assuage. What, at thirty-one, I was evidently still too naive to notice was that she offered that charm and glittering attentiveness to all new acquaintances. But once she felt certain of their attention, she lost interest.

In the three weeks between our first kiss and my separation from my husband, my new girlfriend could not get enough of me. I was the greatest thing that had ever happened to her. But once I was free and clear she shifted into reverse and spent the next year and a half backing out. By the time we began living together, about nine months in, I was contemplating with little amusement the irony of taking so much heat for my wicked, wicked ways while getting so little pleasure in exchange.

Still, she introduced me to lesbian life. For her, a lot of that consisted of going to bars. At first, I enjoyed these excursions. It was 1982, and there were few places where groups of lesbians congregated. I was fascinated by the handsome women in short haircuts and sensible shoes twirling each other around the floor and buying each other drinks. I watched as if my life depended on it, looking for clues that might enable me to find my place on the new planet where I was surprised to have landed.

By the summer of 1983, I realized that hanging out in gay bars with twenty-somethings and watching my girlfriend dance with her exes was not my idea of a good time. I had started out naively believing that the fact we were all lesbians would make us pals, but I gradually realized that some of these women were just plain boring.

I studied the gay weekly newspaper for ideas. There were a few ads for churches that claimed to by gay friendly. I could hardly imagine such a thing. I found an announcement for a lesbian reading group that was forming. The group met once a month in members' homes. Within a few short weeks, I went from having no lesbian friends of my own choosing to having several.

There were maybe twelve of us gathered for the third meeting of the book group when the doorbell rang again. The hosts were busy, so I jumped up to open the door. There in front of me was one of the finest-looking women I had ever seen. She was about my height and build—tall and thin, and her freckled face was framed by soft, brown, wavy hair that fell in layers to her shoulders. She took a forthright step into the apartment and gripped my hand in a no-nonsense shake. Her name was Carol, and she had recently moved back to the Midwest from Maine. She came in and sat down next to me. She was smart and funny. She liked to tease, and when she said something really mischievous she would touch her tongue to the bottom of her front teeth and laugh. I was sure we were going to be friends.

Meanwhile, back at home, my relationship continued to grow ever more miserable. I was in therapy, she was in therapy, we were in therapy. Despite all that, we couldn't connect. When my therapist asked me why I was afraid to have a relationship with an equal, I was shocked. I was paying the bills, cooking the meals, doing the cleaning in the large apartment to which we had moved, and making all sorts of accommodations so we could be together, and yet I still thought my girlfriend was the one in charge.

It's hard to know how I could have thought this. She was young and floundering. Unable to extricate herself from the demands of her needy family. But I was so committed to the notion of a prince that I was still trying to cast her in that role just because she was a few inches taller and a lot more butch than me.

By the time she broke up with me on New Year's Eve, I must have known it was already over. She moved into a different bedroom, and for several weeks we continued as roommates.

Gay people joke quite often about the unlikely characters we sometimes choose to come out with. Perhaps that was part of it. Maybe my unrecognized but no less urgent need to come out, and the limited opportunity I had to do so, caused me to waltz off with the first woman I found.

But the truth is she fit a pattern of mistakes I had made with men. Although I somehow managed to marry honest, honorable men, in between I had fallen hard for a couple of thoroughgoing narcissists who would tell you anything they thought you wanted to hear. On some level, despite all evidence to the contrary, I still believed every song my mother had ever sung. Out there somewhere was a handsome soul mate, the one who would love me and only me. Surely growing up with a mother who was by turns adoring and angry, sane and crazy, a mother who in the end needed help I desperately wanted but did not know how to give, made me hungry for a chance to try again, to bring to someone I loved the healing comfort that I never could provide for my mother. I fell in love repeatedly with people who would never be able to love me back the way I wanted and whose deep hurts were far beyond the reach of my love.

When my mother had careened off into madness, I felt great pain, but I also felt enormously alert and alive. She needed me. I could help.

Except, of course, I couldn't. It was a tired and tiresome drama by the time I finished repeating it in the third of three increasingly miserable and melodramatic romances.

When she first told me it was over, I cried. But even at my most miserable I could see that this breakup was no disaster. Soon I called my friends. Carol from the book group was one of the women I called. We went out for Chinese on a Monday night and sat in the restaurant talking until the waiters began to give us baleful looks and we realized we were

the last diners in the room. She told me how she had headed off to graduate school in Maine with a boyfriend named Loon, living in a tent that
fall until the cold weather forced them to find better shelter. She cooked
over an open fire and showered on an as-needed basis at the home of
friends. She loved the camping more than the boyfriend, and once the
tent was struck and she started going to classes all the time he gave up and
wandered on. I was utterly charmed by the notion of a tent in the woods
as transitional graduate student housing. I concluded that she was, in the
best sense of the words, a wild woman. Not long afterward we sat laughing and talking together in a Greek restaurant when a man approached to
ask if we were alone. "No!" we shouted in unison and burst into laughter.

Shortly after New Year's Eve, I went to a house party for single lesbians. I was determined not to sit at home and mope. When I walked into
the kitchen, Carol was one of the first people I saw. I never got past the
kitchen. I stood and talked to her for an hour and a half. As we talked, I
grabbed her arm. I expected her to be skinny like me, but I felt a big, firm
bicep. "Wow, have you been working out?" I asked. "I swim at the Y,"
she told me.

Pretending to myself that there was no connection, I joined the
YMCA and started doing laps. Predictably, I ran into Carol there. I
would watch her in the next lane over glide effortlessly through the water
with a fluid stroke that made most of us look like turtles paddling alongside a dolphin.

Later we would shower, standing across from each other and talking.
Then we'd stop at the sink to put our contact lenses in. Twenty-twenty
vision restored, we'd sit together in the hot tub before we headed off to
our separate apartments. My workouts grew more and more frequent.

One night, as we walked home from a restaurant, Carol asked me if I
was close to my mother. I said the first thing that popped into my mind.
"I guess you haven't seen the surgeon's scar on my hip. It was painful, but
at least we can now lead separate lives."

She laughed. "So that's a yes?"

"I'm really close to her. I'm too close to her. She can read my mind.
She thinks I'm her. But I'm working on it. The doctors think there's
hope." I'm not sure why it came out quite like that. But the wounds from

our painful coming-out correspondence were still fresh, and my mother and I were in the throes of trying to figure out how we could be so close and yet so far apart.

Carol and I planned more and more evenings together. Theater lovers both, we saw numerous plays. At the Y, our workout schedules magically synchronized. One cold February day, we walked partway home together. At the corner on Sheffield, where I headed north and she south, she said good-bye and swatted me lightly with the brown leather glove she held in her hand. It was like one of those little jock swats that athletes use to show affection for a member of the team who has made a really good play. Her father was a basketball coach. I loved this little jock caress. I was slow, but I was starting to catch on that I wanted to be more than her teammate.

Carol loved language. Behind her quiet reserve, there was an independent and adventurous streak that I relished. She had resisted getting a real job for years and so had pursued an MA in comparative literature in Maine. She had boyfriends and tried to imagine herself married someday. She pictured herself with a sailor or a surgeon. It was, of course, a picture of herself married without a husband underfoot. She found her first feelings for women terrifying. Eventually, she found a group of lesbian friends, found a woman to love, lost that love, and then worked her way into advertising—not exactly what she had intended her love of language to come to, but it earned her a good living. She loved Maine's wildness, its abundance of water, its unpretentiousness. But it was not an easy place to make a living, and when she eventually found herself without either a job or a girlfriend she moved to Chicago and began reaching out for new friends.

I sensed in Carol a solid core of integrity that I valued more than ever after the shifting sands of my recent relationship. She was the sort of person who paid her fair share and followed through on commitments. She maintained friendships from high school, college, and the years in Maine. She was hardworking, responsible, and unflinchingly honest—a person whose opinion was unvarnished. She was gentle hearted and kind but constitutionally incapable of flattery. And she was funny.

On Valentine's Day, I telephoned her at work. I was preparing material for a performance of poetry class I was teaching, and I used that as an excuse to read her an Adrienne Rich poem over the phone, "Transcendental Etude." She knew and loved the poem. "Happy Valentine's Day," I said boldly as I was hanging up the phone. "Happy Valentine's Day to you," she replied.

One night near the end of February we decided to have dinner together and then go to Mountain Moving Coffee House, a woman-run organization that brought folk music and other programming for women-only audiences to a small performance space in a church basement. Although by this time she had told her friends that she was interested in me, Carol had assured them that she did not intend to get involved with someone so obviously on the rebound.

At dinner in a Thai restaurant, the sexual tension was running so high that my mouth kept drying up. Between the spicy food, the white rice, and my own anxiety I couldn't drink water fast enough. Finally, I tackled the subject head-on.

"I'm so attracted to you, I'm having trouble talking. I can't think about anything else."

I looked into her gray-blue eyes. One of them has a brown speck in it. She looked down at the table, then back into my eyes, then away again.

"I feel the same way about you," she said. "Does that make you feel any better?"

It did. She looked terrified, like she might bound from the table if I made any sudden moves. I felt like I was courting a wild deer. She abruptly bolted for the ladies' room, but when she came back to the table we were still falling in love.

We later drove to Mountain Moving, went inside, and tried to concentrate on the evening's program but couldn't. At the first intermission, we left and went for a drive.

"I'd really like to get involved with you," Carol told me, "but you need to know two things. I don't want to get involved with you as long as your ex is living in your apartment. And I don't want to get involved with you unless it's going to be a monogamous relationship."

She was serious about this. She had standards.

"OK," I swallowed. "I can live with those terms." We drove for a while in silence. I reached my hand toward hers. "Can I hold your hand?"

"Yes."

"Can I take your glove off?"

"Yes." Her shy blue eyes brushed over me and back at the road.

I slipped her long, strong, right hand out of her leather glove while she kept the left one on the steering wheel. With naked hands clasped, we drove up Lakeshore Drive into the northern suburbs and then back into the city. We were nervous, happy, excited, and so wide awake and alive. Something was beginning. Something wonderful. Or crazy. You can never tell at the start. You jump and only begin to find out months or years later where you have landed.

9

Marriage of Addresses

During spring break, I visited my parents for the first time since I had come out to them. Mother and Daddy were once again living in Louisville. After twenty-three years as the pastor of First Baptist Church in Somerset, Daddy had accepted a position as Executive Director of Kentucky Baptist Homes for Children. We celebrated Mother's sixty-third birthday. We felt happy to see each other and yet somewhat wary.

Near the end of the visit, we tried to talk about what had happened. Mother said very little. But Daddy returned again and again to his struggle to understand how he had failed as a parent. He catalogued mistakes. He and I had always had difficulty communicating, he thought, and he was trying to figure out why. It wasn't, I thought, so much that we had difficulty communicating as that we often didn't agree. He wondered if it had been a mistake to end so many of our discussions in my childhood with the words, "Don't talk back," or if he had failed me by working such long hours and being absent so often. He believed he had been too rigid in his beliefs. Yet, he insisted, he had tried his best to set a good example.

He kept sifting through our relationship, trying to figure out how his good intentions and devotion could have failed so utterly. He always knew what he believed, he said, and that he was called of God. Somehow he suspected that this assurance seemed to bother Jeannie and me. But he didn't know why. He told me he had given up offering advice and counsel; it did no good unless people wanted to hear it. Then he launched into a long testimony about his faith and how it sustained him.

He wanted me to talk about what I believed. I parried; my spiritual life was important to me but was not a subject I wanted to discuss. I wasn't going to church. I believed there was "something more," something transcendent. I believed we all needed to find ways to care for one another and the world. I believed in talking to Jesus and saying thank you when I did so. I suspected this was much too watered down to reassure him about my spiritual life. He talked about the values he and Mother tried to instill that had taken root—honesty and integrity, concern for social justice, interest in women's rights. He couldn't figure out how it was that they had taught us some of their beliefs but not managed to transfer the whole package. Tears filled his eyes.

Perhaps without meaning to, he circled back to the familiar role of counselor. When he moved to my side, put his arm around me, and began to offer advice, I stopped him.

"Daddy, I need to say something to you. If you want to give me advice, go over there and sit in that chair and fire away. If you want to hug me, come over here and let's hug. But don't do both together. Because when you do I can't figure out whether you're trying to love me or control me."

He was shocked. He had been hugging people and counseling them throughout his whole ministry. He thought giving advice was one of the best gifts he had to bring to a relationship. He would stand at the front of the church and present new members or converts with his arm tight around their shoulders while he told us why they had come forward. People liked the way he loved folks into the church. Church members seemed not to mind an arm around the shoulder while he told them how they should live their lives. But for me it was miserable, and he hadn't even known. For years, I had flinched and said nothing; my objection came out of the blue. My heart was pounding. I loved him so much, and I didn't want to hurt his feelings. But he listened to me (and he never did it again).

After he left the room, I told Mother I wished he would not blame himself and take it all so hard.

"I've learned not to do that anymore," she said quietly. "I just enjoy what we have in common and leave the rest."

"That's it exactly," I said, and we continued on comfortably without trying to figure out where or why I had gone astray. As he drove me back to the train station, Daddy spoke again about his sorrow over having failed me.

"I don't think you failed me at all," I told him. "Don't be so hard on yourself. There aren't any perfect fathers out there. You did the best you could. I think it all turned out pretty well." But that, of course, was a point on which we could not really agree.

At Chicago's Union Station, Carol met me, and our life together began.

We had been dating for several months when we traveled to Kentucky for another visit to my parents. On the drive down Carol had asked if there was anything she should know about them.

"Don't take the Lord's name in vain," I advised.

"I'll do my best," she said gamely.

I seemed to have a knack for finding girlfriends who exclaimed, "Jesus Christ!" within the first half hour of meeting Mother and Daddy. In Carol's case, the ill-fated oath burst from her mouth when my mother asked her to raise the blinds in the kitchen. At her first tug, the blinds crashed to the floor. She stood sheepishly in the bright yellow, sun-filled kitchen. But my parents kindly pretended not to notice that she had broken one of the Ten Commandments.

They couldn't help but like my kind, smart, funny, engaging girlfriend. Carol so clearly matched me in interests and background. By the time I knew her, she neither drank nor smoked, which must have gone some way toward consoling them for the occasional expletive, and if she wasn't raised Baptist she was at least Protestant. Her parents were nominal Methodists. In our family, Methodists were considered about the nearest thing to Baptists, so she got definite points for that affiliation. Mother and Daddy carefully ushered us into separate bedrooms when we visited, but in many ways they seemed to accept us as a couple.

In May of 1985, Carol and I moved in together. Today gay wedding ceremonies have become so common that mainline Protestant churches debate their acceptability. Canada and the state of Massachusetts have legalized gay marriage, and gay weddings have shown up on prime-time television. In 1985, however, gay weddings were almost unheard of. Yet the decision to move in together marked a deeper level of commitment in the life we shared, and we wanted, in some way, to mark that for ourselves and our friends.

We planned a party that mimicked a wedding reception. Our wed-dinglike invitations announced the "marriage of our addresses" and invited the recipients to a celebration of this union. I remember the look of disapproval on the face of the woman from whom we bought those invitations when we told her how they should read. I remember feeling hurt by her response and how Carol and I forged ahead, determined that she would not dampen our happiness.

Our marriage of addresses party was both a thoroughly camp send-up of wedding receptions and an honest and deeply felt public declaration of commitment. The structure of the party allowed us to make explicit connections to heterosexual ceremonies while its tongue-in-cheek tone distanced us from the very ritual we were invoking. It seemed barely possible to us to mark the occasion with a wonderful party. It did not seem possible to do so without offering any friends who wished it some space for ironic distance. I warned a woman I worked with that she would be getting an invitation from me and should remember that it had been issued with tongue planted firmly in cheek. I felt I had to give her permission not to take us seriously at the same time that Carol and I were in absolute earnest about the life we were creating together.

My tastes had gone uptown since the basement wedding receptions of my childhood. We followed the Baptist traditions of my youth by having a three-tiered cake, pastel mints, salted nuts, and a guest register, but we also served a catered buffet. Our mimicking of tradition included a cake topped with the figures of two brides.

The question of what to wear occupied a good deal of our attention. The choices we made signaled our connections to traditional wedding celebrations and our lesbian community and the playful approach we took to the whole event. We wore tuxedo shirts, bow ties, and casual pants (one pair black, the other pink). Shoes for Carol were high-top sneakers; I wore black flats and lace socks.

On the appointed day, our friend Diane arrived early, wearing an aqua chiffon mother of the bride number she had found at Goodwill. Her accessories included white tennis shoes and crew socks and white gloves with the fingers cut out. She played piano for the event, including a lush rendition of "Feelings" that had Carol and me whirling around the living room in our best version of the happy couple's first dance. Lesbian friends joined with work friends. This motley company ate and drank and celebrated for hours.

Even as we made our plans, we felt uncertain about the response our heterosexual friends, families, and coworkers would have to our celebration. Neither of us invited our parents. We did not think they would come and did not want the pain of a refusal.

Although my parents were not there, we were not without family. My sister came to help us celebrate, as did a sister of Carol's. Jeannie stayed the weekend, helping us get ready; enjoying the fun, friends, and good food; and helping us clean up.

In the wedding ceremonies of my youth, showers of rice symbolized the fertility wished upon these unions. In the celebration Carol and I created, nothing foretold the children that would transform us publicly and irrevocably into a family. When we joined our lives together in 1985, the social and legal definitions of family had sufficiently influenced my dreams that I assumed we would not have children. There were no little satin packets of rice.

A few months after that party, Carol's sister gave birth to a daughter with whom Carol fell hopelessly in love. We had great fun being doting aunts. Carol had never really pictured herself as a mother, but her love of Ardyce caused her to begin to think of a child of her own. But I'm getting ahead of my story. It took several years for Ardyce to work her magic. During that time, Carol and I settled into our life together.

My work flourished. For the first time since I had begun teaching at DePaul, my home life was a source of peace and support. I entered a period of scholarly productivity that earned me tenure and a promotion to associate professor. I began writing on the short stories of Grace Paley, stories that had drawn me in with their innovative use of language and narrative structure and their insistent belief that mundane moments in the lives of women and children matter. I loved Paley's voice, at once wise and wisecracking, and her passion for social justice. I loved her invention of narrative worlds that shone a light on ordinary women's lives. I took on a growing leadership role in the university, moving into the position of director of women's studies, a program I had helped create. I was surprised and pleased to discover that DePaul, a Catholic university, had become a place where you could be out without sabotaging your career.

When I first came out, I was not certain that this would be possible. Although I knew other gay faculty members, most were extremely closeted. I soon realized that I would not be comfortable in the closet and made a decision to act as if there was nothing remarkable about my lesbian life. I talked about my partner as casually and comfortably as my heterosexual colleagues talked about their spouses. When university parties or functions included spouses, I brought Carol. Of course, this matter-of-fact approach was a bluff. I didn't feel that casual and comfortable. But I hoped that if I behaved naturally about my choice of a partner others would take their cue from me, and for the most part they did.

By this time, Carol was working as a writer and editor for Lands' End. Whenever we could both get away from work, we traveled. For three or four summers in a row, we spent a week in Maine. Carol loved to return to see her old friends and breathe in the clear and salty air of this state she called home. I had never been to Maine and delighted in being brought into her special world—the rocky coast, beautiful clear lakes, and snake-free northern woods (an especially important point to Carol, who had a terror of snakes), the boiled lobsters and blueberry pancakes. Sometimes we rented a cabin on Pemaquid Point. We would read, hike, canoe around the bay, cook lobster, and entertain friends who would roll in from nearby towns.

In 1988, we traveled with several hundred thousand other gay men, lesbians, and their friends and family to a Gay Rights March on Washington. A few weeks earlier, my parents had visited us. They saw a postcard announcing the march on our refrigerator door and asked if we were planning to go. We told them that we were. "What do you want that you don't have?" my mother wondered.

I mentioned job and housing discrimination, harassment and in some cases assault on the streets, parents denied custody of their own children or turned down for adoption, unrecognized and unprotected relationships, and the lack of funding for AIDS research. Mother began to worry out loud about our safety. I assured her we would be fine.

My father, who, no matter what the topic, always sounds like a preacher, said, "Here's what I can't understand. I can't understand how you could think that this is normal, not against nature."

"Daddy, that's because it's not normal for you; it doesn't fit with your nature. But for me it is completely normal. I think you know that I gave heterosexuality a thorough try. As much as I tried to make it work, it always felt like an effort to me. This feels like the most normal thing in the world."

"I can't understand it," he said. "I guess we'll just have to agree to disagree."

"I guess we will," I said with a sigh. Both of them looked tight-lipped and uncomfortable. I searched for words that could help us find common ground. "Listen," I said after a moment, "I want you all to know how much I appreciate the loving way you treat me and Carol. You really have accepted us and made both of us feel so welcome with you. That means so much to me. I want you to know that I don't assume your fundamental objections to homosexuality have changed."

As I said those words, both Mother and Daddy visibly relaxed. I had sensed over the past several months that they felt I might not understand this. As if I were pressuring them to be not just accepting of but in agreement with us. Their reaction told me I had been right. Now they could be just as warm and loving as they wanted without worrying that I would think they had abandoned their convictions about the sinful state I had elected. Of course, I would have dearly loved for them to agree with me that Carol's and my relationship was as valid and life affirming as their own. On some level, perhaps, they had been right to be on their guard. I'm sure I had been pushing for exactly such full and complete acceptance. But I knew that if I wanted them to accept me as I was I had to accept them as they were. Somehow we all had to love one another in spite of, rather than because of, some of our most deeply held beliefs.

Not long afterward, Carol accompanied me on a visit to Kentucky for the first time in about two years. It was not easy for us to visit my parents all day, with little or no private time, and then spend our nights in separate bedrooms. Carol liked my parents, but she felt in some sense like she was still, despite nearly five years together, the outsider—a good friend, perhaps, but not quite family. We left on Friday after work, and by the time we made the six-hour drive it was almost midnight. Yet when we got there the lights were on, and Mother and Daddy were waiting happily to greet us. They had fixed a substantial snack, more of a supper really. Cornbread sticks and greens and navy beans cooked with bits of ham—a good Kentucky meal. Mother didn't think I ate properly up north. After we'd visited for a bit and eaten more than we could really hold, Mother said, "Well, I expect you all want to get some rest. We should let you get to your room."

They walked us down the hall toward the two rooms they had always given us. But instead of showing us into separate rooms they walked us into one. The lamps were on; the fresh, clean sheets were turned down. There was a little vase on the dresser with two rosebuds from the garden. Two sets of fresh towels were stacked on the chest of drawers. I almost expected to see tiny chocolates on the pillows. The family room with the foldout couch was dark, the couch not made up for sleeping. "Here you go," Mother said. "Everything is all ready for you."

"Thank you," we said. Flabbergasted, we feigned nonchalance. "This looks really inviting. Goodnight, I love you, we'll see you all in the morning." We kissed goodnight. They walked to their room and shut the door. We turned to each other, jaws dropping, grins of amazement and delight on our faces. At last, they had decided to treat us as a couple.

The next morning, when I came into the kitchen, I noticed something I had missed the night before. On the kitchen wall, Mother had always had two small, intricately carved ivory frames brought to her from China by a missionary. One held a picture of Jeannie and her husband. The other had contained a picture of me. Now my picture had been replaced with one of Carol, me, and our cat. I said something pleasant but low key, maybe, "Oh, look, a picture of Carol and me and Louise." But I felt such love.

We never spoke directly about the changed sleeping arrangements. Later I learned how Mother put it when she talked to my sister: "Well, they'll be more comfortable, and we'll be more comfortable, and anyway, why pretend?"

Mother, by this time, had begun to share news with me of gay-related events in Louisville. When the daughter of a wealthy newspaper family in Louisville planned a commitment ceremony with her partner, a local female judge, Mother told me about it. When gay-related hate crimes were reported in the local press, she filled me in. When a particularly interesting gay-related television program was aired on the *Phil Donahue Show*, I heard all about it.

I'll never know exactly how these changes came about, although I suspect my mother led the way. Perhaps it helped when I reassured them that I would not interpret loving treatment of Carol and me as agreement. Of course, I hoped that they had become less certain over time of how God regarded gay relationships, that they had perhaps begun to harbor a sliver of doubt over the absolute rectitude of their earlier judgment, but I had to content myself with the amazing distance they had already traveled. Whatever their beliefs, they welcomed us with open hearts and arms.

10

Expecting

We sat in the November sun next door to the Café du Monde, eating beignets and sipping Louisiana coffee so thick and dark you could almost chew it. I licked the powdered sugar from my fingers and looked out at the river, then closed my eyes like a cat napping in the sun. I had come to New Orleans to deliver a paper at a conference for communication scholars. Carol had flown down to join me, and now, with my conference over, we had three days to enjoy New Orleans and each other. We were nearly five years into our relationship.

"What would you think," Carol asked, "if I told you I wanted to have a baby?"

Suddenly I was wide awake, my heart going kerthunk. "A baby," I repeated in amazement.

We had often talked about my disappointment at not being able to bear a child. Although Carol had never wanted children, each time she assured me she would never stand between me and my desire to be a mother. We could find a way to do it.

"No," I would always say. "If we have a baby when it's not what you really want to do, it could break us up. Now that I've found you, I'm not going to take that chance. Raising a child will just have to be one of those things I wanted in my life but didn't get. This is a good life. It's enough."

But now here we were, in the French Quarter, where the winter sunshine, French architecture, music, narrow streets, bright colors, and moist Gulf air always made me feel like I had entered a magical realm of outrageous possibility. Carol was describing how, as she waited to board her plane, she saw a tiny infant snuggled in its mama's arms and knew, in a swift and sudden flash of insight, that she did not want to miss this.

"I'm thinking I want to be a mother," she told me. "How would you feel about that?"

As if a gunshot had signaled the start of the Chicago Marathon, a whole throng of excited, sweaty feelings came pounding and stampeding into my consciousness from whatever locked-up place I had sequestered them. I felt a rush of longing and delight. I could immediately picture Carol and me and our baby. At the same time, I felt afraid. Too many times my hopes and plans had ended in heartbreak. I didn't want to get back on that roller coaster of baby longing unless there was to be a baby at the end of the ride.

"I'd be ecstatic," I said quietly. "But get back to me when you've made your mind up. I don't even want to think about it unless we are actually going to do it. I can't bear any more losses." As if one could so easily set a limit on loss, as if you get to say when you've had enough.

Of course, this topic was not so easily vanquished. During the rest of our weekend and then back home in Chicago, I was appalled to see how much power Carol suddenly held over my future. I wanted to ask her every few minutes whether she had made her mind up, and yet I was afraid that if I pestered her, I would sabotage the possibility for fulfillment of my no longer dormant desires. Mercifully, she realized rather quickly that she was serious. We were going to be mothers.

With the question of whether settled, we were ready to move on to the question of how. In 1988, there were still relatively few gay and lesbian families that were deciding to become parents together, although there had always been gay parents with children from previous heterosexual relationships or marriages. We were aware that some lesbian and gay couples were becoming parents, via donor insemination, surrogacy, or adoption, but we didn't actually know anyone who had done this. Most such families, at that time, were in a handful of cities on the East and West Coasts. Basically, we saw two options: one of us could get pregnant or we could adopt. Either path would include some hurdles.

A pregnancy for me was out of the question. I had no intention of trying again. Although I often dreamed that I was pregnant or even that I had found a baby on my doorstep, in lucid moments I knew I would never bear a child.

Carol was a few days away from her forty-first birthday. If she wanted to get pregnant, she would have to hurry. For lesbians, pregnancy usually occurs via donor insemination. A decision to inseminate requires choosing between a friend who will agree to donate sperm (with the attendant decisions and legal documents regarding his degree of involvement in the child's life) and an anonymous donor from a sperm bank. For perhaps two weeks, she thought hard about it. During that fortnight, we sized up nearly every man in our acquaintance as a potential donor, unbeknownst to them, of course. This led us to some highly comic considerations of their good and bad points.

Carol concluded that her desire to have a baby had little to do with bearing one and everything to do with caring for one. We decided to adopt not one baby but two. Neither of us could imagine life without siblings. And they would be girls. Although several of our lesbian friends had raised wonderful sons, we felt more confident of our ability to parent daughters.

I was relieved by Carol's decision to adopt. After longing for children for so many years, I didn't want to become the second-string mother, the one without any legal or biological claim. I had worried about what it would be like to watch Carol swell with the child I had been denied. There was no way to embark on motherhood without risking a broken heart, but I wanted, if I could, to protect my heart at least a little.

We researched adoption, contacting agencies and attending information sessions. We sat awkwardly in circles of heterosexual couples and introduced ourselves as single friends both considering adoption. While the other couples held hands or sat with their arms around each other, we carefully avoided sitting close enough to touch shoulders. We tried to remember to say "I" when all our thoughts and plans involved "we." We learned that if we wanted to adopt an infant, and relatively soon, the likeliest route for success was international adoption.

Someone gave us the name of a lesbian couple in Boston who had adopted internationally. I remember the excitement with which I called them and the warm welcome they extended as they shared information about their experiences.

We explored the receptivity of social workers to lesbian parents. Illinois did not explicitly ban gay people from adopting, but the state did not allow both partners to adopt as a couple. One had to be the legal parent. We would have to do two single-parent adoptions. We were strongly advised by a social worker we spoke with against presenting ourselves as a couple.

By February of 1988, we had located an agency that could arrange an adoption of a Peruvian infant. We chose Peru because adoptions there were moving quickly. We probably would not wait long for a referral. Since it was easier for me, as a faculty member on a nine-month contract, to take the summer off, I would apply first. Carol would accompany me but could not stay for the entire six weeks we were told the adoption would take. Sometime after I had adopted our first child, Carol would adopt our second. Now that we had made our decision, I found any wait almost unbearable. I wanted our baby, and I wanted our baby now.

With these decisions made, it was time to tell our parents. Carol called Art and Betty. Her father, a retired high school basketball coach, hesitated then found his voice.

"Who's going to take care of it? You two are—working girls." His concern focused not on the idea of lesbian parents but on the idea of working moms. Someone, he believed, needed to stay at home to raise those children.

"Both of us," Carol answered calmly. Betty, when she heard our surprising news, said little. Was that because she believed firmly that if you couldn't say anything nice you shouldn't say anything at all? Perhaps. But she was also a person who was warmly hospitable to anyone who entered her home. Even if our family came as a surprise to her, she would make our children welcome.

I steeled myself for the call to my parents. I didn't expect them to be thrilled. I anticipated consternation. But my sister had firmly decided years before that she did not want children. I hoped the realization that this was their only hope of becoming grandparents would eventually overcome their qualms. As I had often done before, I underestimated them.

I called on Saturday morning; they both got on the line. We began exchanging news about the weather. My mother knew I had not called to talk about the weather and was trying to get me to move to the reason for the call. I could tell she knew that I knew this. Still, we chatted on about snow and cold. Finally, I took a deep breath and plunged in.

"Carol and I have made a big decision. We're really happy about it and we wanted to share our good news. We have decided that we are going to adopt two children."

Mother spoke first. "Oh, Jackie, we're so glad you have figured out a way to become a mother. We know how much you have wanted that." Daddy chimed in immediately with his own enthusiasm for our decision.

I told them how relieved I was that they were happy. I confided my nervousness about calling. They wondered why I should be nervous to share "this glorious news."

"Oh, I don't know," I said. Could they really find this surprising? "I guess I thought maybe the idea of two lesbians raising children might give you pause."

"Why, Jackie," Daddy instantly responded, "we think you and Carol will be wonderful parents." I couldn't have scripted a more soul-satisfying endorsement.

I had known interracial adoption would present my parents with no problems. Recently retired from his job with Kentucky Baptist Homes for Children, Daddy was wholehearted in his support for adoption and convinced that since God didn't make distinctions based on skin color neither should we. But I had never guessed that my parents would so readily embrace the idea of their daughter becoming a lesbian mom. I was truly blessed.

On February 15, I mailed my application for adoption to the agency. I got physical and psychological exams, submitted financial records, updated my passport, got fingerprinted, filled out endless forms, and wrote a fifteen-page autobiography. It mentioned my divorces and the fact that Carol (described as my friend) and I jointly owned our home.

By April, it was time to meet my caseworker. I was nervous. I had learned that the married couple that headed this adoption agency were religious fundamentalists. They had founded the agency somewhere in the midst of the adoption of their own eight children. I was understandably concerned about a lesbian's chances of adopting through this particular organization. What happened next was too improbable for fiction.

At her home in a small town an hour and a half south of Chicago, the caseworker, a friendly woman maybe half a dozen years younger than I, opened the door. She was an adoptive mother herself, with a year-old daughter from Guatemala. She pulled out a photo album and began showing me pictures of her trip to bring home her baby.

She interviewed me about my house, work, child care plans, theories about child rearing and discipline, and much else. After about forty-five minutes, she stopped her tape recorder.

"I'm going to turn this off now for the next part of this interview," she said.

I waited.

"My boss thought after reading your autobiography that you might be a lesbian. She told me that was one of the things I would need to find out in this interview." I braced myself, fearing what might come next. "I told her I didn't know how I could find that out unless you told me, and I didn't know why you'd do that. I said to her, 'That's not really what you want me to find out, is it? I thought what you wanted me to find out is whether or not she would be a good parent.' 'Oh, well, yes,' she said, 'I guess that is what I need you to find out.'" Inside I was shouting hallelujah and doing backflips. It took all my self-control to maintain an expression of pleasant attentiveness. "So now I want to ask you a few questions as if you were a lesbian."

"OK," I agreed.

"I need to know how committed you and Carol are to each other and whether you think the two of you would ever separate."

I had no idea how to negotiate this land mine of a question. "Carol and I are both happy with the situation we are in right now. Neither of us has any intention of changing it. We can't see ourselves in any other situation."

"Let me tell you what I want to hear you say," my interviewer prompted. "I want to hear you say, 'Carol and I are going to be together until we die.'"

"Carol and I are going to be together until we die."

"If you were a lesbian, and Carol were your partner, which one of you would be the mother?"

"We both would be mothers," I said. "We would raise the child together."

"But would one of you be the main mother?" she pressed.

"No, I don't think so. We would mother together."

"But wouldn't the child need to know which one of you was really the mother?"

I explained that we wouldn't dictate to the child how she should relate to us, but we would care for her together. If when she grew older she wanted to have only one of us show up at school, we would respect her wishes. We wouldn't want our child to have to carry some sort of banner for us. But we would both be mothers.

"What would the child call each of you?"

"Mama-Jackie and Mama-Carol."

"Would you tell your child that you are lesbians?"

"We wouldn't have to tell her because she would just grow up knowing it. We don't think it is good for children to grow up with a secret in the family, and so we would just be ourselves."

"Would you show affection in front of the child?"

"I don't think parents should engage in hot and steamy behavior in front of the children, and neither would we. But if you mean would we ever hold hands or hug each other or kiss each other hello or good-bye, yes, we would."

Each of these questions led to a fuller discussion. We disagreed on a number of points, including whether or nor it was a good idea to spank children (she said yes, I said no) and whether or not children needed their gay parents to be out (she said no, I said yes). This was a conversation on which Carol's and my future hung. The social worker and I did our best. But we were constrained by the hypothetical nature of our conversation and her apparent difficulty in imagining a world in which a lesbian parent could be matter-of-factly visible in her own family.

I liked this smart, gutsy woman who didn't have to stick her neck out for me but did. When her employer told her she needed to find out whether or not I was a lesbian, she could have just agreed. But she acted on her principles to reframe the employer's goals and then signaled me with perfect clarity what could and could not be said on the record and off.

As I drove back to Chicago, I found myself giving thanks to a God I hoped, in the absence of the gift of unshakable faith, was listening. If there were no miracles, then where did this woman come from, the evangelical Christian from the little country town who was not afraid to champion the out lesbian feminist Christian from the big city?

At the end of June, we received our referral. There was a baby waiting for us, an eleven-month-old girl named Laura. I was told to book a flight to Peru for five days later and to pack my bags.

Our friends had helped us prepare by giving us two baby showers. From our freshly stocked nursery, we culled baby clothes big enough for an eleven month old. We loaded an entire suitcase with large diapers. We set aside most of the bottles and all the formula, for this baby was already beginning to drink milk from a cup. We located the various gifts we had been instructed to bring to encourage our Peruvian attorney, the judge, and anyone else to expedite our adoption. We packed and repacked, trying to cram into the limited space everything we might need.

Then the agency called again. "There has been a slight change," we were told. "Laura is no longer available for adoption. Her mother changed her mind. We've assigned another baby to you, a three-month-old girl who weighs about ten pounds. She's waiting for you, so get here as soon as you can."

We unpacked and repacked, replacing large clothes with smaller ones, adding formula and bags of smaller diapers. I was secretly happy about this change. I didn't want to miss any more of my baby's life than I absolutely had to. At the same time, I worried about Laura. Would she be all right? Had her mother made the right decision? And I worried about our new baby. Would she really be the one we got? Would her mother change her mind?

I hoped with all my heart that some higher power was at work in this, guaranteeing that the baby we would receive was intended for us all along. I wanted to believe, and I did believe, that we were all in the hands of destiny. I hoped destiny wasn't just a story we told ourselves.

At 5:00 am on July 7, 1989, we headed for the airport. Our bags bulged with diapers, formula, bottles, clothes for the baby, clothes for ourselves, and a small library of books we hoped would tell us everything we needed to know about how to take care of a baby. Between us, we had about seven thousand dollars tucked into money belts strapped under our clothes. Most of this would go to the Lima lawyer handling the adoption. The rest would cover living expenses while we remained in Peru.

Sometime after 11:00 pm, we cleared customs and were greeted by Pepe, whose sister Ana Maria would be our Peruvian attorney. He ushered us quickly past small children with their hands out, tiny children who worked the streets until well after dark trying to earn a few cents to help feed their families. We brushed past dozens of eager young men offering us rides in the rusting and decrepit Volkswagens that served as taxis. Pepe whisked us to our apartment in Miraflores, on the outskirts of Lima, where another American mother and her Peruvian baby were already asleep in the other bedroom. Worn out from the trip, we soon slept, too, despite our excitement.

Around noon the next day, Pepe drove us to the home where our baby waited. The foster parents supplemented their income by caring for several babies, all awaiting adoption. They brought out our daughter and laid her in my arms.

"Here you are, Mom," they told me. The bright-eyed baby (Maricruz was the name her mother had given her) looked me right in the eye and smiled a great big, dancing smile. She was a charmer. She seemed to know it was time to shine. Her scrumptious-looking round cheeks begged to be kissed. "Cachetes," said the foster father, giving one of those beautiful cheeks a gentle pinch.

As I held her, I felt my heart melting into hers. By my side, Carol reached over to take her hand. Our daughter curled a tight fist around Carol's long finger.

"Doesn't your friend have a beautiful baby?" the attorney asked Carol. I passed little Lucia Maricruz (for we had added our name to the name her birth mother had given her) over to Carol. She held Lucy close and covered her with kisses. She, too, was meeting her baby for the first time. But no one called her mother.

After a few moments, the foster mom took Lucy back to diaper her afresh for the trip to our Miraflores apartment. The foster papa demonstrated how Lucy liked to be bounced before going to sleep and how she liked to have her head scratched. We hoped all these kind attentions meant that she had known only the best of care during her stay with them. They placed her in my arms, telling her good-bye over and over. Then we were on our own. We headed back to the apartment to begin the process of turning ourselves into a family.

Lucy arrived in our lives with an air of authority and presence I have never seen in another baby. She was three and a half months old but had none of the vagueness, the out-of-focus fuzziness of most infants. Babies often seem to occupy a blurry kind of dream world. They blink around in a befuddled way, their little fuzzy heads wobbling on their necks, not quite sure what's going on. Only gradually do they wake up and enter into the life buzzing around them.

Not Lucy.

She had a head of thick black hair, already so long it looked like the hair of a two year old. But her expression also made her look old and wise. She would fix you with a penetrating stare that seemed to say, "I'm back, and I'm in charge." She was here on a mission. She couldn't say yet just what it was, but she was sizing you up to see what your place in it would be.

Within the first two days, Lucy learned to roll from her back to her stomach. This made her happy for a moment, but then she noticed that she couldn't crawl. This aggravated her. Later, when she learned to crawl, she was frustrated because she couldn't walk. When she walked, she wanted to run. And when I plucked her from the top of a six-foot stepladder at twelve months I could have sworn she was on her way to higher ground so she could turn around and tell everyone in the hardware store a thing or two about how it was going to be from now on.

Carol and I spent two wonderful weeks together in Peru caring for Lucy. Although having to pretend in public to be the helpful friend instead of the parent was a strain, in private Carol was a full-fledged mom and we were knitting ourselves into a family. We could see we made a great team. Reluctantly, after two weeks, Carol returned to work. She cuddled Lucy close and kissed her good-bye, then caught a late evening plane for the States.

The next day Lucy was disconsolate. She slept that Sunday in fits and starts. When she did manage to drift off, she would startle awake after a few minutes, as if terrified. Awakened, she would fuss and cry until she eventually fell briefly asleep again. In this way, she managed, through a series of twelve or more agitated naps, to sleep for about an hour and a half. When she cried, she wrung her little hands and tiny sweat beads formed on her forehead. It was an exhausting day for both of us, and I was convinced that her obvious distress was related to the pain of separating from Carol.

Fortunately, the next morning my parents arrived at our little apartment in Peru. Almost immediately, Lucy calmed. She seemed to recognize Granddaddy and Grandmama as family from the beginning. She stretched out and napped on my father as if he were her favorite La-Z-Boy recliner. He tossed her gently into the air, and she shrieked with delight. When Mother sat Lucy on her knee, raised her eyebrows, and talked to her new granddaughter, Lucy gazed into my mother's eyes with such a look of eagerness and understanding that I almost expected her to reply in complete sentences.

Daddy worked tirelessly to help me with the shopping, cleaning, and baby care. I was surprised to see that my mother was unable to be of much help. She tired easily and preferred sitting and talking to all other activities. Although she was only sixty-eight, she had become an old woman. She dozed off frequently and would sit upright in a chair, snoring softly, her head bobbing down toward her chest. When she lay down to nap, the snores grew louder, rattling the loose windowpanes. This was a revelation to me. Over all the years and Mother's difficulties and illnesses, I had persisted in thinking of her as my all-powerful mother, the one who would swoop in whenever I had a child of my own and, with an air of calm authority, teach me what I needed to know. When she pinned a cloth diaper on Lucy so loosely that my robust little kicker had flung it off within ten minutes, I began to wonder about my version of the past. Mother had always laughed about the time Jeannie, at age two, walked right out of her diapers on the streets of Cleveland at the Southern Baptist Convention. In Mother's recounting, this was a funny caper of Jeannie's. Now, I wondered. Had she never known how to pin a diaper on? Had I partly made her up? Yet her sweet, calm, loving presence and her confidence in my capacity to mother were enormous comforts. She beamed love, sympathy, and encouragement my way and sweet talked and cuddled Lucy while Daddy and I buzzed around cooking, cleaning, shopping, and fixing bottles. Nor was Daddy content to stop with housework and child care. He located two families of Southern Baptist missionaries who worked in Lima. We took them out to dinner, and he secured their promises to help when he was gone. I was grateful to have help from any quarter.

When Mother and Daddy left after ten days, Lucy and I entered the longest, hardest stretch of the adoption. In the end, we would spend sixty-one days in Peru as we continued to work our way through the bureaucratic process of completing the adoption. Sometimes the mom with whom I shared the apartment and I walked the neighborhood together, our babies resting on our chests in their Snuglis. On other days, Lucy and I went to the courthouse or the police station or the doctor's office or the social worker's office pursuing the various steps of the adoption. We could not leave the city because, although I had temporary custody of Lucy, her birth mother, Maria Chacpa, had not yet fully relinquished her.

I longed for Carol and grew tired of trying to communicate in my fractured Spanish. I wearied of the uncertainty about how much longer all this would take. Despite the loneliness and hardships, it was wonderful to have so much uninterrupted time with my new baby. It was also a gift to learn a little bit about the country where my daughter was born. When we were not busy, we would wander around, strolling through shops. As I practiced my Spanish, I began to be able to make myself understood and to understand in turn.

In the last few weeks of our Peruvian stay, I secured the remaining paperwork. In the final days, someone had to take the adoption decree back to Huasahuasi, where Lucy was born, and secure a new birth certificate with my name on it. Esperanza, a relative of the birth mother, Maria Chacpa, made this trip. Esperanza had spoken to me at the courthouse one day to say that Lucy looked happier than she had ever seen her. When she was with her mother, she said, she had cried all the time. It was Esperanza, I learned, who had brought Maria Chacpa down from Huasahuasi and introduced her to the attorney, Ana Maria.

Carol returned for the last week and a half of our stay. When she arrived in Lima, Lucy crowed with delight and leaped into her arms. Within the next two hours, she began to cry and wring her hands with the same pattern of distress she had exhibited the day after Carol left. But this time Carol comforted her. Pained at the separation, Lucy was ecstatic to have her other mama back.

The adoption papers were signed, but we still had to wait for the new birth certificate and Lucy's green card. During the wait, we took a four-day trip to Cuzco and Machu Picchu. We were thrilled to be together again at last, and this part of Peru is beautiful beyond description. Yet Carol was no more capable of stepping into the part I had scripted for her than my mother had been. I wanted a perfectly joyous reunion, one in which we would all instantly meld into a perfectly happy family. Instead Carol grew annoyed at my attempts to proffer too much advice about how to care for Lucy. She described, with what seemed to me altogether too much satisfaction, her own personal growth during our weeks apart. I began to repeat stories I had already told her about some of the difficulties Lucy and I had lived through, believing that she did not yet realize how hard and lonely it had been and how much I had done for us all. We grew cross with one another.

The physical and emotional separation we had endured during these crucial weeks of our new life had exacted a price, although we didn't yet fully understand this. While the heterosexual parents around us had been nourished as couples throughout their adoption struggles, our partnership had been driven underground; the impact of this new life on our relationship had been denied. In a way that had the potential to become either a blessing or a curse, we found we had no scripted parenting roles to guide us in the division of labor. Both of us fully expected and intended to be Lucy's mom, with all the primary responsibility that the role implies. But we saw right away that figuring all this out would take some adjustment. At times, then, and for the next several months, I wondered if we had traveled across an ocean and into another hemisphere in search of our daughter only to lose one another.

When we deplaned in Miami on September 6, I wanted to kiss the airport carpet. In Peru, I had insisted I would never complain again if I could just eat a salad without getting sick, mix formula with water straight from the tap, wash clothes in my own machine, and get my diapers from the diaper service. That promise, of course, would be quickly broken, but it was more than good to be safely home.

11

Are You Listening, God?

It might have been sensible to stop with one daughter for awhile and adjust to our new life. But happily we didn't. Carol believed our family would not be complete until we had adopted a second child. "Three," she insisted, "is not a good number. We need our other daughter." I had learned that when Carol insisted she was usually right. So almost immediately we began the paperwork for the second adoption.

We were tired all the time, and we found ourselves with neither the time nor the energy to be sweet to one another after we had finally gotten Lucy to sleep. We took to mothering wholeheartedly, but learning how to find each other in the midst of all that responsibility and constant care took some effort. More effort, at times, than we could manage. Patient with Lucy, we were frequently cranky with one another. Easily, it was the most difficult year of our lives together. Despite all that, we forged ahead, persuaded by Carol that this was the right thing to do.

By June of 1990, nine months after we brought Lucy home and just a few days after Carol had express mailed the last of her paperwork to Peru, the call came from Ana Maria, our Lima attorney. She had a beautiful two-month-old baby waiting in an orphanage, a baby with no name. "Can you be here in three days?" Ana Maria asked.

"Of course I can," Carol answered. "Tell her Mama's coming." She hung up the phone, bought her plane ticket, packed her bags, and headed for Lima.

At the orphanage, Carol was told to expect a baby who was beautiful and ate a lot. A smiling woman brought her out and laid her in Carol's arms. "Hello, Gracia Esperanza," Carol said, naming her at last. "Mama's here, Gracie. Mama's finally here."

True to her reputation, Gracie was a fine-looking girl who vigorously drank every bottle she was offered. Drinking her fill was a new experience. Carol learned that the orphanage had fed Gracie a certain number of ounces of reconstituted powdered milk. If she was still thirsty, she got sweetened herbal tea. The babies in the orphanage were clean and conscientiously cared for but spent much of their days in their cribs. That first day Gracie seemed subdued. Carol took her to a pediatrician, Dr. Arribas-Plata, who found her healthy but a little slow to respond to stimulation. But within two or three days she opened like a little flower to the love and attention Carol showered on her. At her second examination, the doctor exclaimed over the rapid progress she had made and pronounced her "a showcase baby." When she turned her bright smile on him, he added, "Oh, Gracia, with that smile and those eyes, you're going to be able to get anything you want!"

Gracie's adoption took two months. Carol spent most of that time in Lima, flying home once to keep from losing her job. While Carol was gone, Gracie spent a week with the same foster family that had cared for Lucy the year before. When Carol returned to Lima, she brought her mother along to help. Betty, who had said so little when we first announced our adoption plans, was steadfastly at Carol's side during the remaining four weeks of the adoption, lending daughter and granddaughter her quiet, calm assistance. Their sojourn in Peru was fraught with all the ups and downs and challenges that typified these adoptions.

At one point, Gracie got quite sick with a nasty intestinal bacteria. Carol had to learn to give her a daily shot of antibiotic. She practiced by injecting water into an orange. When she was as ready as she knew how to be, she injected tiny Gracie. Carol felt that this was the most difficult thing she had ever done. One frightening night, she stood on a darkened street corner in desperate need of a bottle of Pedialite (an electrolyte-balanced drink that prevents dehydration in sick babies). She had tried several stores and pharmacies to no avail and had no idea how to find what she wanted in a city where a can of formula (on some days even a box of matches) could be scarce. Not knowing what else to do, she prayed, and an atypically new and immaculate taxi appeared before her. She told the driver what she sought, and he, in what seemed a miracle, drove her to a large pharmacy amply supplied with the necessary drink.

Carol and Betty also fought intestinal bugs—Carol with a daily dose of antibiotic and Betty by carrying her own fork with her to every meal and washing it herself with her own antibacterial soap. Betty was the only adult in a hostel full of American adoptive parents who never got sick.

One Sunday Carol and Gracie visited an English-language church service attended by a small group of Americans. The hymn that morning was "Amazing Grace," which seemed to Carol, holding our daughter, like some sort of special blessing. She created a new set of lyrics to this old hymn.

> *Amazing Grace, how sweet the sound,*
> *It suits a girl like you.*
> *We wished to have a girl so fine,*
> *And now you're here, we do.*

Lucy and I waited at home. Lucy was fifteen months old when Carol left and a fearless climber. She took only the briefest of naps and slept about two hours less each night than the books predicted. I had a full-time job that summer just trying to keep her from walking off a table or electrocuting herself.

Finally, in August, Lucy and I met Carol and Gracie at O'Hare Airport. Carol was skinny, pale, and exhausted but at the same time quietly triumphant. She placed in my arms our beautiful new daughter. We all hugged and hugged. As we walked from the airport, Lucy peered over at her new sister with a mixture of delight and concern. It would take her a little time to get used to the idea of another baby in our arms.

For the first few weeks, Lucy became upset every time Gracie got a bottle. Whenever one mom began to feed Gracie, Lucy would start to wail. She would run to the kitchen and, racing from chair to chair, hurl each one to the floor. We didn't have to guess what she was feeling.

Whichever mom was not feeding Gracie would go to the kitchen and take Lucy in her arms. "Lucy," we would murmur, "Mama-Carol loves you. Mama-Jackie loves you. Granddaddy loves you. Grandmama loves you. Grandma Betty loves you. Grandpa Art loves you. Dee loves you. Aunt Jeannie and Uncle Doug love you. Aunt Sue and Aunt B. J. and Uncle Dave love you. Your cousins, Ardyce and Evan and David and Colette and T. C., love you." Gradually she would calm down and let herself be held. When the storm passed, we would help her set the chairs upright again.

Carol and I brought to our planning for parenthood the same egalitarian model we had used to structure the rest of our relationship. We would both, we were certain, be equally involved parents for each child. We made these plans without considering the preferences and needs of the actual children. Like a lot of new parents, we inclined toward the tabula rasa theory of parenting, expecting our daughters to be shaped almost entirely by their environment and, most particularly, by us.

In practice, it soon became clear that both girls believed they had a first mom and a second mom. The number-one mom was the one who had come to Peru and remained throughout the adoption. It was to this mom that each girl turned first when she most needed comfort and this mom who, as the babies grew older, received the brunt of any attempts to separate.

With Lucy, we tried at first to resist the distinctly different demands she made on each of us. We were sure we were each going to meet her needs equally. But as time went by we learned that we did not, in fact, possess identical gifts to bring to these children. Each of us had her own parenting strengths and her own way of doing things. And we learned that even babies have something definite to say about how a pair of humans will relate. At the same time, we came to understand that the mom who had been there first had to make room for the second mom to develop her own bond with the new baby. For two strong-minded women like us, it took some careful negotiation, but gradually we figured it out. By the time Carol brought Gracie home, we had learned that we would need to be there for each girl without trying to control how close either of them would be to either of us. All this was made much easier by the addition of Gracie to the family and by the symmetry of each girl having her own mom number one. Over the years, the preference for a mom number one would fade into a distant memory, but we couldn't know that then. At the time, the important lesson for Carol and me was to find ways to respect the connections we all shared without competing for top billing or control.

Carol had been right. Gracie did indeed complete our family.

The arrival of the children demanded of us a new level of public comfort about our lesbian lives. When we first brought Lucy home, we didn't guess how out we would have to be if we wanted our daughter to be comfortable with her family. We didn't realize just how quickly this baby would be repeating, commenting on, and questioning everything she heard us say. We knew we were both mothers to this daughter; we knew she would call us Mama-Jackie and Mama-Carol. We just didn't realize how quickly it would all become public. I'm embarrassed to admit it now, but in our first weeks at home we introduced Lucy to some of our neighbors as my daughter rather than our daughter. Soon, however, we recognized that unless we were going to begin our children's lives with impossible explanations about how wonderful our family was but how embarrassed we were about claiming it in public we would have to get ourselves entirely out of the closet and stay there. Small children don't understand homophobia, and they don't make refined distinctions between what you tell your best friend and what you tell the meter reader, but they do understand when they have a mother who is not claiming them or seems ashamed of her family.

After a while, we came to believe that as lesbian parents and adoptive parents we had a certain advocacy role. Whether we liked it or not, when we walked out the door people looked at us as different. We became, with or without our assent, ambassadors for different kinds of families.

Like other adoptive families, we quickly developed expertise in responding to intrusive questions and comments. In the park, people would look at us in surprise and ask, "Are they adopted?" "Yes," we would say, and sometimes we would add, "they're Peruvian." One stranger horrified me by saying through pursed lips, "They're really brown, aren't they?" "Yes," I answered, smiling calmly, although I wanted to bonk her on the head, "I can't get over how beautiful they are. I never get tired of looking at their gorgeous brown skin." "Which one of you is the mother?" others would ask. "We both are," we would say. "We adopted them together."

A taxi driver surveyed me and my beautiful baby and asked, "Is your husband Japanese?" "I don't have a husband," I told him, doing nothing to clear up his confusion.

As the importance of educating people in our community became clear to us, we began to welcome opportunities to let the world know that families like ours not only survive but thrive. So when someone from WBEZ, the Chicago affiliate of National Public Radio, called to invite our participation on a program about single-parent adoption, we accepted without hesitation.

During our interview, we told stories about the barriers we faced as lesbians wishing to adopt. Adopting as a couple had not even been an option, and the process required us to act as if we were single parents. We also talked about how we worked with and against the grain of the systems put in place to support adoptions by heterosexual parents. A social worker on the program with us explained why she and many other adoption workers opposed lesbian and gay adoptions. The gist of her explanation went something like: "Adoption is designed to serve the needs of the children. Adopted children have already suffered at least one trauma—the trauma of losing their birth parents. Placing them in a lesbian or gay household exposes them to the risk of further trauma—societal homophobia. In addition, the agencies seek stable families, and a union not bound by marriage is inherently less stable than one that is."

I talked about the impossible bind such reasoning creates for lesbian and gay couples. First, there's the illogic of the argument that we can protect children from homophobia by keeping them out of gay families rather than by eliminating homophobia. Second, there's the marriage Catch-22. You must be married to demonstrate a truly committed and stable relationship, we are told. OK, we say, we'll get married. No, we're told, you can't get married, it's illegal. Meanwhile, children who need families go unadopted.

During the phone-in portion of the show, one caller expressed horror at the notion of "perverts" adopting. Other callers were supportive. Lucy and Gracie climbed in and out of our laps as the adult talk eddied around them.

For Carol and me, that radio interview was an important coming-out ritual. We left the station with a deeper sense of commitment. In the absence of other defining rituals, it helped us in the ongoing project of defining ourselves as a family. For the next several days, we encountered neighbors and coworkers who had heard us on the radio. We're all the way out now, we said to ourselves and each other.

We used language consciously with the girls to nourish their conception of their kinship ties. "Family," we said over and over. "Thank you for carrying that package. You are helping our family." "This party is just for our family." "In our family, we don't hit." "I don't care what anybody else's mother does, in our family, we don't start the car until everyone is wearing her seatbelt."

It surprised me to learn that people often act as if walking, talking toddlers cannot hear. "Are the girls sisters?" strangers at the playground asked us again and again. Again and again we answered yes. "Real sisters?" they would sometimes continue. Patiently, wearily, we answered, "yes, real sisters," as the girls roared past us to clamber up the slide. Biologically they were not sisters. And legally they were not sisters, for we had each adopted one of them. But in the reality of our daily lives they were most certainly sisters. "Hermanas de corazón," one of my friends explained to me was the Spanish term for biologically unrelated girls raised in the same family. "Sisters of the heart."

Sister was a word that had a clear and specific meaning for both girls. One day when they were three and two, we were out in the backyard planting a row of Kentucky Wonder beans. I was digging the trench for the beans, and Lucy and Gracie were dropping the seeds into the ground and patting the earth over them. "Girls, be careful, you're planting the beans too close together," I admonished.

"We have to," Lucy explained to me patiently, as if to someone not too bright. "They're sisters." Beside her, Gracie tucked another white bean into the rich black soil. She nestled it snug up against Lucy's bean in the little trench I had prepared.

"Oh," I said, "OK, then." We had plenty of seeds. Beans can be thinned.

A few days later Lucy sat on a bench, barefoot, her knees bent out to her sides and her two feet touching each other sole to sole. "Look at my feet," she cried, "they're sisters!" Gracie peered over at Lucy's feet and then arranged her own to match. A sister, it was clear, was someone exactly like you, someone who grew out of the same soil as you, someone who must be kept close enough to touch.

In the early years of our relationship, Carol and I made Sundays our day. The chores were done, the papers graded or put aside for awhile. We drank coffee, read the Sunday paper, made elaborate breakfasts. We lounged around. We talked and talked.

Then Lucy and Gracie arrived. And, like all other parents who have moved away from their religious upbringings, we had to decide what we were going to teach the kids. Had they remained in their native Peru, they would probably have been raised Catholic, a version of Catholicism enriched by Quechua beliefs in the sun and the natural world as crucial sources of the divine. But that is not our heritage, and we would have been ill equipped to try to offer it to them.

Our first effort to take them to church met with mixed results. We tried a Chicago neighborhood United Church of Christ with a congregation so tiny that they met in the basement of their building. We brought Lucy and Gracie dressed in the black patent Mary Janes that I grew up calling Sunday shoes. They were only two and three and didn't know much about sitting still. They slid off our laps and clattered about the concrete floor in their patent leather shoes. We decided we weren't quite ready.

Carol and I, each in our own way, had at this time an uneasy relationship with the notion of organized religion and were hard-pressed to find a church that we found spiritually nourishing. But for all its faults, the church of my childhood had provided a solid foundation for many of my most cherished beliefs and values. I thought perhaps the same could be true for our children. I struggled in my own mind with what and how to teach the girls. I wanted them, as adults, to have access to the transcendent, to believe there was something larger at work in the world than the self or even a collection of selves, to have recourse to the strength and comfort faith can bring.

When the girls were small, I began their religious education by answering their questions and talking to them about the world the way I would have wanted someone to talk to me. Gracie, a present tense, here-

and-now girl, showed little curiosity about these subjects. Not so Lucy. "Is God a man or a woman?" she asked when she was three. "Both," I said, "and neither. God is a spirit and includes both male and female." Perhaps, I might have said, had I known how, God is the name we give to what shines out among and between us, what binds us into the mystery and power of life.

Just as we thought we might be about to settle down after all the changes we had introduced into our lives, Carol's job at Lands' End moved out from under her and up to Dodgeville, Wisconsin. A move for the whole family seemed impossible for us at this time, so Carol began working for the company part time, spending two days of each week in Dodgeville and one day working from home. Despite the challenges of a four-hundred-mile round trip and weekly two-day absence, this arrangement allowed her to spend more time with the girls and to postpone a decision about moving.

Eventually, pressured by the company to come back to work full time, Carol decided she needed to do so. When we look back now on how we tried to solve this problem of two satisfying but demanding careers in cities two hundred miles apart, we think we must have been crazy, but at the time it seemed to us our best course of action. I was willing to do almost anything to accommodate Carol's work short of leaving my tenured position at DePaul. So in the summer of 1992 we retained an apartment for my use in our two-apartment building in Chicago, bought a house in Madison, Wisconsin, and prepared to move our family there.

The girls were too little to have any worries about a move. We had told them what our plans were, and it sounded to them like a great adventure. At dawn on moving day, Lucy roused us to action with, "Moms! Wake up. It's moving day!"

For our first six weeks in Madison, I was on summer break. After that, I left our girls at day care each Monday morning and returned to Madison each Thursday in time for supper. From Monday through Thursday, Carol was a single mom, one who had to commute forty miles to work every day. I applied for a research leave for the following year, and we hoped we could manage this disjointed arrangement for nine months.

The Preschool of the Arts, where the girls spent their days, was really their first foray into the public world. They had been home with their moms and Delia, a wonderful in-home day care provider, until the move to Madison. For Carol and me, it was a new experience to have to explain to the teachers who worked with our children that we were, in fact, a family.

Our adjustment to our new community was eased considerably by the existence of a large, vibrant, lesbian moms group. We learned about that group from a Chicago friend who knew one of the moms even before we moved. Word of our arrival preceded us to Madison, and on our first Saturday in town one of the moms approached us at the Farmers' Market and asked if we were Carol and Jackie. "How did you ever guess?" we kidded, knowing that once anyone had our description—two tall, thin, androgynous-looking moms with two tiny, black-headed, Peruvian girls—they could pick us out of most any crowd.

Soon we were spending one Saturday a month with the moms and kids group. There were a few other families with adopted children, but most of the children were biological. In any case, we had a lot to talk to each other about as we navigated what often seemed the uncharted seas of raising children in a lesbian family. At our meetings, the moms spent the time talking about parenting while the children played together. We quickly made friends.

Shortly before Christmas, I heard one of the little girls in this group say to Lucy, "You didn't come out of your mom's tummy." I held my breath and listened intently, wondering what Lucy would have to say to that.

"That's right," she agreed. "I came out of Maria Chacpa's tummy. But my moms were waiting for me." What a gal, what an answer.

Lucy's preschool class was hard at work on a holiday program, the focus of eager anticipation and weeks of careful rehearsal. Lucy danced around the house for several weeks singing "Here Comes Susie Snowflake," complete with a whole series of choreographed hand movements. She brought home a copy of a carefully crayoned invitation to the "Moms and Dads." At last the long-awaited performance date arrived. Carol took the day off work, and we both arrived, equipped with a regular camera and a video camera, just like every other pair of parents in the room. Every child but ours seemed to have a mom and a dad, and all the parents looked at least ten years younger than Carol and me. We sat down on our tiny chairs with all the other parents and clapped for our happy, busy children. I videotaped it all. I guess this made me the butch that day since all the other video camera operators were dads. Lucy and all her friends, it goes without saying, were magnificent, brilliant. The teacher thanked all of us "moms and dads" for coming, and we joined our budding performers for some snacks.

In the kitchen that night, as I prepared supper and Lucy and Gracie colored and drew at their little table, Lucy suddenly announced, "My mom and dad came to see my Christmas program today."

I was dicing an onion. I paused, raking onion bits onto the cutting board from the side of the chef's knife as I turned toward Lucy and blinked against the sharp scent of the onions. "Oh yeah?" I grinned at her. "It looked like your mom and mom to me."

"No," Lucy said firmly. "Carol was my mom and you were my dad." She studied me to see what I would make of this.

"Sweetheart, any time you need me to be your dad, you just say the word, and I'm your man or woman or whatever. When you need me for a mom, I'm your mom. When you need me for a dad, I'll be your dad."

Lucy said nothing to this, but I saw her face relax. She was relieved, perhaps, that I hadn't launched into some technically accurate but emotionally irrelevant speech about the fact that she had two moms, not a mom and a dad.

Again and again when we filled out forms, Carol and I crossed a line through the word "father" and replaced it with "parent," before writing down the second mom's name. In that split second between Lucy's assertion of a mom and dad and my reply, I wondered what on earth I should say and why in all those shelves of parental advice there wasn't a manual for any of our situations. Her look of relief assured me that through some special grace extended to lesbian and adoptive parents I had found the words she needed to hear.

That spring Lucy began coming home from her preschool complaining about her brown skin and black hair. Although Madison prides itself on its diversity, in the girls' preschool there was such a preponderance of blond children that diversity seemed to mean a child with brown hair. There were at most two or three other brown-skinned children in the entire preschool. One night, when Lucy said yet again that she hated her black hair, I said, "Oh, I love your black hair. I wish I had black hair.

Wait," I commanded and ran from the room. I dug a pair of black leggings from my dresser drawer and returned to the living room wearing them on my head like a hat. The long black legs hung down over my shoulders. "What do you think? I have black hair now, too." Lucy started laughing.

"Don't laugh at me," I said in mock dismay. "I want long black hair and this is as close as I can get."

"Mama-Jackie, you look ridiculous. You're wearing your pants on top of your head."

"Oh, OK," I said, pulling them off. "I thought it was worth a try." After the girls were tucked into bed that night, Carol and I talked about Lucy's worries. "We've got to get outta here," we said to one another, "and back to the city where we belong."

It was not just Lucy's remark about her hair and skin that worried us. None of us seemed quite able to find her place in this new community. Carol's company had grown larger and gone public. The easy collegiality of her early years there was no more. We missed our old friends and, although we attended a church in our neighborhood, continued to feel like outsiders. And it was hard on all of us to have me gone from home so much.

In December, Carol resigned from her job, and we sold our Madison house and moved back to Chicago. On a bitterly cold day just after Christmas, I was driving the girls to the dentist. During the holidays, we had talked to the girls about the importance of giving gifts as well as getting them. We had told them that part of our Christmas celebration is to share with people who do not have as much as we do. We had explained about the money we send to organizations working to feed hungry people in Chicago and Peru. We had carried cans of food to the preschool and put them in food drive boxes. Suddenly, Lucy piped up from the back seat. "We should send a check to Maria Chacpa." Her birth mother had been in her thoughts often that year.

"That would be a great idea, but we don't know her address. We're still trying to find out how to get in touch with her." I waited for a moment. "Lucy, are you worried that Maria Chacpa might be hungry?"

"Yes. We need to send her some money."

"I wish we could, sweetheart. We will have to keep working on finding a way to write to her."

At dinner, I mentioned Lucy's concern to Carol. Carol brought out a brochure for a food kitchen in Peru. People in the pictures were lined up to get food. "We sent some money for these people," Carol explained.

Lucy scrutinized the faces. "Maria Chacpa is there. She's getting food," Lucy announced with glee.

There was no one in the picture who looked like Maria, but Lucy so wanted there to be. She wanted to take care of her Peruvian mother.

"Let me tell you something, Lucy," I said. "Your birth mother is a smart, strong, resourceful woman. She is a survivor. She will find a way to take care of herself and get the food she needs whether or not we are able to help her."

An hour later, I checked with her again. "Are you still worrying about Maria Chacpa?" I asked.

"No," Lucy told me. "I thought about what you said, and I knew that it was right."

"There is something we can do for Maria Chacpa even when we do not know how to send her money. We can say a prayer for her."

"And for my daddy," Lucy suggested.

At bedtime, we said our goodnight prayers, especially remembering Maria Chacpa and Lucy's daddy. "What is his name, God?" Lucy asked. Then she said, "I know his name. Mr. Man-Man."

"That will work fine, for now. Anyway, God knows his name even if we don't."

Lucy continued with her prayer. She included a petition on behalf of Aladdin and the two hungry children he shared his bread with. She put in a word for children everywhere. Her heart held so much, I worried that it might burst.

"Goodnight, God," I said.

"What are you doing, God?" Lucy asked. She was going to have the last word. "Are you listening, God? Why are you listening, God?"

12

*Baby Can't Remember
How to Sleep*

Gracie, from the very beginning, was a championship sleeper. She floated into slumber each night with enviable ease, sleeping soundly, albeit with both eyes only partway closed. Not for her the long prelude of stories and songs. If she was sleepy and found herself in the bed, she slept.

Lucy, on the other hand, was never a big sleeper. Carol and I had dutifully researched infant sleep patterns before adopting her, but she seemed to come with her own (unpublished) instructions. After a nice warm bottle and a somewhat extravagant amount of singing and rocking, she would usually go to sleep. She just wouldn't stay asleep. After a few hours, our bright-eyed three-and-a-half-month-old would wake up ready to party. She didn't care much about the midnight bottle. She just wanted to play.

Nor did she nap much. Oh, she would doze off in the Snugli for a few minutes, but she had little aptitude for the long morning and afternoon naps the books had forecast. By eighteen months, no bed could hold her. She would scale the bars of her crib and drop to the floor ready for action. By age three, naps were a thing of the past. She had finally learned to sleep through the night once we quit running to her side at the first yelp. But she could not get to sleep until we had all but sung ourselves hoarse. Once, a worn-out babysitter, having rocked, sung, and patted well beyond what must have seemed to her all reasonable limits, asked a wide-awake Lucy, "How long does this go on?"

"Until you get tired," was Lucy's perceptive reply.

Perhaps it was coincidence. But it was almost as if Gracie, who Carol had adopted, inherited her ability to sleep well, while Lucy had absorbed a kind of fitfulness that I sometimes felt I had inherited from my mother.

That last summer in Madison, the summer of Lucy's fourth year, her restless energy seemed to reach new heights. Each week I had traveled down to Chicago to teach my classes. By the time the academic year ended and I came home full time, Lucy was furious. I had left her too many times. Whenever I reached out for Gracie, Lucy walloped her or tried to clamber over her into my lap. She threw tantrums. She refused to cooperate.

Perhaps, I thought, we needed some alone time. One Saturday morning she and I said good-bye to Gracie and Carol and went to the Farmers' Market. She loved our private outing and, expansively, chose for me a pair of handmade earrings from a street vendor. I paid for and accepted her gift with many thanks. It was a magical morning, but Lucy was not about to forgive me that easily. Back home the tantrums, the jealousy, the anger continued.

What to do now? I talked to a therapist who had been helpful to me in the past. "You need to tell Lucy the story of her adoption."

"She knows the story of her adoption," I protested. We had consulted those books, too. We were the conscientious sort of parents who make adoption story scrapbooks and page through them with loving recollections of how this particular family came to be.

"Well, tell it to her again, and make it as rich and detailed as you possibly can."

Coming, as I do, from a long line of storytellers, and with the creating and teaching of autobiography a cornerstone of my life's work, I didn't need to be persuaded of the healing power of narrative. So, weaving together all that I knew and what I could imagine, I made a story for Lucy. During a quiet moment, I told it to her.

I told her about Maria Chacpa, the nineteen-year-old mother who had birthed her alone in her one-room house in the mountains of Peru, naming her Maricruz. I explained that this mother, young, poor, and single, knew she needed to find a family who could care for her baby and decided, at her Aunt Esperanza's suggestion, to travel to Lima to arrange an adoption.

"Two months after Maricruz was born," I said, "Esperanza, Maria Chacpa, and Maricruz boarded the bus to Lima. Maria Chacpa carried the baby on her back in a blanket. She also carried a change of clothes for herself and the baby and food to eat on the way. The bus was small and the ride bumpy. People of all ages were crammed onto the bus. There were even some goats and chickens. All the women carried brightly colored woven blankets filled with food, clothing, artwork, or, as in the case of Maricruz, children." Although I couldn't know with any certainty how mother and baby had made this trip, I fashioned the story based on what seemed likely.

I told Lucy how, back in Chicago, Lucy's two moms had begun to prepare to bring a baby into their family. Here I emphasized, as adoptive parents regularly do, the intentional and loving welcome in store for her. Our hope, I suppose, is that the deep purpose and love with which we greet our children will soften the pain of that first abandonment. And perhaps it does soften what it cannot erase. I told of the excitement with which we boarded the plane, the thrill we felt when we held our daughter for the first time. She heard how she had been named Lucia Maricruz, keeping the name given her by Maria Chacpa and adding one from her two new moms. The story of our two-month sojourn in Peru to complete the adoption ended with our safe arrival back in Chicago, where we would "live together as a family forever."

Lucy listened deeply. "Lucy," I said quietly, "you can hear that story any time you want to. All you need to do is ask."

"Right now."

"You want me to tell it again right now?"

"Yes."

I began again. About a third of the way through the story, Lucy popped *Peter Pan* into her tape player and began to page through the accompanying picture book.

"Shall we finish the adoption story another time?"

"No. Both at once. I want to hear both."

So I told the story of her adoption in one ear, while with her other ear she listened to the tale of Peter Pan, the lost boy, the boy without a mom, the boy who wants a mom so badly he teaches a young girl to fly off to Neverland with him. From time to time, I paused to ask Lucy to supply a name, a destination, or some other piece of the story. In truth, I was checking to see if she was really listening. Each time she responded instantly. She was right with me, listening intently to every word, even as she was right with Peter Pan, off in the magical world of Neverland.

After the story, Lucy appeared more relaxed and happy, even peaceful. But over the next two weeks the angry tantrums and jealous rages toward her little sister continued. Once Lucy lay on the floor kicking and crying. As I approached her, she jabbed her legs in my direction, trying to kick me. "It looks to me like you have a lot of kicks in there," I said, firmly grasping each ankle. "I'm going to help you get them out." Moving in concert with her, I bent her knees up toward her chest and pulled them back in the kicker's version of riding a bicycle. She looked surprised for a moment and then began to laugh. Within minutes, the storm, with its anger, was gone and she had returned from her baby tantrum to her four-year-old self. I was astonished. This was one of a hundred strategies I had tried at such moments but the only one that had ever worked. Yet the significance did not yet register with me.

About a week later, in the midst of yet another intense tantrum, I popped a pacifier into Lucy's mouth. She spat it out. I had tried holding her to calm her, but she was all fight. Suddenly, I remembered. "Lucy, you are very angry," I said. "I am going to lay you down on the floor and help you get your kicks out." As I began to join her in her kicking, Lucy's crying evolved into a combination of crying and laughing. Soon she was simply laughing. Within a matter of moments, she had left her rage behind. I began to slow the kicking and then moved into a gentle scissors kick.

Lucy was calm, but where had three-year-old Gracie gone? I found her curled up with her special pillow on the screened back porch, sucking her finger. She ignored me. "Gracie, I know it's scary for you when Lucy has these storms. I just want you to know that I can take care of

Lucy and I can take care of you." This was another story, one I hoped was true. It often seemed that even two moms weren't enough. She put her head on my leg and continued sucking her finger as I stroked her hair. Lucy walked into the room and snuggled onto my other leg. She began talking sweetly to Gracie. I sat for a long time, holding these two precious girls, stroking their hair, speaking soft words of love.

We could see that Lucy sometimes got stuck in a baby rage, a rage that carried her back to a wordless infant fury. And when the rages swirled around her, Gracie retreated into a private world of her own, waiting for the storm to pass.

It was the day before our Chicago neighborhood's stupendous block party, and we had traveled down from Madison to be part of it. I was weeding and edging the front yard. Lucy and Gracie, on their tricycles, pretended to travel to various destinations—New York, Milwaukee, New Jersey. Lucy carried a small notebook. Suddenly, Gracie snatched it.

"Gracie, NO!" Lucy shouted. "That's my directions to Peru, and I can't remember how to get there."

"Lucy," I asked, "does that little notebook have your directions to San Martín?"

"Yes," she said.

"Gracie," I explained, "that paper is very important to Lucy. It tells her how to get back to the village where she was born. You must give it back."

Gracie handed it over, and calm was restored.

That night Lucy could not sleep. The noise on our block was deafening, as our excited neighbors decorated their houses and checked out the sound system for the next day's fiesta. Carol and Gracie were sound asleep by 9:30 despite the commotion, but Lucy and I could not rest. We walked the block at 10:15, admiring the decorations and enjoying the warm greetings of various neighbors. We went back inside and read books. At 11:15, Lucy was almost beside herself with exhaustion, but still she could not sleep. I had tried singing to her, rubbing and scratching her back, and lying quietly beside her, but despite my efforts, she only grew more agitated. Finally I asked her if she would like me to kick her legs. She nodded and then fell asleep in midkick twenty seconds after I began.

The next day, while Carol took the girls to the end of the block for pony rides, I called the therapist again to describe Lucy's anxiety. She suggested that Lucy felt angry with her mother for giving her up for adoption. "Tell her the story again. And this time you must tell her that her mother loved her and was sad to give her up."

The therapist offered insights about Gracie, as well. "Whenever Lucy has a tantrum, Gracie goes back to the orphanage. You cannot let her get lost. You have to help her stay in touch with her own story. She has less of her birth mother in her since she spent no time with her after birth. She will let you know what she needs to hear. But she needs her own birth story, including the loneliness and anger she felt as she waited for you in the orphanage. She needs that lost part of her story."

That night, full of candy that had rained down from the piñatas and worn out from dancing, Lucy fell fast asleep by 10:00. Three-year-old Gracie, carried inside over her protests, partied on alone. At 10:30, with Lucy asleep beside her, she danced on the bed, punching her fingers into the air and singing along with the music blasting from the street, "Do it, do it, do it!"

On Sunday, tired but happy, Lucy and Gracie were playing quietly in the living room. This peaceful moment seemed an opportune time to follow the therapist's advice. I sat beside Lucy. "I want to tell you something about Maria Chacpa," I said. Gracie continued playing, but she glanced toward me, and I could see she was listening, too. Lucy climbed into my lap. I held her like a baby as I began to tell her how sad Maria Chacpa was to tell her good-bye.

"Why?" Lucy asked with surprise.

"Honey, she loved you so much."

"Tell me my story," Lucy demanded. And so we began again.

I added new details. I told Lucy how her mother had named her Maricruz Fiorella, the name of a young woman she had watched in a Mexican *telenovela* (soap opera). Maricruz Fiorella was the star, the one everyone most admired. Maria Chacpa chose this name for her baby because she wanted her girl to have a life as wonderful as the one the character on the program enjoyed. In truth, I do not know why Maria Chacpa chose this name. I only know that the translator laughed with delight when she heard Lucy's birth name and explained its origin. I imagined Maria Chacpa in front of the television, perhaps in the home of an aunt or cousin, watching the unfolding story of the beautiful Maricruz Fiorella as her own belly swelled with her pregnancy. Years later, while traveling in Mexico, I would learn that the *telenovela* was called *Quinceañera* and that the character Maricruz Fiorella was a maid. But I knew none of this then.

I continued relating how glad Maria Chacpa had been to see Lucy once again at the courthouse when we finalized the adoption and how she had held her and given her a bottle. How we all went to lunch afterward and then drove Maria Chacpa to her friend's home. I recounted Maria Chacpa's final instructions, "Take good care of her. Just don't make her cry." I explained how we went at once to develop our film with double prints. Three hours later the photographs were ready, and our attorney, Ana Maria, delivered a set to Maria Chacpa, identical to the ones in our adoption photo album.

Lucy looked at me in wonder and amazement. "Maria Chacpa has those same pictures?"

"Why, yes, honey, they are a great treasure to her. She thinks of you every day." Lucy looked at me and let out a deep breath. "Your birth mother took those pictures back to San Martín and showed them to all her friends."

Lucy looked at her sister. "Now tell Gracie's story," she demanded.

"That story belongs to Gracie. We can tell it if you want to hear it, Gracie, or we can go eat lunch."

"Tell my story," said Gracie. And so I did. Because we never met Gracie's mother, because she disappeared without a trace soon after Gracie was born, this was a sparser tale, constructed out of details passed to us by the folks at the orphanage.

As she sat on my lap, I told Gracie of the young woman in Lima who came to the hospital Sergio Bernales to give birth. Her name, she said, was Elba Rosario, and she was nineteen years old. On April 11, 1990, she gave birth to a beautiful baby girl. Soon afterward, she left the hospital. I described this disappearance as a plan, emphasizing the woman's belief that the hospital would care for her baby.

Gracie, who didn't yet have a name, began waiting, first at the hospital, later at the orphanage. There were many other babies in the orphanage and not always enough workers to pick the babies up as often as the babies would have liked. "Sometimes," I said, "Baby Gracie was lonely, sometimes she was angry, and sometimes she was bored, wondering when her life would really begin."

"Why?" asked Gracie.

"Because even though the workers at the orphanage fed you and took care of you the best they could, they were too busy to give you the attention and holding that you needed and wanted."

I described our preparations for her in Chicago, Carol's trip to get her, and the moment they met. How Mama-Carol held Gracie in her arms and said, "Her name is Gracia Esperanza. Grace and Hope."

I added more details about the two-month wait in Peru for the adoption to be completed and then told of our meeting in Chicago. "At the airport, Lucy and Mama-Jackie met Mama-Carol and the new baby. Everyone hugged and hugged. And that is the story of how Gracie came to be in our family forever.

"Mama-Carol can tell you that story again. She can tell you more than I can about what your time together in Peru was like because she was there." Gracie looked pleased. Carol came in, and we all sat down to lunch.

That afternoon we went swimming. Lucy announced that she wanted to be my baby. I carried her around for ten or fifteen minutes at the public pool. She enjoyed all this babying to the hilt, spicing her four-year-old chatter with "gagagoogoos" and crawling or walking with stiff legs, when I sat her down while I showered. As we headed toward the parking lot, my beach-towel-blanketed baby wrapped her arms around my neck, looked deep into my eyes, and pronounced, "You're my mama, FOREVER."

"Yes, Lucy love, I'm your mama FOREVER." I hoped that deep in her heart she could begin to believe it.

Unfortunately, an hour or so after Lucy declared our forever connection, I had to say good-bye for another few days as Carol and the girls headed back to Madison. I returned on Wednesday afternoon and picked the girls up at preschool. Lucy appeared quite matter-of-fact about my return and then, at our house, threw a major tantrum about getting out of the car. She struck out at Gracie and me, then remained screaming in the yard as we went into the house. Little by little, she calmed herself. After ten minutes, I saw her picking raspberries in the backyard. Soon she came inside. Yet at suppertime Lucy, who was usually attached to me like one of those little sticktights you pick up on your socks when you walk through a field in August, did not want anything to do with me.

"Go away," she said firmly. "I want to eat by myself. Gracie can stay. But not you."

"OK," I said. "I'll be in the next room." After a few minutes, I was invited to return. I could come back to Lucy. But only at her bidding.

At bedtime, Lucy was full of what looked like good cheer. She seemed to want to party. I was reminded of the almost manic merriment with which she greeted Carol and me in the middle of the night when we were first together in Peru. We thought then that we were being worked, but, happy to be at her beck and call, we didn't mind. It was as if she were determined to charm and distract us so that she would not have to sleep— a tactic she had never entirely abandoned but one I hadn't seen in such force in some time.

I offered to tell her a story. That was how my mother always calmed me. "Tell about Casper," she said, requesting a story from Carol's repertoire.

"Mama-Carol tells that story. Let me see. I'll tell you a story about when I was a little girl."

"Tell a story about when I was a little girl. Tell my adoption story."

"Is that what you want to hear?"

"Yes."

This time, when the story ended, Lucy had questions. "Where is Maria Chacpa now?" she asked.

"Well, honey, she was planning to go back to San Martín. I think it's likely she's there, but I can't be sure. It's possible that she returned to Lima. I've written her a couple of letters, but I've never heard from her. I don't know whether she got them."

"Will she have other babies?"

"I don't know, but I imagine so. She was very young when you were born—only nineteen."

"Will she take the other babies to Ana Maria to be adopted?"

"I don't know. She might." Behind that question were the unspoken, unspeakable questions: "Am I the only one she gave away? Will she love some other baby more than me?"

"She doesn't have money or much family or many resources. It's almost impossible for her to take care of a baby," I said.

"Let's find her," Lucy said eagerly. "We could go to Peru and find her and she could come and live with us. We have plenty of food."

"Oh, honey," I sighed, "wouldn't that be wonderful?"

"Will we go to Peru?"

"Someday when you are bigger."

"Could I go by myself?"

"Do you want to?" I asked, surprised. Lucy nodded. "Would you be scared?" I asked. She nodded again.

"Maybe," she suggested, "Gracie and I could go by ourselves when we are bigger."

"Of course you can if you want to. And if you decide it is too scary to go by yourself, Mama-Carol and I will go with you."

"We could all go!" Lucy exclaimed with delight and relief. She thought for a moment. "I want to sing Maria Chacpa a song."

"OK," I said, "what do you want to sing to her?"

Lucy answered with our family's well-worn adaptation of "Normal American Boy" from *Bye Bye, Birdie.*

> *We love you Maria Chacpa,*
> *Oh yes we do.*

I joined my voice with hers, fighting back my tears.

> *We don't love anyone,*
> *Like we love you.*
> *When you're not near to us,*
> *We're blue.*
> *Oh, Maria Chacpa, we love you.*

I was all choked up, but Lucy laughed with pleasure. "Now," she said, "let's sing to Elba Rosario." This was the name by which we knew Gracie's birth mother.

"OK," I said again. I marveled at her ability to navigate her way through this terrain of rage, grief, loss, and integration as she enfolded each of the birth mothers into our family and her circle of love. We sang to Elba Rosario. And then, one more round, this time to both birth mothers and Gracie together.

> *We love you Maria Chacpa and Elba Rosario and Gracie,*
> *Oh yes we do . . .*

Now everyone she needed to integrate into her family had been sung together into a necessary whole, sung together with the song we used to enfold one another—especially when we were about to be parted. At last her work was done for the night. She curled up against me and let me sing her to sleep. At nine-thirty, well past her usual bedtime, I felt the tension and constant motion leave her muscular little body.

An hour and a half later, just as Carol and I had turned out our light, she awakened, sobbing. We both leaped from the bed. Carol took her in her arms. Huge sobs wracked her little barrel chest. Carol sat on our bed with her and rocked her with her body. "It's OK, Lucy, baby, your mamas are here."

Lucy was crying as if her little heart would break. There was a desperate edge to these painful sobs, as if she were searching for someone, something. "You're so sad, honey," Carol murmured, stroking her hair, "It's OK to be sad. Do you want Mama-Jackie? She's right here."

Lucy, whose eyes had not yet even opened, sought me out by smell and touch and crawled into my arms. She snuggled against me and stopped crying. I carried her back to her bed. As I settled her in, she clutched at me. I lay down beside her. My hand brushed her cheek. Her face moved toward my fingers in the instinctive rooting motion of a tiny baby searching for the nipple. I cuddled close and held her tight. She clung to me and settled again into a deep sleep.

The next morning I sat at our cherry dining table drinking tea and looking out at the birds busily harvesting berries in the backyard. Lucy walked stiff-legged to the top of the stairs. "It's Baby Lucy," she announced.

I knew this already, for that stiff-kneed walk always signaled the return of the baby. "Come on down here and crawl in my lap, Baby Lucy." She toddled down the stairs and into my arms. I cuddled her up close and we talked baby talk to each other. Lucy, not usually much of a cuddler, was all snuggles that morning.

"You woke up crying last night. Do you remember?"

She did not.

"I thought maybe you weren't completely awake. You were so sad. So sad. You cried as if your heart were breaking."

She said nothing, but she was listening closely.

I invented an explanation, the best one I could think of. "I think maybe you were mad at me yesterday for going away when you need me with you so badly right now. Were you mad at Mama-Jackie?"

She nodded solemnly.

"Baby, I'm sorry I had to be away when you needed me here so much. I love you so."

From upstairs, I could hear Gracie beginning to stir. After a few minutes, Carol, who was on her way to work, carried her down. "You have another baby," she told me.

With a grumble, Lucy moved over to the leg I always told her was hers and made room for Gracie, who climbed into place and cuddled close. Later that day I would hear from Carol how Gracie had come to the top of the stairs, looked at Baby Lucy in my lap, let out a whimper, and run to our bed. She had burrowed under the covers and begun sucking her finger. Carol scooped her up. "Come on, Baby Gracie. Mama-Jackie has room for you, too. Come in my arms and let me carry you down to be her baby."

After a few more minutes of cuddles, we moved to the kitchen to start breakfast. "Tell Gracie's adoption story," Lucy commanded.

"That story belongs to Gracie," I replied. "We tell it when she wants to hear it."

"No. I don't want it," growled Gracie. Unlike Lucy, she liked to ease into the day.

"Then tell my story," said Lucy, coming by this indirect route to her real agenda. "I want to hear mine."

"You want to hear it again? OK." And so, for the third time in five days, I told Lucy's story. At its conclusion, Lucy began to sing again what she had selected as the ritual song for bringing Maria Chacpa into our family. Gracie and I joined in as the Rice Krispies snapped, crackled, and popped a gentle percussion. It was a satisfying moment, and one I suspected I had better enjoy, for if the past held any clue to what lay before us the next storm was already gathering on the horizon.

I scrambled all that summer to give Lucy the narrative tools with which to shape her own story. It occurred to me to wonder whether I was leading her where she needed to go or simply where I imagined she needed to go. Or, worse, someplace I needed her to go. Yet she persistently returned to the subject of her adoption.

One weekend our family attended a Peruvian picnic. Entering the park, we saw the Peruvian flag waving over a crowd organizing picnic tables and choosing teams for a soccer game. Peruvian music blasted from a loudspeaker. About two-thirds of the families at the picnic were Peruvian. The other third were families like ours, with American-born parents and Peruvian adoptees. We enjoyed the gorgeous weather, the friendly people, the delicious food, the music. Driving home, we asked the girls what they thought of the event.

"Good," Lucy pronounced. Then, after a moment, she added, "One of the women looked like Maria Chacpa."

Surprised, I followed her lead, "Which one?"

"The one with the headband," Lucy replied.

"Yes, she did look something like Maria Chacpa," Carol agreed.

Neither of us had guessed that Lucy would go to the picnic looking for her birth mother. But she did. And in her determined fashion she found her.

When a friend was leaving for Peru at the end of August as a Fulbright teacher and scholar. I asked whether she would be willing to carry a letter to Peru for Lucy, explaining that the mail is unreliable and we had no address for her birth mother. Characteristically, she offered more than I asked, promising to find someone from Tarma who could try to get the letter to San Martín and to deliver a copy to our attorney, who might know Maria Chacpa's whereabouts.

I hung up the phone and told Lucy.

"OK. Great!" She grabbed colored markers and paper and set to work. She invited her sister to join her, and Gracie, who loves art projects, happily complied. Soon Lucy had the two of them singing, "We love you Maria Chacpa and Elba Rosario, Oh yes we do-ooo," as they busily colored and drew. Within minutes, Lucy presented me with a brightly colored abstract shape, a construction paper flap pasted over it. Lucy explained that you could lift the flap for a surprise.

"Beautiful!" I said. "She'll love it. Would you like to write her a letter?"
Lucy nodded. "Yes."
She began dictating immediately, the words tumbling out.

> August 1, 1993
> Dear Maria Chacpa,
>
> I love you. There is so much I like in Madison. I like everything.
> I like you too. Best of all, I like you very much. I like my raspber-
> ries outside in my garden. Everything in Madison, I like. I got a
> drink of apple juice on the way home from the farmers' market. I
> have a nice house in Chicago. I have a nice garden, there's so
> much, there's flowers. I like all my neighbors. I like ponies.
> Someday, when I get bigger, I want to ride a horse all by myself.
> I love you very much.
>
> Love,
> Lucy

I read Lucy's dictated note back to her and she approved. I wrote one
of my own to enclose. I invited Maria Chacpa to write us back, assured
her that Lucy was doing well, and expressed my hope that she, too, was
well. As I sealed up the packet of letters, artwork, and Lucy's school pho-
tograph, I felt a little bit like I was preparing a message in a bottle. I could-
n't know if our missives would ever find Maria Chacpa.

With the letter sealed, we hit one of those good patches that I always
hoped were the way it was going to be from now on. I wanted Lucy's pain
and worry to be something we could fix. For the moment, it seemed so.
Lucy's face relaxed, and she grew more peaceful and happy.

When I asked her to brush her teeth or wash her hands or pick up her
toys, she said "OK" and went and did it. She seemed older, like children
do when they have been raising hell and then suddenly take one of those
giant steps forward. Of course, easier times are never a destination, just a
stop on the journey.

One hot afternoon, the girls asked if they could get out their watercolors and paint each other. They had had a rollicking good time doing
this once before, but the washable watercolors ended up rubbing off on
the furniture. "OK," I agreed, "but you must take a bath as soon as you
finish."

They agreed, but when they finished painting Lucy threw a fit. Once Gracie was clean and dry, I dunked furious Lucy into the tub, becoming pretty thoroughly drenched in the process. Ensconced in a towel and sucking a pacifier, she still raged at bath's end, picking on Gracie and yelling at me. I was baffled.

"Lucy," I said in exasperation, "you cannot be this angry about the bath." Lucy usually enjoyed baths and calmed down in the water. "What on earth are you so mad about?" Even as I asked, I wondered if I was ascribing too much meaning to her bath resistance. It was not as though she was ordinarily an easygoing child. But if I was imagining a larger significance, so was she.

"I'm mad because you didn't meet the bus," she shouted.

"What bus?" I asked, confused. There was no bus to preschool.

"The bus Maria Chacpa brought me to Lima on."

"Well, that makes sense. You needed me to meet the bus. And, honey, if I had known you were on that bus, I would have been there."

"And I'm mad because I didn't grow inside your body," she was still yelling out her answers, but there was less steam behind the words now.

"Of course you are." I ventured a pat on the back and then a hug. "I would have loved to carry you inside my body. Honey, we can't go back and make it different, but we can imagine what it might have been like if you had grown inside me." I helped her get dressed and we moved to a table on the screened back porch. I pulled out some art supplies for her and for Gracie.

Lucy began drawing on one of those erasable tablets.

"Why don't you draw a picture of you growing inside of me?" I suggested.

"I can't draw that," Lucy said impatiently. "You draw it."

And so I sketched myself with the big pregnant belly I never had and Lucy visibly curled up inside me as she never was.

"That's so cu-ute!" she exclaimed, drawing *cute* out into a two-sylla-ble replication of my own Southern accent. "Now draw Gracie growing inside Carol."

Alongside my pregnant figure, I added Carol's.

"Oh, that's so cute! Gracie! Look!"

Gracie glanced up and then returned to her own artwork.

Lucy had more ideas. "Now draw you and Carol holding me and Gracie as tiny babies," Lucy instructed. For a moment I started to object that they were not tiny babies at the same time, but this had nothing to do with a linear view of history. I drew as instructed. "Cute!" she pronounced again and again invited Gracie to look.

"Now," she said with growing authority, "draw me by myself as a tiny baby."

I drew a Lucy-like baby sitting up and looking at us. But of course that was wrong, for Lucy did not sit up until several months after we had her.

"No," she said, frustrated by my obtuseness, "a tiny baby, lying down, wrapped in blankets."

"Oh," I said, "of course. A tiny baby," and I drew as directed. By this time, we were drawing on sheets of paper. She held up the picture of the two pregnant mamas and the tiny baby with satisfaction.

As soon as Carol walked in from work, Lucy ran to her with the pictures. "How wonderful," Carol said. "But Lucy, I, too, would have loved to have you grow inside my body."

"My feet can grow inside your body," Lucy told her, "and the rest of me can grow inside Mama-Jackie."

"That would be perfect," Mama-Carol agreed.

Lucy actively reshaped her earliest history through these drawings, urging me to create the missing family photographs—the ones that pictured her and her sister growing inside their moms, rocked by their moms from earliest infancy. She calmed still further after the pictures were completed, lulling me, once more, into the fantasy that we had finally told the story or drawn the drawing to calm all hurts. If we hadn't, it is because our hurts never can be quite that simple, and yet each retelling soothed and calmed if it could not entirely heal.

I suppose I should not have been altogether surprised, on the day in July that began with Lucy and Gracie perched in my lap declaring themselves babies, to find that they had not miraculously matured into three and four year olds while at preschool. When I picked them up that afternoon, Lucy announced that she was a baby and could not walk to the car. I suggested that I carry her and hold Gracie's hand, whereupon Gracie also sat down and refused to move. She held the position of baby by birthright (adoption right?) and wasn't about to relinquish it.

"OK," I said brightly (too brightly). "One of you can sit here in the hall, while I carry the other to the car, and then I'll come back." I was glad no other parents or teachers were listening. What if my narrative theories were all askew and I was in reality just one more overindulgent baby boomer who didn't know how to control her children?

Neither daughter was having any of my idea. Neither wanted to be the baby left behind. I could see only two alternatives. I could drag both daughters kicking and screaming to the car (seventy-five total pounds of active resistance, two lunch boxes, and assorted artwork), guaranteeing a spectacle, or I could sit down with them in the hall until they got sufficiently tired of waiting to walk.

I stood there, feeling frustrated and inadequate. A better mother would know what to do now. A better mother never would have gotten herself into such a pickle. Fortunately, a big-hearted preschool teacher happened along at that moment and put Lucy on her back while I carried Gracie. As we headed at last toward the door, Lucy's teacher paused to ask whether Lucy might be anxious about anything. "Yes," I replied, unable to provide details with both girls in earshot, "she's got a lot on her mind right now. Why?"

"She's tearing her nails down to the quick and she's even more restless than usual," she explained. The restlessness was literal. Lucy did not rest. She was the only child in the class of three and four year olds who never took a nap.

"She's not much of a napper," I said. "You might want to let her lie quietly and look at a book. Maybe we can talk about this some more tomorrow."

Back home I parked the girls in front of a video while I started supper. I could see that they were much too tired to play together without bloodshed. By the time the video ended, the spaghetti was ready and waiting. But suddenly Lucy was enraged, insisting that she could eat only if Gracie were not there, screaming and crying and trying to hit her sister. I sat on the floor and held her in my arms, so she could not hurt anyone. I told her I could see she was feeling angry and sad. "I know you're having a tough time, honey," I tried to soothe. But Lucy could not calm herself, and my attempts to calm her only seemed to make her angrier.

"I'm too tired to eat!" she wailed. Spaghetti was her favorite meal, so I knew she was in desperate shape.

"I'll put you to bed, honey. Gracie, do you want to pet Louise while I put Lucy to bed? We can finish our supper in a minute." Gracie adored the cat and always sought her out the moment we returned to the house.

I lay down with Lucy and began to sing, but she soon decided she was hungry. "I'm too tired, and I'm too thirsty, and I'm too hungry." That sounded right to me. It had been days since she had slept well.

While Gracie lay on the floor petting Louise, I fed Lucy, spoon by spoon, like a baby. She calmed. For her second and third platefuls, Gracie and I joined her. After supper, I lay down with her again. Gracie came and sat on top of me. Lucy began fussing. She wanted to be my baby alone. I hugged Gracie tight and told her I was glad she came to join us. I sang to Lucy and held her hand. But, tired as she was, she could not go to sleep. We gave up and went back downstairs.

Carol was late getting home. She was recovering from foot surgery. Because of complications from the surgery, she had to go for physical therapy a couple of times each week. When she walked in at 7:30 from a full day of work followed by the therapy, she took the tired Lucy back up to her bedroom without even pausing to get herself a bite of supper.

I turned my attention to Gracie. "Now where were we?" I asked as I lay down beside her on the living room floor where she had made a nice nest for herself with her pillow and a blanket. "I know," I said, "we were just getting ready to put on our shoes and sneak out of the house for a walk."

"Right now?" Gracie, already bathed and in her pajamas, wasn't expecting this.

"Right now," I said. I tiptoed up to the girls' bedroom and returned with a sundress and shoes. We got ready quickly and snuck out the back door so Lucy would not hear us leave. With her hand firmly in mine, Gracie led me on a brisk walk around the block, pointing out the moon in the dusky sky, the cats sitting in neighbors' driveways, the big kids playing basketball in the park. We felt the thrill of escape, confederates on an illicit after-dark walk. I am sure no one wanted to get out of the house more than me. The pressure of the afternoon and the past few days had been overwhelming. As I clung to Gracie's hand and listened to her happy conversation, I hoped that what we had to give to each of these precious girls would somehow be enough.

Our escapade at an end, we stole into the kitchen and swore ourselves to secrecy. Carol came downstairs to tell me that Lucy was still wide awake and she had to stop and get some supper before she dropped. She looked exhausted. I wished her swollen stiff foot could be the only thing our family needed to take care of just then.

I headed up to Lucy, who was in bed looking at a book. She glanced up eagerly. "I've come to help you get to sleep," I said, returning the book to her shelf.

"Baby can't remember how to sleep," Lucy explained, with an uncanny accuracy.

"I'm going to teach you," I said, curling up beside her.

Lucy began bouncing on the bed. She displayed a spirited determination to stay awake by any means necessary.

"I'm going to name you some feelings," I said, as I lay down beside her, "and I want you to tell me which ones you have right now. Sad. Lonely. Mad."

With each feeling that I named, Lucy nodded her head. "Yes," she said, "yes, yes."

"What are you mad about?"

"I'm mad about Gracie. She didn't share with me this afternoon." Could it be that simple, I wondered? Somehow, I doubted it. Lucy's tendency to blame her younger sister for every unwanted emotion was automatic but not, I thought, the real issue.

"Maybe you're mad at Maria Chacpa. Could that be?" No answer. I worried. Was I helping her shape her narrative or starting to impose one? I tried a less leading question.

"What are you sad about?"

"I'm sad that people in Peru give their babies to foster families."

"Oh, honey, it is sad. Do you wish Maria Chacpa had just given you straight to me?"

"You could have met the bus."

"Oh, how I wish I could have met the bus. If they had called me and told me, I would have been there to meet the bus. Me and Mama-Carol."

"You could have ridden the bus. You could have come to San Martín."

"And I would have. We would have. If we had known you were there waiting for us."

"What would Maria Chacpa have said?"

"She would have said, 'Here is my beautiful daughter, Lucia Maricruz. Now she will be your beautiful daughter. Take good care of her. Just don't make her cry.' Then we would have taken you in our arms, said good-bye to Maria Chacpa, and taken you back to Lima with us."

I waited a moment. "Why do you feel lonely?"

"I feel lonely because of all the strangers in Machu Picchu and Peru."

I thought about this. Perhaps it made her lonely to think of being related and connected by blood and nationality to people she did not know. "It's hard to be connected to people you don't really know, isn't it? Who are you lonely for?

"For Mama-Jackie and Maria Chacpa." She paused. "For Mama-Jackie and Maria Chacpa and Mama-Carol." It somehow made sense that you could be lonely for the mom lying beside you, the one who bore you, and the one downstairs in the kitchen with your sister.

"Oh, sweetheart, it's so hard when your own mamas and the mama you grew inside of and were born from are not the same."

"I wish I could have grown inside your body," she said softly.

"Oh, baby, I know. I wish it too. But I couldn't love you any more, if you had."

"I wish my feet could have grown inside Maria Chacpa's body and the rest of me could have grown inside of you."

"Lucy, that would have been such a good solution. Then you could have come from both of us. But in a way you did. You came from Maria Chacpa's body but from Carol's and my hearts."

"I want to be a tiny baby again. I want to grow inside you," she said, curling closer against my belly.

"You can be my tiny baby," I promised.

"If I was your tiny baby, what would I do?"

"You would sleep in my arms, I would rock you and cuddle you and feed you."

"Would I drink milk out of your breasts?"

"Of course, my baby. Is that what you want to do?"

Lucy nodded. She cuddled close to me and nestled into my arms like a nursing baby. She fixed her eyes on my face with a look of such love as she drank imaginary milk. After a few moments I nestled her head back on her pillow.

"Now, baby, your tummy is all full of warm milk. You can go to sleep." She curled against my belly as tightly as a cat, as if she would crawl inside my body and be born again. And, like a contented cat, she went to sleep at once. I lay there marveling at the complexity and strength of these ties to her various mothers, the one who gave her life and cared for her for her first two months and the two who had mothered her every day for the past four years. As well, I marveled at our search for the story that would, if only for a moment, quiet our fears and bring us home to ourselves.

13

Some Glad Morning

When I was about three years old, Daddy bought Mother a second-hand car, an old black 1941 Chevy sedan with a standard transmission. Mother was a tentative and somewhat nervous driver, although I didn't know that then. She had the general idea of how to put in the clutch and shift gears, but she never quite mastered the stick shift. With characteristic good humor and love of alliteration, she christened her car Leapin' Lena. In this way, she made the jerks and shudders with which each ride began seem to inhere in the vehicle. Each time she started the engine and let the clutch out too fast, she would sing out, "Off we go with a buck and a jump!" Jeannie and I would grab the back of the front seat and hold on for dear life as Leapin' Lena, Mother's fractious black mare, bucked her way down the road.

The truth is, Mother was scared, not just of stick shifts and driving but of so much else besides. "For God hath not given us the spirit of fear; but of power, and of love, and of a sound mind" (II Timothy 1:7), she quoted again and again. I figured out only after I got older that she was trying to encourage herself not just us kids. Almost every favorite scripture passage noted on the flyleaf of her Bible dealt with overcoming fear or coping with infirmity. Beautiful and brilliant, she never developed an accurate picture of her own strength and power.

In the public life into which Daddy's career catapulted her, Mother graciously played her part. But, despite the carefully composed public persona, she remained, to a large extent, the scared, shy, country girl of her youth. She never ceased to remark in awed wonder on the distance she had traveled from a childhood of kerosene lamps, wood-burning stoves, outhouses, and horse and buggy transportation to the 747 jets that carried her and my father on travels around the globe. She often felt, I think now, a bit like a befuddled time traveler who finds herself dropped unexpectedly into a future landscape she can scarcely fathom.

Mother maintained a great sense of nostalgia for the world of her childhood. A collection of stories she wrote about those days is entitled "Dear Days beyond Recall." She filled thirty pages with lively accounts of the toys and games of her childhood, of dogs they had owned, of Christmas celebrations. But when she reached the Great Depression years she stopped writing. Those years of want and hardship were not the dear days she wanted to relate. Despite her title, the happier days she did chronicle were not yet beyond her recall, but she must have felt on some level like the lone survivor of a vanished world. I'm inventing explanations, of course. Trying to account for the fearfulness in the life of this woman, who seemed to me such a bulwark.

As a young adult, I realized that my mother was afraid of many of the experiences and ideas her grown daughters brought into her world. I began to suspect that she could not teach me much of what I needed to know as a woman living in the seventies and eighties. Women of my generation were searching feverishly for strong role models, and I grew frustrated that my own mother, who had seemed, as parents do, omnipotent to my childhood self, couldn't be the powerful trailblazer I needed her to be.

In the fall of 1993, just a couple of months before Carol and I moved back to Chicago, Mother was diagnosed with non-Hodgkins lymphoma. Not long after she told us she was sick, Mother and Daddy came up to spend Thanksgiving with our family. They were both extraordinarily calm and philosophical about what lay ahead. Or perhaps it was not so extraordinary but rather a manifestation of the depth and reality of the faith they had spent their lives proclaiming. To me, anyway, it was marvelous and comforting to see the peace and confidence with which they met the approach of the unknown. Mother was scheduled to begin chemotherapy a few days after our visit. One morning while she and I sat on the couch visiting over coffee, I asked Daddy to take our picture. I knew exactly what I was after. We were both looking alive and healthy and happy. I wanted to hold on to that. I wanted to freeze the frame. I wanted the last possible picture of the two of us laughing and talking together with full heads of our own hair.

Losing her hair was about the only part of the experience lying before her that Mother worried about out loud. Not long after our visit, she told me that she was getting ready to buy a wig. "I've always hated my hair. I always wished I had a beautiful head of blonde hair like Marilyn Grissom. Now I'm sorry I ever talked bad about it," she told me.

Mother thought her hair was too straight. Her older sister had had soft brown curls but not she. "Straight as a stick," she would say with disgust, "and look at all these cowlicks!" At the nape of her neck, her hair grew into a long, sharp point. On each side of the point, the hair grew up and in. None of this was right. Hair was supposed to grow down, curl softly, and stay off your neck. If she hated her hair, she hated mine, too, for I had inherited her hair right down to the exact position of all three cowlicks.

"Well, Mother," I replied, "this is your chance. Just march yourself into that wig store and tell them you'll take one of those big, fluffy, platinum numbers. It's now or never." Still, when it came time to make a wig purchase, she bought a sensible silver-gray number with a touch of salt and pepper to it that looked so much like her own hair you almost couldn't tell she was wearing a wig except, perhaps, for the bangs.

In January, in the midst of her chemotherapy, Mother experienced a small strokelike episode known as a transient ischemic attack, or TIA. In the hospital, her stroke symptoms diminished, but her blood pressure remained dangerously high. Her white cell count had been brought so low by the chemo that she was at serious risk of infection, and so the hospital placed her in reverse isolation. Hence everyone who entered her room was required to wear a mask. My father was beside himself with worry. They needed me. I booked a flight.

It had only been two weeks since we moved back to Chicago from

Madison, and the girls had just started attending their new preschool for two and a half hours a day. They rode the school bus to and from school. Riding the school bus had been one of the chief ambitions of their short lives, so they were thrilled to achieve this important goal at such an early age. But it was all rather a lot to get used to.

While Gracie's focus was on helping our cat Louise adjust to the move, Lucy was not happy with my decision to go to Kentucky. "You told me that when we got back to Chicago we would all be together," she complained. I had said that. I couldn't think of any way to explain this that would make sense to a four year old. But I tried.

"Lucy, baby, I'm not going to travel back and forth all the time like when we lived in Madison. But Mother and Daddy need me right now. I have to go help them for a few days. Mama-Carol will be right here, and I'll be back soon. If you were an adult and I were sick, wouldn't you want to come and visit me?" Even as I said that, I could hear how ridiculous it must sound to her with all those ifs and a hypothetical faraway time in which I would need her to mother me, a time she could not imagine.

"I couldn't leave Gracie," she said. "And our animals." Their current plan was to live together on a farm with dolphins and dogs and cats and blue horses. "Don't you have a sister?" she asked. She knew perfectly well that I did.

"Yes, but she doesn't plan to go right now. I'm the one who feels like I need to be there to help."

"Well, your sister's in Kentucky."

"I know, honey. I'm sorry this isn't good for you. I'll hurry back as quick as I can."

I arrived on the second day of Mother's hospitalization and went straight to Baptist East Hospital. She was still wearing the gown they had put her in on Monday, and no one had washed her or combed her hair or brushed her teeth. I got her cleaned up and gave Daddy a list of things to bring from home. Jeannie's husband, Doug, was in town for a meeting. Back at my parents' house that night he took down the outdoor Christmas decorations and set up Mother and Daddy's new answering machine while I did some laundry and cleaned the house.

Mother was tired and weak but surprisingly calm and cheerful. She had accepted her hospitalization with admirable grace, but she objected to the masks we wore when we entered her room.

"You don't need to wear that old thing," she protested when I entered her hospital room for the first time. "Your little old germs couldn't hurt me." It was characteristic of my mother's encompassing love that she extended her conviction of my basic goodness right down to my germs.

I stayed four days. I persuaded Daddy to line up someone to clean the house. They had been trying to do it themselves, and it had been getting more and more difficult for them. Now it would be impossible.

In the hospital, I read to Mother from the Bible and her well-thumbed copy of *101 Famous Poems*. I bathed her weak, tired body, carefully covering with the sheet any part I was not washing. I polished her fingernails, washed and set her rapidly thinning hair, fixed her lipstick the way she liked it, and just held her hand. Her hand had the prominent veins that I have inherited. I ran my hands along those veins, like I used to do years ago when we sat together in church. I gently pinched a bit of the loose skin between my fingers and watched it stay there, the elasticity gone. My own skin still pops back into place, but more slowly now. We held our hands together, finger to finger. They were exactly the same size. Our fingernails had the same shape. We had the same little hills on the pads of our fingers. We entwined our fingers; we rubbed and stroked one another's hands. Hard as it was to see her so sick, there was an extraordinary richness in those precious hours. My mother was just plain happy to be with me. I was just plain happy to be with her.

I was surprised. When she told me in November that she had lymphoma, I thought I knew for sure this was bad news. I thought her lymphoma would be something we would just have to get through. But sitting on her bed in the hospital, I began to realize that her lymphoma was not just something to get through. It was something to be in. There was an astounding sweetness to living together in the knowledge that our time for loving each other in this life was short. In a funny way that I never would have expected, this cancer brought us the chance to be together in the full light of our mortality but without having to experience just yet the final separation.

As we sat together, I didn't feel there was anything I needed to hear her say that she hadn't already said. Nor did I feel there was anything I needed to tell her that hadn't been told. Instead, I felt a kind of deep peace and a powerful connection flowing between us. Holding hands with her was like a prayer.

As her days in the hospital wore on, her situation deteriorated. On my third day there, she developed pneumonia, an especially dangerous disease for someone with few white blood cells, and then, as I sat on her hospital bed on January 13, she started to experience chest pains. My father had driven down to Somerset that day to keep a speaking commitment. When Mother complained of chest pains, I told her I was going for the nurse. "Don't go get the nurse," she objected. "She'll just want to do a bunch of tests."

"I certainly hope so," I said.

I told her she'd have to try and stop me and headed to the nurse's station. The nurse came on the run. She placed nitroglycerin under Mother's tongue, and the chest pains eased. Heart disease. Cancer, diabetes, stroke, hardening of the arteries, pneumonia, and now heart disease.

That night Daddy returned and the family doctor came by. Daddy mentioned that the shaking in her hand might be, according to the neurologist, the beginnings of Parkinson's. "I reckon if anybody's going to get Parkinson's it's going to be me," Mother said with a wry smile.

Right now we had much bigger worries than Parkinson's disease. The doctor looked grim. "She's a fighter," he told us, "but she's got a lot against her. It's impossible to tell what will happen." After he left, my mother, too weak to lift her head from her pillow, began to sing an old country hymn from her childhood: "Some glad morning when this life is o'er, I'll fly away."

"Mother," I scolded, "don't sing that." She stopped.

"You don't want me to sing that?" she asked, with a quizzical lift of her eyebrows.

"It's a little too realistic under the circumstances, don't you think?"

She smiled and waited. After a few minutes, she tried again, "So you don't want me to sing 'I'll Fly Away'"?

"No!" I insisted.

A few more minutes slipped by. "So you don't want me to sing that?" she asked once more, an amused smile playing around her mouth.

"Mother," I asked, "do you want to sing it?"

"It ends happy."

I thought I should humor her. I was too inexperienced to recognize that she was bearing gifts.

"OK, then, if you really want to sing it, you go on and sing it." And so she did. Lying flat on her bed, she sang it all the way through.

> *Some glad morning when this life is o'er*
> *I'll fly away.*
> *To a home on God's celestial shore,*
> *I'll fly away.*
>
> *I'll fly away, O glory,*
> *I'll fly away.*
> *When I die, hallelujah, by and by,*
> *I'll fly away.*
>
> *When the shadows of this life have gone,*
> *I'll fly away.*
> *Like a bird from prison bars has flown,*
> *I'll fly away.*
>
> *Just a few more weary days and then,*
> *I'll fly away.*
> *To a land where joys shall never end,*
> *I'll fly away.*
>
> *I'll fly away, O glory,*
> *I'll fly away.*
> *When I die, hallelujah, by and by,*
> *I'll fly away.*

That night at home Daddy and I were scared. We laughed about her song, about her amazing spirit. We touched on his fears of a life without her. He told me he knew it would be difficult, but he knew that somehow he would find the strength to go on. "You know," he said, his eyes wrinkling in a soft smile, "Marjorie has been pointing out first one and then another woman at the church that she thinks would make me a good wife." I wasn't all that surprised. It sounded just like her to want to make things as easy on him as possible. She couldn't really see him managing alone. "Finally," he said with a laugh, "I just told her, 'Marjorie, I did a pretty good job picking out my first wife, and if it comes to that I can pick out my second one, too.'" Still, it was nice to know she was so set on taking care of us, whichever side of the grave she might be on.

When Mother sang "I'll Fly Away," it wasn't the first time she had comforted me about her death. A year or two earlier I had come home for a visit. Mother told me that she and Daddy wanted to drive over to Cave Hill Cemetery to show me the plots they had recently purchased. In truth, I had not been sitting at the breakfast table that morning hoping for a trip to the cemetery. But I figured cemetery plots were probably an inevitable gathering site among my parents' age group. I was a grown-up. I could feign a gracious interest.

It was a glorious spring morning. As we stood on the hillside where Mother's and Daddy's plots were located, the flowering trees and bushes blazed in the bright light of the sun. Mother was radiant, too, as she talked happily about how much she loved this beautiful cemetery and described the features of this particular spot. She mentioned some friends with nearby plots, and we joked about how they could run back and forth and visit one another. Then she looked at me. "Jackie, I wanted to bring you here on this sunny spring day, when the birds are singing and the flowers are blooming and we're all together, to tell you how happy it makes me to think about being buried in this beautiful spot. Someday, when you come back here to bury us, I hope you will remember this day."

By the time I flew back to Chicago after four days at Mother's bedside, I was starting to rethink my notions of what constituted fear and courage and my ideas about who was caring for whom. I hated to leave her. And yet I was glad to point my face toward home.

Carol and the girls picked me up at the airport. All of them were tickled to see me, but Lucy grinned so hard she looked as if she might pop. She talked rapidly all the way home from the airport, trying to tell me everything that had happened while I was gone.

A friend came by that day for lunch. Lucy told her, "First we were in

Madison and Mama-Jackie was always going to Chicago, and then we moved to Chicago and Mama-Jackie went to Kentucky." Over the course of the weekend, she repeated that same account to two more visitors. It was impossible to ignore the theme of betrayal and abandonment not far below the surface in this tale.

Each night Lucy prayed for Grandmama. "Will Grandmama die?" she asked God. "What will happen to Granddaddy without her?" I wasn't sure when or whether God would get back to her, so I did my best to answer these questions. I told her that Grandmama would surely die, just as every living creature eventually dies, and that we didn't know when it would be but hoped it would not be for a long time. Each morning Lucy got up asking whether this would be the day Grandmama would come home from the hospital.

Because the following Monday was Martin Luther King Day, there was no school. When I tucked the girls into bed that night, Gracie fell asleep the moment her head touched the pillow. "Lucy," I said, as I settled her in, "it was great to spend the day together. Didn't we have a good day?" I thought I was asking a rhetorical question.

"Not that good," Lucy replied.

"What was wrong with it?"

"No special time with you," Lucy fired back immediately.

"You're right. We haven't had that since I got home. Tomorrow when you get home from school you can come with me to Timothy's for my haircut, and then we'll go out for a treat." She liked the sound of this and fell right to sleep.

But the next day, January 18, the temperature plummeted to twenty-five degrees below zero and all the Chicago public schools canceled classes. I canceled my haircut as well, and Lucy and I had to make do with an hour of reading on the sunporch.

School remained closed yet another day, but when it warmed up to only single digits below zero, Lucy and I headed to a neighborhood café for a treat. The waitress brought Lucy a place mat for coloring and a small box of crayons. Lucy reciprocated by telling the waitress all of our business. "My sister Gracie wanted to come with us and she was crying, but she couldn't come because I needed some special time with Mama-

Jackie." She beamed as she explained all this. She wiggled with delight when we got our matching cookies and our matching glasses of water. We're the same. We're connected. We're together.

My mother came home from the hospital one week after I returned to Chicago. She was still weak but making progress.

It was during this month of January, the month of the new school, the month of my mother's hospitalization, the month of our adjustment to our Chicago return, that Gracie invented a new game. Lucy and Gracie each, in turn, would crouch in the back of the pantry, meowing. The sister not in the pantry would go to the pet store to find a new kitten. She would invite the kitten into the family. We listened to the conversation. The kitten's mother was dead. The kitten needed to be adopted.

After a few rounds of this, they enlisted our help. We were the mothers. We must come to the pet store to find a kitten. Sometimes there were two waiting kittens. Sometimes, one girl was our kitten already and would accompany us to the pet store to look for a sister. Each time we encountered a girl huddled in the pantry, we would exclaim over the beautiful, special kitten who was oh so right for us. We would invite her into our family. She would nod her little kitten head and jump into our arms.

The game evolved again. Now the kittens waited in the closet at the back of the pantry. With the pantry and closet doors closed, it was quite dark. I wondered at their willingness to crouch there on the floor of the closet in the dark, waiting to be reborn into their adoptive family.

Gracie played this game with particular urgency. She wanted to play it all day long. She hid in the closet again and again, meowing. Again and again, we walked away from the dishes, the cooking, the newspaper, the work due the next day, to come to the pet store and discover the perfect kitten waiting to join our family. The kitten was curled in a ball at the back of the closet, her face buried. "Oh, look," one of us would say. "Look at the little sleeping kitten."

We would lift kitten Gracie into our arms, and she would begin to purr. "Why, she's a beautiful little kitten! She's just the kind of kitten we've always wanted. Let's adopt her. Kitty, sweet little kitty, will you come home with us and let us take care of you? We've always wanted a kitten just like you."

Gracie would purr even louder and nuzzle her face against us in a happy kitten nod. We would stroke her black hair and scratch her softly under her chin.

A few days after she came home from the hospital, Mother fell and cut her leg badly. Because of the risk of infection, she was readmitted to Baptist East.

Each day I talked to my parents. Mother was less patient with the hospital stay this time. Stubbornly independent, she walked to the sink one night and, as all the long-legged Taylors do when we want clean feet, lifted her foot up and stuck it in the basin. Except now she was seventy-two years old, recovering from a TIA and weakened by chemo, and the sink was a high hospital sink. So she fell backward, banging her head and skinning a place on her hip. I began to talk to Carol about whether I should go down again when Mother got out of the hospital.

One night I walked into the kitchen as Gracie nestled in Carol's arms, talking about how she came into our family.

"Where was I?" Gracie wanted to know.

"You were in the orphanage waiting with the other babies for your family," Carol told her.

"And what were they doing with us there?"

"They were feeding you and changing your diapers and cuddling you and taking care of you."

But Gracie persisted. "But what were we doing?"

I thought I knew what she wanted to hear. "You were mad sometimes and bored sometimes and lonesome sometimes because they were so busy they didn't have time to pick up any of the babies as much as you would have liked. You were waiting and waiting for your moms and wondering when your family life was going to begin."

Gracie accepted my contribution with a satisfied look. "And what did I do when you came?" she asked Carol.

"I took you in my arms, and we gave each other a big hug, and you said, 'Chchchchc,'" replied Carol, imitating one of Gracie's favorite mouth noises. "And I said, 'you don't say, Gracie, tell me more.' And you said 'Cchhhh.'"

"And then you taked me to the doctor?"

"Yes, and he liked you. Doctor Arribas-Plata. He said you were a showcase baby because you became so alert and lively after we had a few days together. And he gave me some medicine so I could get you all well."

Half an hour later Gracie and I lay sprawled on the big bed, coloring. Gracie had placed our gray and white cat, Louise, on the bed beside us.

"Louise," she told her, accompanying her story with a series of loving pats, "you were waiting and waiting and waiting at the pet store for someone to come and buy you and you were waiting and waiting for a long time, and then Jackie came and taked you home."

"Ahhhh," I said softly, "yes, of course."

Mother was out of the hospital after a ten-day stay. My father realized that she was not safe at home alone, and yet he didn't have anyone to take care of her when he left the house. Over the phone, his voice cracked with fear and worry and exhaustion. I realized he needed help making decisions about how best to care for her. I made a reservation for the next week.

Lucy and I went downstairs to borrow half a teaspoon of thyme from our neighbor, Beth. We sat for a few moments and talked about my mother. "I don't think she can be left alone anymore," I said. "They're going to have to have some help."

"Not you," protested Lucy.

"I can't be their help all the time," I responded, "but I am going to have to go down again soon for a few days to help them make some plans."

"You promised you weren't going to do that anymore," Lucy accused me, indignation ringing in her voice.

"No," I said. "I never promised that. I have to go for a few days, but I'll be right back. I have to come back to you. We belong together." I gave her a tight squeeze.

"You do belong together. You make a great pair," Beth assented, trying to ease the moment.

After the girls were in bed, Carol and I talked about Lucy's distress. Carol reminded me that when we moved back to Chicago I promised Lucy that I would not go anywhere for a long, long time. The purpose of the move, I assured her, was to bring our family together in one place so that we would have no more of the frequent separations that characterized our commuter arrangement. The distinction between my weekly commutes and what had suddenly become monthly visits to my parents was a subtle distinction even to our adult minds.

The next morning, right after my first cup of tea, I asked Lucy to come and sit on my bed so we could talk. "I thought about what you said," I told her. "I did tell you that once we moved to Chicago I would not go anywhere again for a long, long time and that we would be together without separations."

"I was right; you were wrong. I knew I was right," Lucy crowed.

"Yes, honey, you were right. Listen, Lucy, I am not going to go away each week for my job. That will never happen again. But when we talked about how I would not go anywhere for a long time I didn't know my mother would get sick. This is an emergency, and I have to go and help them for a few days, but I will hurry home to you."

We were still playing Adopt a Kitty several times a day. Gracie had created yet another variation. Costumed in a hot pink bandanna tied babushka style—except backward, with the point coming over her forehead—and with a long swath of hot pink lace forming a shawl around her shoulders, Gracie would knock and then meow at the kitchen door. Carol or I would open the door to find Gracie crouched in the dining room, mewing softly.

"Why, it's a kitty!" we would exclaim, opening the door wider. "Come in and let us take care of you. Where have you been?"

"I've been lost in the woods. My mama died."

"Oh, poor kitty, won't you be in our family? Come in to our nice warm house and let us love you forever. Can we take your scarf and your shawl?"

The well-brought-up kitty would hand us her wraps and jump into our arms for a few good cuddles. Sometimes she asked to be introduced to her sister kitty, Lucy, or to our other kitty, Louise. Sometimes she explained sadly that there were bears in the woods and she'd been out there for a long, long time. We would cuddle her more tightly when we heard about the bears, and stroke her back, and she would burrow her face into her new mama's neck.

Before catching my plane to Louisville on the morning of February 17, I walked with Lucy to the school bus corner. We always held hands on the way to the bus. "Lucy," I said, "just remember while I'm gone that I love you forever!"

"Me too," she replied in a quiet little voice.

"We love each other!" I proclaimed, swinging her arm.

"We love each other, we love each other!" she sang, skipping beside me. "We're walking to the bus, and we love each other!" She sang this through two or three times as we skipped down the street to the bus stop. I, at least, felt comforted. Her happy song gave me hope.

In Louisville, my feeble, worn-out, and addled mother struggled to navigate more safely with the help of a four-footed cane. She seemed muddled in her thinking and uncharacteristically querulous. I suspected from her demeanor that she might be entering a manic episode. The easy connection we shared on her hospital bed a few weeks earlier seemed far away. She knit her brow together in a worried frown and fussed about her hair, which in the past three weeks had fallen out by the fistfuls. I cast about for a way to connect with her.

I went to the hall closet, where she kept all her old hats, and began pulling them out and piling them, hatbox after hatbox, on the brightly colored cross-stitched quilt that covered the guest bed. She followed me into the bedroom, tapping clumsily with what she referred to as "that pleckit cane." *Pleckit* is the shortened form of *plague-taked* (a Baptist way to swear).

"What are you doing with all my old hats?" she asked.

"Let's try them on," I said. "Let's see which ones still look good. You might want to wear some of these again now that you don't have much hair."

Mother always loved hats. She had boxes and boxes of beautiful hats, spring hats, fall hats, winter hats, straw hats, felt hats, and peacock feather hats, hats she had shopped for in Louisville's and Somerset's finest dress shops throughout the forties and fifties and into the sixties. Back when accessories meant a hat, white gloves, and matching purse and pumps, Mother knew how to pull an outfit together.

We started opening boxes. We pulled out each hat, one by one, all lovingly wrapped in tissue paper. There were big straw boaters in black and red and navy. An elegant black straw with a stovepipe shape. Another wide-brimmed straw, this one bought in Egypt to shade her face when she rode on a camel to the pyramids. A little jewel-colored whimsy in iridescent shades of turquoise, green, purple, blue, and violet. Two Borsalinos bought on separate trips to Rome—a wine-colored beret with her initials in its band and a black one with a brim. She had been so proud of each of these, pronouncing their name, Borsalino, with relish and showing me how they folded up in their neat little boxes and then popped back out again to assume their saucy shapes. They were great hats. You could squish them, squash them, sit on them, and still they bounced back. And of course there was the brown, gold, and turquoise peacock-feather pillbox with the brown velvet piping that she bought in Louisville in 1960, the day she and Daddy found out that an anonymous donor had given them a forty-two-day trip to Europe and the Middle East.

We tried on every hat. We divided them into piles: the hopelessly out-of-date, the could come back any minute, the goes with anything, and the perfect for covering a bald head. We were like two girls playing dress up.

Later, after Mother had gone down for her lengthy afternoon nap, Daddy cried on my shoulder. "She's not making sense so much of the time." This worried him terribly. He felt her beginning to slip away, and he thought if he could just get her to straighten out her facts he could keep her with him longer. He was correcting each misstatement so emphatically that he was starting to make her jumpy.

"I know she's not," I said, "but you have to quit worrying about whether she's making sense or not. Here's what we have to worry about now. Is she safe? Is she having a good time? If she's safe and having a good time, then you've done all you can do." He grabbed that thought and held on.

"We just have to keep her safe," he repeated, "and make sure she's having a good time."

But the truth was that when he left her alone she was not safe. She fell easily. She could not keep track of the many medications she took throughout the day. She was confused and disoriented. We talked about a neighbor, a friend of Mother's, who could be hired to stay with her when Daddy went out. Mother didn't think much of the idea when we presented it to her. She liked her privacy. But Daddy and I insisted, and, trusting us, she acquiesced.

Flying home, I ached with love and sorrow. She was still with us, but she was already slipping away. Caring for my parents brought me such a bittersweet mix of joy and grief. Mother was still here to give to, and yet she was drifting out of my grasp just as I was finally able to fully comprehend how truly precious she was.

When I washed her off or helped her dress, I couldn't escape the connections with the daily care I gave my own children—children who would one day grow too big to need my daily ministrations. My mother would need me more and more until she ceased to need anyone. I thought of all the care she had given me, care I was now returning to her and passing on to my own daughters. I didn't know how I would find the energy to keep giving in both directions with my heart aching like this. Sometimes I couldn't breathe very well. If I hadn't had daughters of my own, I don't think I could have kept breathing at all.

But just as I felt I might be pulled in two Mother began to get better. She was not yet ready, after all, to fly away. She made it through the final course of chemo with her cancer in remission. She began to recover some of her strength. Her hair grew back, short and curly. The curls were common in the first growth after chemo. There was even a name for this: the chemo curl. "What a way to get those curls I always wanted," she joked. She was happy to discard the turbans she had worn for weeks and to get her own hair back on her head. She welcomed it, curly or straight, cowlicks and all, and in any color.

"Thank God you made it through all that," I said when she phoned with the good news of the remission and the end of the chemotherapy. "You must be so relieved."

"Oh, it wasn't so bad," she replied breezily. "The worst part was losing my hair."

I snorted. "Oh, I thought the worst part was when you almost died."

"You and Eldred probably remember it better than I do. I didn't think it was so awful." Stick shifts and highways terrified her, but when my fearful, anxious mother encountered her own death she was as solid and serene as a burr oak.

14

Destiny

Christians raised, as I was, in an evangelical fundamentalist tradition must, at some point, choose between the clear-cut, rule-bound but essentially ahistorical and anti-intellectual worldview these religions offer and something more complicated. The fear of many fundamentalists is that any step away from a belief in the Bible as inerrant, as literally true in every respect, is a step away from belief. My father was a long way from the Southern Baptist preachers he refers to as "the fundies," who have dominated the denomination in the past three decades. He believed in and taught biblical study based on knowledge of the original texts and on historical scholarship. He taught me to ask hard questions and recognize scripture as open to interpretation in light of ongoing revelation.

Yet he never could have anticipated nor prepared himself for some of the directions my quest for a faith of my own has taken. Where he has remained Baptist (even while embarrassed about some of the recent shenanigans of the Southern Baptists), I have abandoned not only my denominational roots but, at times, organized religion altogether.

I felt, in adulthood, as if I hadn't so much left the church as been left by it. I had been raised in a religion in which, at a certain point, if you believed women were truly equal to men and if you believed God made gay people and therefore must love us, something had to give. "Trust in the Lord with all thine heart, and lean not unto thine own understanding" (Proverbs 3:5) was a favorite verse of both of my parents. They offered it up to me time and again as advice worth heeding. This passage of scripture must have provided deep comfort to both of them, an assurance that God would be actively present, caring for and guiding them, but I always bristled when they quoted it to me. I heard the verse with special emphasis on the words "lean not unto thine own understanding," and for this reason, I grew to hate it. Shut down your mind, don't think, don't ask questions, don't try to understand is what I thought I heard. I was having none of that.

Church hadn't been prominent in Carol's childhood. She was raised Methodist, but in practice this meant that on many Sundays her parents dropped their three girls off at church and headed home for a little relaxation. Carol and her sisters were a brazen lot. They often took their offering money to the drugstore to buy comic books. One Sunday, unwilling to get dressed up, they simply buttoned their coats over their underwear. The Sunday School teacher couldn't figure out why those Sadtler girls refused to hang up their coats.

By the time Carol and I became a couple, neither of us was involved with any church. I missed it enough to have visited a couple of Baptist churches in Chicago. There I found a style of worship familiar to me but a theology that I could not accept. My longing for a "church home," as my father would have called it, was not nearly acute enough to cause me to search further. But then the girls came into our lives.

As our children began to talk and ask questions about the world, I often found myself speaking about God and God's love and care for the world and each of us. Carol and I began talking about whether we wanted a church for our family. We decided that if we could find a church that would not simply tolerate our family but welcome it, a church that would celebrate all of the gifts God has given us, including our sexuality, we would like to make that part of our lives. We were not interested in taking our daughters to a church that would teach them there was something fundamentally wrong with their family. Also, we decided, there needed to be a good music program since we both agreed that had always been one of our favorite parts of church. It took us awhile to find the right fit, but eventually we found Broadway, a United Methodist church that was intentionally inclusive in its welcome to gay and lesbian Christians and that had, as well, a great choir and lots of spirited hymn singing. At home, we talked about God in whatever ways seemed appropriate to the moment. Gracie rarely showed any interest in theological discussions, although she liked some of the art projects in Sunday School. But Lucy plowed into such conversations with gusto.

One day, when she was five, Lucy, who has always hated rodents, looked at me over her cereal and asked, "Did God make rats?"

Ah, I thought, the question of evil. I tried my best. "Yes, just like God made all things, God made rats."

"God didn't make me," Lucy asserted.

"Oh, no?" I replied. I was surprised. "Who made you?"

"Maria Chacpa," she answered definitively, naming her birth mother.

The girl had a point. "Well, you're right, she did do all the real work. You came out of her body. She gave birth to you. But in the sense that we speak of all life coming from God, God as the author of life, in that sense God made you." I suppose I was seeking an answer that didn't claim more than I myself believe and yet was simple and clear enough for a five year old. Our theological conversations often found me sifting through the answers from my childhood for something suitable and then improvising a murky path between the concrete and the not yet known. But Lucy would not be brushed off. I had not touched her real question.

A few days later she circled back to it. "Mama-Jackie, why did God make rats?"

Why, indeed? Who can answer a question like that? Are five year olds supposed to be thinking about these kinds of questions? "Lucy," I said, "that is a really profound theological question. Rats are creepy, and they don't seem to be much good. Why, indeed, would God decide to make such a thing? Maybe you should ask our pastor." I could have said God sets the world in motion and then lets evolution take its course. Some of what evolves is pretty ugly. I could have said I wonder, too, about why a supposedly powerful God leaves evil loose in the world. I could have said I don't know and sometimes it makes you wonder what on earth or in heaven God is up to.

One morning not long after the rat discussion, Mother and I were on the phone. Lucy came pounding in. "Is that Grandmama?" she wanted to know. I nodded. "Ask her," she commanded.

"Ask her what?"

"Ask her about the rats." Lucy had decided that as a seminary graduate Grandmama was as good a source as any pastor.

"Mother," I said. "Lucy has a big theological question. She wants to know why God made rats."

Mother answered immediately. "Well, when Eve ate the forbidden fruit, sin and suffering entered the world: thistles and disease and snakes who crawled on their bellies and everything evil." I was surprised she didn't mention cramps and the pain of childbirth.

"Mother," I protested. "She's five years old. I can't give her the Fall. Help me here. What else have you got?"

She didn't point out that she had begun teaching me the story of the Fall and its attendant evils long before I turned five. Instead she gamely tried again. "Well, let me see. God made rats so the hawks would have something to eat."

"Ah, the circle of life," I said. *The Lion King* was Lucy's favorite movie. "We can work with that." I passed Grandmama's second answer along to Lucy. Her doubts were temporarily assuaged, though her terror of rats abided.

About a year after we returned to Chicago, Lucy, who at age five could have gone to the nursery, opted to sit in church with me so she could "sing songs with all the peoples." Christmas was approaching. Our pastor preached about how young Mary was when she got pregnant, only thirteen or fourteen and not married. Yet God chose her to bear his son. God's call can come to young people, just as it comes to adults, the pastor wanted us to know.

As we walked home from church that unseasonably warm December morning, Mary Alice, one of our neighbors, burst eagerly onto her porch. "I think today may be the day," she exclaimed. "Today or tomorrow. Karen has begun to have contractions."

Karen and Mary Alice are two friends who were expecting their first child. They had enjoyed meeting Lucy and Gracie and talking to us about our family when they were planning their own.

The girls and I walked on toward home. "Which one is having the baby?" Lucy wanted to know.

"The one you didn't see. Karen, the one who is pregnant."

"How did she get that baby?" Lucy wondered. This question had recently begun to interest her as she came to realize that not all children join their families through adoption.

"Donor insemination," I told her. "Just like in *Heather Has Two Mommies.*" The book tells the story of two women who want to have a child and eventually do so through donor insemination. The story dwells on the process of insemination with a level of detail unnecessary for preschoolers, but it's one of the few books out there that make a lesbian family sound almost ordinary. So, despite what was, to my mind, a bit more anatomical detail than we really needed, we had read this book. Lucy loved it, requesting it again and again.

That night Lucy could not sleep. We had run through our usual extensive bedtime routine—tooth brushing, bedtime stories, a few songs from one of the moms, and then soothing music on the cassette player. In the top bunk, Gracie was sleeping soundly. Lucy kept popping up to go to the bathroom, to get a Band-Aid, to see what we were up to in the living room, to ask if she could turn on the light and read a book, to let us know she was still awake.

Tucking her in yet again, I asked her what was the matter.

"I can't stop thinking about it," she told me. "How does the doctor get the sperm from the man to put inside the woman?"

Heather Has Two Mommies, voluble on so much else about the insemination process, is mercifully silent on this point. But I believe with all my heart in honest answers to honest questions.

"The man touches his penis with a back and forth motion of his hand, and the sperm comes out into a jar," I explained.

"But how does the doctor get it from the jar into the woman's body?" Lucy relentlessly and logically persisted.

"The doctor puts something like a turkey baster inside the woman's vagina and squirts the semen in."

Lucy thought about my answer for a moment. She was silent as she considered this new information. "How did Mary get pregnant from

God?" There it was. The crucial question that had been keeping her awake.

I thought for a moment. I tried an easy answer. "The Bible tells us that God's spirit came on her and she conceived Jesus."

Lucy was having none of this. "But how?"

"It's a mystery, Lucy. There are no sperm in this story. No one can explain it except as a mystery. Some people think that Mary and Joseph were the biological parents but that Jesus so fully expressed God's spirit that he came to be called the Son of God. Others are certain God is the biological as well as the spiritual father. I wasn't there, so I can't tell you exactly how it happened. But, however this story is told, there are no sperm in it."

In my heart was the hope that this answer would leave room for her to hold onto faith even when, as an adult, she began to see the story of the virgin birth as a myth tacked onto the Jesus story by overzealous writers of the gospels who wanted to appeal to the broadest possible array of converts. I wrapped the kernel of the truth I had come to, that Jesus walked so closely with God that he came to be called the Son of God, in several layers of what various interpretive communities believe about Jesus' parentage.

"So," Lucy said, after a pause. "Adam and Eve had children and they had children and they had children and they had children and they had children and eventually they had Mary and she had Jesus."

"That's right," I said, admiring her synthesis of the genealogical information contained in the opening chapter of Matthew.

"OK," said Lucy, "but tell me this. If God was going to send Jesus, why did he wait so long?"

Why would a God who has a great gift to give withhold it for generations? Why, indeed? "In the fullness of time," my father would have said. I said something different. "Lucy, love, that is a profound theological question. There are adults who spend their lives studying the Bible who do not have a good answer to that question. I can't possibly answer it. Maybe, when you grow up, you can study all this some more and maybe you can figure out an answer to that question." Or maybe, I didn't add, you'll find behind your big questions only more big questions. I tucked the covers around her and patted her chest right over her great big heart. "Try to sleep."

But she wasn't ready to sleep. "Mama-Jackie?" she said, as I started to tiptoe from the room. "How did Jesus get his helpers?"

"The disciples?" I asked.

Lucy nodded. I sat back down beside her on the bed, tucking my head to fit in under the top bunk, nestling down beside her to share her pillow.

"Well, he saw them at their work, and he spoke to them. He said, 'Peter, follow me. Mark, follow me. Matthew, come with me.' And they stopped what they were doing as soon as they heard his voice, and they followed him."

"Why?" Lucy wanted to know.

"Because it was their destiny. When they heard the voice of Jesus call their name, they recognized their destiny, and they followed him."

"How can you recognize your destiny?" Lucy wondered.

It is a question I have often asked myself, a question at the core of this very book, yet as I sought an answer for her I found myself saying, "You have to listen to your inside voice. If you listen to your inside voice, you will know."

"Is that how you came to Peru to get me?"

"Yes, exactly." And as I spoke these words I knew that they were true.

"Did God tell you to come?"

"Lucy, honey, God has never spoken to me directly like that. I just listened to my inside voice and knew what I had to do."

Lucy folded me in a huge hug. "You're my destiny, you're my destiny, you're my destiny!"

"Oh, baby," I said, hugging her back with all my might, "you are so right."

15

Which One Is Your Mom?

With the move back to Chicago, Lucy and Gracie had begun public preschool at Chicago's Inter-American Magnet School, a wonderful place with a bilingual Spanish-English curriculum and an emphasis on Central and South American culture and history. It seemed ideal for our girls, and we were thrilled that they would have the opportunity to attend. They were thrilled to be riding the bus with the big kids, where they had a chance to learn a whole range of vocabulary and behaviors we probably weren't ready for them to know.

Not quite two months after Lucy and Gracie started school, the girls and I were crammed into our small bathroom getting ready for bed. Gracie and I were brushing our teeth, while Lucy finished up her bath.

"Mom," Gracie asked me, from her perch atop the toilet seat, "are you a lesbian?" She couldn't say her els yet, so "lesbian" came out as "wesbian."

I spit out a mouthful of toothpaste and looked at her. I was surprised but feigned nonchalance. "Yes," I nodded, "I am."

Gracie looked pleased.

"Who asked?" I said, as neutrally as I could manage. "Someone at school?"

"A boy on the bus."

"A big boy?" I asked. My heart was pounding.

Gracie nodded. "He asked me if my moms were lesbians."

"What did you tell him?"

Gracie gave me a self-satisfied look. "I said yes."

"Well, you were right!" I took a deep breath and tried for a look of tranquil interest that my inner turmoil belied. I was interested, all right, but definitely not tranquil. I kept my voice calm. "And what did he say then?"

"Nothing."

Phew, I thought to myself.

"Was it the big boy who helps you off the bus?" He was the one, I figured, who got the best look at the two middle-aged, short-haired women in comfortable shoes who took turns waiting at the bus stop.

"Yes."

"Gracie," I asked then, "what does it mean, to be a lesbian?"

Gracie thought for only a second. "It means you're magic!" she pronounced triumphantly.

Well, I admit it; I was pleased. "Good answer," I said. "What else does it mean?"

Gracie fixed her face in the happy expression of a girl who knows she knows. "It means you're smart."

I took proper note of this fleeting moment when my three year old thought both of her moms were magic and smart. Such confidence in our powers was bound to fade. Before another ten years rolled by, she would lose her belief in our magical powers and develop serious doubts about our intelligence.

"Oh, Gracie, I love your definitions. Let me tell you another one. When people say that I'm a lesbian, they mean that I'm a woman who fell in love with . . ." In the brief pause in which I searched for the next word, Gracie triumphantly completed my sentence. "Carol!"

"Well, yes, precisely. I fell in love with Carol. A lesbian is a woman who falls in love with a woman. A gay man is a man who falls in love with a man. A heterosexual is a man who falls in love with a woman or a woman who falls in love with a man."

"I'm a lesbian," Gracie announced.

167

"How do you know?" I asked.

"Lucy!" Gracie replied. "I'm married to Lucy. Lucy, do you want to pretend that we're married?"

"I don't know," said Lucy languidly from the bathtub. "I might marry Ana. Then again, I might marry Raul."

I knew Ana, a dear friend with the most immense Barbie collection Lucy had ever seen. "Who is Raul?"

"Someone in my class," Lucy replied breezily.

"Well, there you are. You can't tell whether you're a lesbian or not until you see who you fall in love with."

Gracie thought about it some more. "I can't marry Kame or Julia Frances," she stated confidently. These girls had been her two dearest friends in Madison.

"Why not?" I asked. Because they're girls? I thought to myself. Different religious backgrounds?

"Because they're in Madison," Gracie sensibly replied, extending her palms and shrugging her shoulders in a "why else?" gesture from her perch atop the toilet seat lid. She leaned over the sink and rinsed her toothbrush clean.

"Come to your mama," I said, and I held my arms out to Gracie. She jumped into them and wrapped her arms and legs around me in a big hug.

"My magic, smart mama," she said as she cuddled close.

"Exactly," I agreed.

A few days later I was in the kitchen pouring the last of the Cheerios into two cereal bowls. Somehow, we had omitted this staple from the grocery list. As I fished around in the Cheerio dust at the bottom of the package, trying to sift out a few strays, the girls protested loudly.

"That's not enough!" wailed Lucy, indignantly.

"I need some more!" Gracie complained.

"I'll give you whatever I can find here," I said, still excavating the bottom of the package. "We're out," I concluded in defeat, and fixed them with a sorrowful look.

But they were unresigned. They roared their disapproval. I grew exasperated. "I can't make Cheerios out of thin air!" I barked. This line had echoes of my own mother and was tinged with the same indignation she must have felt when she had done her best for us and come up short. For some reason, this statement struck Lucy's funny bone.

"Yes, you can," she said, laughing. Her laughter shifted the mood.

"Oh, well, maybe I can. After all, Gracie tells me I'm magic. She told me a few days ago, and I've been feeling special ever since."

Gracie beamed. "You're a lesbian!"

"That's right. I'm a lesbian. I'm a lesbian because I love Carol."

"And I'm a lesbian because I love Jackie," Carol chimed in from the sink, where she was mixing the orange juice.

"What would you be if you were a man and you loved Carol?" Lucy wanted to know.

I resisted the impulse to reply "On the way to divorce court" and said instead, "I'd be a heterosexual."

"And if you were a man and Carol was a man?" Lucy continued.

"If there are two men? Gay men."

Lucy thought this over. I continued. "But, whether you're a gay man or a lesbian or a heterosexual, when you see the person you love you see hearts."

Lucy looked pleased at this image. "Just like I see every time I look at you," I added.

"I don't see any real hearts," Lucy said.

Ah, an empiricist. "They're not real hearts," I explained. "They're metaphorical hearts, hearts in your heart."

In the pause that followed, I asked myself whether it was time to mention that not everyone would be as thrilled about lesbians as we are in our family. What can you say to protect your children from prejudice, I wondered, and when do you say it? How do black or Jewish parents talk to their children about the comments or ridicule they might encounter from classmates? Do they have models for this sort of talk learned from their parents? Or do they just make it up as they go along, always improvising? I have a recurrent dream in which I am driving but I cannot see the road. I steer madly and hope for the best. It is, I suppose, a metaphor for modern life, especially the modern life I am living on a road far different from the one on which I first learned to drive. This felt just like that dream.

"You know," I ventured, "sometimes when people hear that your moms are lesbians they won't think it's wonderful. Some people might say mean things about lesbians."

"Why?" Lucy wanted to know.

"Because they're ignorant," Carol explained, as she poured the third can of water into the orange juice pitcher.

"Sometimes they might say 'Ugh,'" Gracie suggested.

"Did someone on the bus say 'Ugh'?" I asked. I could feel the hair on the back of my neck stand up, a vestigial trace of an ancient protective instinct.

"No," said Gracie.

"Some of my friends said 'Ugh,'" Lucy told us, "but they're still my friends."

"They can be your friends whether they say 'ugh' or not," I assured her.

"That's right," Carol said. "Some people are ignorant about some things, but that doesn't keep us from being friends with them."

For the moment, everyone seemed satisfied. Carol poured the juice.

The following year Lucy was in kindergarten. One Friday afternoon the girls invited two sisters home to spend the night, a classmate and close friend of Gracie's and her older sister, who was in second grade. Carol picked them up, and they arrived full of excitement at the adventure before them. Gracie's friend had met both Carol and me during previous visits, but her older sister had not spent any time with us. When the seven year old walked into the living room and I came out to greet them, she began what would prove to be a major struggle to get her bearings in our household. "Which one is your mom?" she asked Lucy.

"They're both my moms," Lucy explained. "I'm adopted."

This didn't clear up much for our visitor. She had never before encountered either two-mom households or adoption. The questions kept coming.

"Where is your real mom?"

"These are my real moms, but I have a birth mom in Peru. I'm adopted."

"Why did your mom give you away?"

"She didn't have very much money and she wasn't married and she made a plan to find me a family that could take care of me."

The puzzled seven year old could not have been comforted by this explanation. Her mother was not married and had very little money. Lucy forged ahead, trying, time and again, to provide a satisfactory explanation. At last, she grew exasperated. She marched over to me and placed her short, brown arm beside my longer, paler one.

"Look," she commanded. Do you see our skin tones?" She gestured emphatically with her free arm. "I'm dark; she's light. Do you see our hair? She has brown hair; I have black hair. Do you see how we don't look alike? I'M ADOPTED."

I'm not sure, even after that, if this new family configuration made any sense to our overnight guest. Her life had done nothing to prepare her for this moment, and her skin was a shade or two darker and her hair considerably curlier than her biological and only mother's. But I saw I could have absolute confidence in Lucy's grasp of who and where she was.

The four of us challenged people's notions of what a family should look like. A couple of years after Carol and I became mothers, I was ranting to one of my lesbian friends about the ignorant, insensitive, and sometimes downright obnoxious and offensive things that strangers would say to us—regarding adoption, skin color, ethnicity, or the curious spectacle of two mothers mothering together. My friend gave me an indulgent smile. "Jackie," she said, "you're exactly right. And, of course, I agree with you completely. But you must admit you are asking people to take in an awful lot all at once." She was right, of course, and her gentle dose of reality helped me temper my impatience at the ignorant responses we encountered. And yet, I still insisted, I was right, too. We're here, we are one of many answers to the question of what a family looks like, and whether or not that pleases everyone we encounter the world is going to have to make room for us.

We knew this would mean that we would have to help Lucy and Gracie find ways to talk about these differences. We couldn't always anticipate what others might say, but we worked at giving them a vocabulary and a consciousness that would equip them for whatever might be coming next. Often our efforts seemed to be working.

One Sunday, after church, we went to a favorite Indian restaurant. The girls loaded their plates with naan and tandoori chicken. They pulled up to the table and tucked in with gusto. After a few moments,

Gracie had taken the edge off of her hunger sufficiently to have a look around. The restaurant bustled with families and waiters. Indian people predominated, although there were several African American families as well. Gracie surveyed the crowd. "There aren't too many plain people in here," she observed.

"Plain people?" we asked.

"Like you," she explained, indicating both moms with a nod across the table. Gracie's strong interest in visual detail had already become manifest. She loved to draw, and she didn't think anything should ever be left plain if it could possibly be decorated with designs or brightened up with color. It was clear, in that moment, that she had come to regard brown skin as a wonderful alternative to the plain, pale condition of her moms.

"You know, you're right," Carol agreed. "There are hardly any plain people in here except for Mama-Jackie and me. Almost everyone else has beautiful brown skin."

The girls complained to us at dinner one night that their classmates sometimes asked them questions they didn't want to answer. We asked for examples. They had plenty. Is that really your mom? She doesn't look like you. Where were you born? Where is your real mom/dad? Why don't you live with her/them? Why did your mom give you away? Don't you want to see your relatives? How can you have two moms?

Sometimes we don't know what to say, they told us. Sometimes we don't want to answer these stupid questions. You don't have to, we told them. It's your story, and you can tell it or not. And so, for the next half hour, we invented possible answers to intrusive questions.

"Where were you born?" we asked Lucy.

"I was born on Pluto," Lucy replied. "Or maybe it was Mars. I was born into a royal family there. I arrived here in a spaceship."

"Who is your real mom?" we asked Gracie. "Where is she?"

"I'll tell you," said Gracie, "but not today. Ask me again tomorrow."

"OK, it's the next day. Where's your real mom?"

"Ask me tomorrow," Gracie said again. She liked the potentially endless loop of this polite demurral. Tomorrow never comes, so you never have to answer if you don't want to.

Gracie, with her great gift for living in the moment, said much less

172

than Lucy about her biological mother. She had little desire to disc
her status as an adopted child. Her one expressed curiosity was to kno
what her birth mother looked like. This was a natural question, but one
with no answer. We don't know what she looked like, we would tell her,
but we know she was beautiful. Gracie was the evidence for this claim.

One afternoon Lucy climbed off the bus shaking with laughter. We
wanted to know what was so funny.

"A girl on the bus wanted to know which one of you was my mother."

"What did you tell her?"

"I told her you were both my mothers."

"What did she say?"

"She wanted to know which one of you I live with," Lucy said, laughing again at the memory of these questions. "So I told her I live with you
both."

"What did she say then?"

"She wanted to know which one of you I liked best. I told her I liked
you both the best." Lucy's voice rose higher and higher in amazement at
the absurdity of these questions.

"Then," Lucy said, with a "you're really not going to believe this one"
air, "she asked me how you got together."

"And you told her?"

"I told her, 'I don't know. I wasn't there when they fell in love and got
married.'"

It was abundantly clear from Lucy's demeanor as she told this story
that the joke was on this silly girl and her ridiculous questions.

Lucy discovered the Meg Christian recording of "Leaping Lesbians"
tucked away in some forgotten stash of women's music tapes. She found
this spoof of the irrational fear of lesbians as hilarious as I had more than
a decade earlier when I was first coming out. Christian warns the listener
to beware of the dreaded leaping lesbians because "We want your loving,
that's our plan." Her teasing send-up echoes the cadences of spooky Halloween music.

> *AH-ah-ah*
> *Don't look in the closet.*
> *AH-ah-ah*
> *We're creeping down the stairs.*

AH-ah-ah
Sneaking up behind you.
AH-ah-ah
Watch out, better beware.

...sition of people's fears with her own familiar mommies was ...arious to Lucy. She played the tape again and again.

As time passed, she began to understand that even her own dearly beloved grandparents had struggled with the notion of a lesbian daughter. On a trip to Kentucky, not long after she had begun to make this connection, she popped "Leaping Lesbians" into her tape player as our car approached the bridge over the Ohio River that led into Louisville. Here was courage from an unexpected quarter: my own daughter providing the ironic soundtrack for my visit home. She liked the joke so much that she played the tape again the next time we crossed the river into my home state.

We longed, as I suppose parents always long, to protect our girls from any pain. We didn't want them to ever have to fight our battles or take a beating from peers because of their moms. Yet, as I worried about what might lie ahead for them, I couldn't help thinking about the pain and social ostracism I had experienced as the preacher's daughter. Despite the well-known difficulties of the preacher's kid role, it is unlikely that my parents ever questioned whether they should bring a child into a situation in which she would have to encounter that kind of prejudice. They just counted on providing me with the necessary strength of character to play the hand I'd been dealt. And they rested easy in their right to become parents.

There is no such tolerance for lesbian and gay parents. In some states, it is still illegal for lesbian and gay parents to adopt at all; in most others, we cannot adopt as a couple. Hefty percentages of the U.S. population do not believe gay people should raise children. Some believe gay people are living immoral lives. Others simply don't think that children should be subjected to homophobia. The fact that the homophobia comes not from the family but from society is not considered an indictment of society but of the couple that wishes to become parents.

Had Carol and I not been possessed of a rock-solid belief in our right to be parents and ample confidence in our ability to be good ones, we never would have had the courage to commence. For me, I think some of that confidence came from the knowledge that I had been well loved by two fine parents and would know how to pass on my own version of what was given to me. However we came by our audacity, Carol and I never doubted that we could make a family by heart. But we realized that at times all four of us would be up against it. Although the number and visibility of gay families has grown dramatically in the past decade, at the time we adopted Lucy and Gracie we knew no other families like ours in Chicago. We kept talking to our girls about who we were and what we believed and hoped that when the time came Lucy and Gracie would have the resources they needed to carry them through.

The more the girls moved out into the broader world the more complicated became the situations they faced. Carol spent a year interviewing gay and lesbian parents and researching the kinds of support that various families managed to put in place. She wrote an article reporting on some of this and proposed a book to several publishers, but a book on lesbian families had come out the year before, and most publishers felt that the one already out there had, if not covered the subject, saturated the market.

Determined to use some of what she had learned to help others, Carol offered to do a presentation for the Inter-American teachers on how to provide support for children who have gay families or might themselves turn out to be gay. Not long after her presentation to the school, Lucy's first-grade teacher reported the following encounter.

Lucy and her classmates were seated at their tables working on a project. Apropos of nothing, one of the little boys in the class, whom we will call Miguel, suddenly piped up with an announcement: "Lucy, I know something really bad about your two moms."

"What?" Lucy asked.

"Your two moms have sex." A hush fell over the room. Lucy, rarely at a loss for words, looked puzzled.

"I don't know what you're talking about," she said quietly, when she found her voice.

At this point, the teacher came to Lucy's rescue. "Miguel," she said gently, "everybody's parents have sex." If Miguel's announcement had created a shocked silence, the teacher's claim was even more startling. Who knew? All of them?

"Well," Miguel said, trying to regain his lost footing, "I know one thing. Your moms can't get married."

"Yes, they can," Lucy said. The fine points of legalized marriage were not yet clear to her, but she had seen the pictures of our cake with the two brides on top. She had helped us celebrate our anniversary. She figured she knew all she needed to know.

"Well, anyway," said poor Miguel, backtracking yet again, "two men can't get married."

"Of course they can," said Lucy, with a look of exasperation. "I know lots of men who are married to each other."

That night at the dinner table, Lucy recounted her version of this exchange. Then she turned to me. "Here's the thing I still don't get. What's sex?"

"That's when two people who love each other and want to be partners with each other kiss and cuddle and use their bodies to express their love," I said, hoping this would be enough detail for a first grader.

Lucy had seen something like this in the movies. "Like in *The Sound of Music,* when Maria and Captain Von Trapp are in the garden under that little shelter and he asks her to marry him and they kiss?"

"Yes," I said, smiling with relief. "Like that."

"I still don't get it," said Gracie.

"You will," I said.

Gracie's kindergarten teacher asked us if we could recommend a book about a lesbian family she could read to the class. We recommended *Asha's Mums.* In this picture book, a little girl is reprimanded by her teacher when she brings her field trip permission slip back signed by two moms. The teacher tells Asha that she can't possibly have two moms and that she must get the form signed correctly. Asha's moms eventually show up and straighten the whole thing out, the teacher apologizes, and order is restored to Asha's world. In the storybook classroom, the children quickly accept Asha's family. When one of Asha's moms shows up at school, a boy from the class asks, "Which mom are you?" and she replies, "Mom number one." A few days later, the second mom visits the class and the boy repeats his question, "Mom number one," the other mom cheerily replies.

Gracie's teacher asked her if it would be OK for her to read this book to her class, and Gracie agreed that it would. We really appreciated the teacher's effort to make Gracie's family visible and ordinary. The children took their cues from the teacher. Not long after they had listened to the story, Carol visited the classroom. "Which mom are you?" asked Santino, one of the boys in Gracie's class. "Mom number one," answered Carol. From that day on the joke was set. Year after year, Santino would greet us on the playground or at the door of the classroom with this ritual question, and each time whichever one of us had stopped in would laughingly reply, "Mom number one."

We could see that such complex negotiations of the encounter between our family and the school were bound to continue. In the third grade, Lucy's classmates would begin a new game. As they sat in the noisy lunchroom, someone would call out, "If you're gay, sit down." All the children within earshot would stand up, and then the instigator would point and laugh at the still-seated children. Lucy would be appalled. She would go to her teacher, Mr. Emmer, to tell him about this development. All year long the class had studied discrimination and the civil rights movement. Lucy's sense of justice and fair play, already finely honed, had grown even stronger under Mr. Emmer's instruction.

When the class reconvened, Lucy would raise her hand, intending to say, "I don't think some of you know that my moms are gay, and when you make jokes about gay people in the lunchroom it makes me feel really bad and makes me feel like I don't want to be here anymore." But before she could say any of this, Mr. Emmer would speak.

He would tell the class that he understood some of them had been making jokes about who was gay or not gay. He had been teaching them about social justice all year. This, he would explain, was no different. Maybe not everyone in the class realized that Lucy had two moms who were gay. They had a right to be a family and love each other. When the class made jokes like that, it didn't make Lucy feel very welcome. These jokes were not going to be acceptable, and if he heard of another incident there would be an automatic parent-teacher conference. As he spoke, Lucy would begin to relax. She would pull her hand down.

That same year, just before school let out, we would read one morning in the *Chicago Tribune* and the *New York Times* that the Southern Baptist Convention had passed a resolution demanding that wives graciously submit to their husbands. It was not enough that they had to submit, but they had to be gracious about it. Uncertain whether to laugh or cry, I would choose to laugh.

"What does it mean to submit?" Lucy would ask.

"I'm not surprised you would ask," I would say, "since not a single person in this family has a working knowledge of the word. It means you let another person be in charge of you."

"I submitted to you," she would claim.

"What? When? Was I asleep? I have no memory of this."

I would call my father to see if he had read the story. He would not share my amusement, sick at the direction his beloved denomination was taking. More and more he distanced himself from the national denomination's machinations, focusing his energy on the Kentucky Baptist Convention and the work of his own church.

That evening, I would return from work to find a message from Mr. Emmer: "Well, there's another Lucy story every day, and this one was just too good to keep. At school this morning, Lucy sidled up to me and said, 'Mr. Emmer, did you hear that the Southern Baptists have passed a rule that wives must graciously submit to their husbands?' I told her, 'No, Lucy, I hadn't heard that.' 'Well, they have,' she told me, and then she gave a big pause for dramatic effect. I waited. 'Fortunately, at our house, this is not a problem, because we have all girls.'"

Later, when I talked to Mr. Emmer, I would say, "Lucy is an incipient feminist."

"Check again," he would tell me. "There's nothing incipient about it."

On a sweltering day in July 1995, I picked up a copy of the *Chicago Tribune* and started to toss it into the back seat. My eye snagged on the headline: "State Court Says Gays Have Right to Adopt." Two women had decided to have a child together. One mother gave birth, and the other, her partner, raised the child with her but had no legal standing in relation to the child or her partner. Thus, the second mother could not legally make decisions for or represent the child in school or medical settings, nor would she have any recourse if the partners broke up and she was denied access to her daughter. They had petitioned the court to allow the nonbiological mother to legally adopt the child as a second mother. This is called a coparent adoption, and stepparents engage in this sort of adoption regularly. The judge who heard their case turned them down, but they had appealed. The headline announced an appellate court ruling holding that the best interests of the child, not the parents' marital status or sexual orientation, should be the basis of any adoption decision. The women's coparent adoption petition had been approved. The newspaper didn't name the family involved, but we later learned that two lesbian couples had joined in this appeal. One of these families was the one in our neighborhood that we had passed on our way home from church the day of their daughter's birth.

What this meant for our family is that for the first time it might be possible for each of us to adopt the daughter originally adopted by the other mother. I quickly called Carol and then our attorney. She assured us that with our long history as a couple and as mothers, and with our original adoptions long since complete, we made what she considered an ideal test case. Ever the careful lawyer, she warned us that, although the door for coparent adoptions appeared to be open, the state legislature or a ruling by a higher appellate court could close that door at any time.

"Then let's move quickly," we told her.

"OK," she said, "but I want to be sure you understand that a positive ruling now could be reversed in the future."

"We'll take that chance," Carol insisted.

"We don't know how long this opportunity will last," I said. "The door is open. Let's see if we can get through it." Within days, our attorney entered our petition for coparent adoptions for each of our daughters, a petition that, if successful, would convert our two single-parent adoptions into two-parent adoptions.

Although we had completed the required home studies (to determine the suitability of the adoptive parents and home) when we originally adopted our daughters, the court appointed a guardian ad litem to make a recommendation on the basis of the children's best interest. This court-appointed attorney contacted us and arranged a time to drop by our house and meet all of us.

To say that we cleaned the house and spruced ourselves up would be a grave understatement. We cleaned that house right down to the inside of the cupboards, the backs of the closets, and the dust-bunnies under the beds. We were shameless in our blatant emotional appeals. We filled the living room and dining room with fresh flowers. Carol, whose homemade piecrusts are legendary, baked an apple pie. By the time the attorney arrived, our house was filled with the irresistible aroma of cinnamon, apples, and butter. He stayed just long enough to have a piece of the still-hot pie and to meet us all. He never even peeked into our closets or under our beds. He was warm and friendly and seemed relaxed with our family, so we felt optimistic. To the extent, that is, that lesbians approaching any sort of adoption proceeding can ever be said to feel optimistic.

We knew we were a family before we arrived at the Daley Center shortly after lunch on a hot August afternoon and made our way to family court. We knew we were both mothers to both girls, we knew they were sisters, and we knew we were forever joined. We knew it because our hearts told us. We believed it was the daily act of mothering that made us mothers and the daily acts of sisterhood that made our girls sisters on a level more fundamental than any law can reach. Still, when we entered Daley Center dressed in our best, it was with a powerful sense of excitement and anticipation and, yes, anxiety. What if the judge saw our petitions for coparent adoptions and decided to block them? Our attorney assured us we had little to fear, but paranoia dies hard for lesbians used to dealing with a homophobic world and for adoptive parents who have weathered the vagaries of Peruvian adoptions.

Along with several other families awaiting their turn, we gathered in a toy-filled waiting room that adjoins Family Court. After twenty anxious minutes, our names were called. We stepped into the courtroom, each mom holding a daughter by the hand. The judge was a kind and intelligent-looking African American woman about our age. After a brief conversation with Carol and me, she began to talk to the girls. To get the conversation started, she asked them what school they attended. "Inter-American Magnet School," they answered solemnly. "Are you girls sisters?" she asked next. Carol and I stopped breathing. She was trying to find out whether they understood themselves to be related to one another. "Yes," Lucy and Gracie answered clearly and firmly. Of this answer both girls were comfortably, happily certain, so certain, in fact, that a year later Lucy recalled the judge's query with the words, "What a ridiculous question! Why would a judge ask such a ridiculous question?"

And yet it was not until we walked from the court a few minutes later with our temporary custody orders that the law began to catch up with reality.

A few weeks later our final adoption orders for each girl arrived in the mail. We lit candles and cooked a special dinner to celebrate. We were each moms to each; they were sisters to one another. Our hearts had told it, and now the law declared it.

Family of the heart, family by the state's decree.

16

We Went to Church on a Saturday

A lmost two years had passed since Mother was diagnosed with cancer. Although she had beaten it, either the cancer or the chemotherapy set in motion a process of inexorable decline. She spent a lot of time sleeping and, as little strokes damaged her short-term memory, her grip on the present slipped away. She often seemed to be floating out of our grasp. Yet, though much was taken, much abided. No matter what course her health took, she held steadfast in her capacity for pleasure in the present moment and her calm, even joyful, acceptance of the approaching end. "For I have learned, in whatsoever state I am, therewith to be content" (Philippians 4:11), she quoted with Paul.

I took nothing for granted. When she began her battle with non-Hodgkin's lymphoma, I understood, for the first time in my life, that Mother was going to die. In the nearly two years that she lived beyond that diagnosis, I reveled in every telephone conversation and every visit.

Although she was only seventy-four, there was no longer any doubt that she was an old woman. Whenever she sat down for more than a few minutes, she fell asleep, sometimes snoring softly. She moved more slowly and with more effort than ever before. Yet in the summer before she died she continued to take an interest in her beloved family, rejoicing with us when our coparent adoptions were approved. She felt good enough and was getting around well enough to plan a trip with Eldred.

In early August, the two flew to Portland, Oregon. They had always loved travel, and Daddy wanted Mother to see this beautiful place, which he had once visited without her. They had a grand time. On August 4, 1995, they stood at a lookout with the ocean at their backs and asked a stranger to take their picture.

Daddy stands with the sun reflecting just a bit off of the top of his bald head. He weighs only ten pounds more than he weighed the day they married. He still has the broad shoulders and strong forearms he earned hanging tobacco all those years ago. His left arm firmly encircles Mother, just an inch or two above her waist. Her shoulder tucks into his, and one of her arms reaches behind him. With the other, she braces herself lightly on the weathered wood of the fence post that edges the lookout. She looks magnificent. She wears purple slacks and a short-sleeved white blouse embroidered with purple and pink flowers. The blouse is a favorite. It reminds her of Switzerland and the fields of beautiful wildflowers high up in the alpine meadows. Her full head of salt-and-pepper hair sweeps back from her forehead and curves softly behind her ears. She wears just a hint of lipstick. The kindness you can only wear on your face at age seventy-four if you have earned it brightens both of their beautiful smiles. The sky is blue. The sand is gray, a gray turning to taupe. The water is gray below the blue sky, gray mixed with the white of a gentle surf. I know the date because it is etched in little digital orange numbers in the lower right-hand corner of the picture.

The woman who took their picture was young and beautiful, with blond hair like Marilyn Grissom's. Mother told me later she was convinced that this pretty young woman was flirting with Daddy. Mother was inclined to think everyone was flirting with Daddy. She found him so irresistible that she assumed he had much the same impact on every female he met. I suspect that pretty young woman did enjoy her brief conversation with the friendly, confident, handsome man and his charming wife. But I don't think she was flirting. I think she was just happy to see this older couple so alive and in love. Just before she snapped the picture, she asked them if they were newlyweds. This tickled them both, although it was a question they had heard often over the years. She was astonished to learn they were fifty-three years married. "You can't be that old," she said. And, indeed, the two smiling people in the picture I have here on my desk look nothing like most of us imagine seventy-four year olds ought to look.

Later that same day, Mother had some kind of ministroke. At first, Daddy couldn't figure out what had happened. Suddenly, it was much harder for her to walk, and she grew confused. It was perhaps the next to the last day of the trip. They flew home. Doctors couldn't tell them much. Nothing showed up on the brain scan. Mother began to show signs of the onset of a manic episode, and as she came under the influence of the antipsychotic medications her thinking became still fuzzier. Her balance was poor, and her short-term memory was damaged. When Daddy walked out of the room, she could no longer remember whether he had left the house or simply gone to the bathroom. She didn't know whether she had eaten or not because she could not remember what had happened that day or even in the last few minutes. She would often ask when they were going to eat lunch right after they had gotten up from the table and cleared the dishes.

My family was vacationing at a little cabin on a lake in northern Wisconsin. That weekend, because I had always talked to my parents on Saturday morning, I walked over to the bar and office. There was a pay phone on the little wooden porch. I stood there in the cold morning air and dialed their number. My breath was visible in cloudy puffs.

That's when I learned they were having trouble. I could hear the worry in Daddy's voice as he described what was happening. I could hear the mania and paranoia in Mother's. We were near the end of our vacation. We packed quickly, drove back to Chicago and caught a flight to Kentucky.

I wondered if I should go alone. I wanted to be a help, not an added source of stress. But school was starting in another week, and it would be difficult for us to visit once it began. There was a chance the girls might never see their Grandmama alive again unless they came with me. So we planned a two-day stay. Not long enough to wear out our welcome, we hoped, but long enough to give us all a chance to be together.

Daddy met us at the airport in his big white Cadillac. Driving home, he told us that Mother's memory had not improved. She could no longer keep track of the dozens of medications she needed to take. Her balance was shaky, and she was in constant danger of falling. He had installed a grab bar in the bathtub, but now she could not pull herself out, even using the bar. Some nights she had accidents on her way to the bathroom or while she slept. When that happened, he got up and cleaned up the mess and put on fresh sheets.

"How are you doing?" I asked, reaching over and rubbing his tight shoulder. He glanced at me and then back at the road. His eyes gleamed with tears. "I've been trying to figure out what it is that I am feeling," he told me. "I think it's grief. I see her slipping away from me. I want her to get better. I hope that she will get better. I pray that she will get better."

"Perhaps she will," I said. "But then, after that, she will get worse again."

"I'm afraid that's right." Tears began to roll down his cheeks. "I'm losing her little by little."

I couldn't think of anything to say. I rubbed his shoulder again.

This visit was a painful one. It hurt to see Mother so confused and weak. She was sometimes querulous in a way I had never seen before. The girls' noise bothered her, and she fretted when they buzzed back and forth between the living room and the sunporch, never once moving at less than a run. I began to fear that bringing them had been a mistake, but then in the next minute she would happily read them a story, the memory of her passing irritation gone without a trace.

The first afternoon we were there she decided she wanted popcorn. She was determined to make it herself. Unsteady on her feet, she had no business making popcorn. "I can make it," I protested. But her determination surpassed my own. She might indeed fall and break her hip or cut her head open and bleed to death, but she was, after all, an adult. She seemed, on this point, to know what was left of her own mind. As I stood to the side to let her cook, she reached for the can of bacon drippings she had cooked with all her life and spooned a great gob into her popcorn pan. No wonder she had been so insistent on doing it herself. No one else would ever have prepared the popcorn the way she wanted it. No one else, in fact, was even able to eat the greasy stuff when she was finished. But she relished every salty, greasy mouthful.

She was cheerful about her memory lapses. She would often say something that showed plainly how far her mind had slipped. But if she realized her mistake, as she often did, the realization seemed to leave no shadow of self-consciousness or embarrassment. Certain ideas held such power for her that she repeated them over and over. For instance, the first time someone mentioned the name Jim, she exclaimed, "Jim! We're surrounded by Jims. We've always had Jim Strause over here next door to us on the south. He's the one that does all that pretty needlepoint. Then Jim, the banker, moved in across the street. And now we have another Jim next door to us on the north side. That Jim's a plumber. So we have Jim on the south, Jim on the west, and Jim on the north. Jim, Jim, Jim. If we can just get a Jim to move in behind us, we'll have Jims in all four directions." A few minutes later, when one of the Jims was mentioned again, she repeated her Jim speech verbatim, as if she had just that minute thought of it. Because the neighborhood was chock-full of Jims, she must have made the same speech at least eight or ten times during our short visit.

The last night we were there Daddy needed to go to a meeting. We stayed home with Mother. Carol and I were in the yard on one side of the house practicing tai chi. The girls were with Grandmama out by the vegetable garden. Suddenly, they came running. "Come quick!" they shouted. "Grandmama fell down!"

We ran. We found her sitting in the garden with a big smile on her face. "I toppled over," she said cheerfully. "I was trying to pick this little ripe tomato, and I guess I lost my balance." She held the tomato up triumphantly. "This would taste mighty good if you washed the dirt off and put a little salt on it," she advised. Carol and I each took an arm and, using all our strength, hauled her back to her feet. Her legs didn't seem to have too much push left in them.

"Mother," I tried to scold. "I don't think you're supposed to be picking tomatoes right now."

"Oh, probably not," she said calmly. She was someone who would just as soon agree as not. "But it was perfectly ripe. If I had left it there, it would have fallen on the ground and the squirrels would have ruined it."

She showed no remorse. I could see that she was going to do just as she pleased with whatever time she had left. We might as well save our breath.

I hated to leave Daddy alone with this load. I worried about Mother's safety and how much time she had left. But over the next few weeks she began to improve. In early October, right around Daddy's birthday, they drove up to see us.

Mother looked great. She was back. She had a little trouble climbing the steps to our second floor, but once up there she had no trouble keeping track of what was going on. They were both really happy about the progress she had made. I had just started a new job as an associate dean in arts and sciences. I took them to see my new office and meet my dean. They wanted to see where I spent my weekdays, but the walk from the car to the office and back wore Mother out. Still, in the three days they visited, we all had a wonderful time. When they headed home early Monday morning, the girls leaped out of bed to see them off. Lucy and Gracie, barefoot and wearing their "sleepy shirts," walked with me off the porch and out to their Cadillac. We hugged good-bye, and then they climbed into the car and pulled away. Lucy and Gracie ran all the way to the end of the block in their bare feet, waving and blowing kisses. They gave their Grandmama a royal good-bye. It was the last time they would see her alive.

On October 21, Mother awakened before dawn to find that she could not get out of bed. Daddy called at once for an ambulance. At the hospital, she learned that she had a brain hemorrhage but one that was not yet dangerously large. She squeezed Daddy's hand.

"Honey," she said, "I'm afraid I've really messed up your Saturday."

"Oh, good grief, you haven't messed up anything," he replied, giving her hand a squeeze in return. She told him she loved him. He told her he loved her. She closed her eyes and slipped into a coma.

The hemorrhage grew rapidly. The doctors operated, but they were not able to prevent massive damage to the brain stem. By the time Jeannie and I arrived at the hospital Saturday afternoon, Mother's wrecked body lay almost lifeless in the hospital bed. She was in the intensive care unit (ICU). She was fitted with oxygen and a breathing tube. An intravenous tube pumped fluids into her slack body.

In between our brief visits with her, we sat in the ICU waiting room. As the word got out about what had happened, the waiting room began to resemble a gathering place for impromptu Southern Baptist prayer meetings. Daddy, Jeannie, her husband Doug, and I sat around and talked about Mother. Every few minutes someone would stop by. There seemed to be about a 75 percent chance that the person would be a minister of some sort.

The visits followed a predictable pattern. First, we would fill our visitors in on what had happened and how Mother was doing. Then, we would sit around and tell stories about Mother for twenty or thirty minutes. Many of these stories were funny, and we laughed a lot. The stories brought the living Mother into the room much more powerfully than standing beside her slack body tethered to life-support machines ever could. After the storytelling round, the minister would say, "Well, I need to be going, but before I do I'd like to lead you all in a word of prayer." We would all hold hands and bow our heads. The preacher would ask for healing for Marjorie if it be God's will, for guidance for the doctors, for strength and comfort for Eldred and the family, in Jesus' name, Amen. Then the visitors would say good-bye. A few minutes later someone else would arrive, and we would repeat the sequence.

By Sunday night, it was obvious to the doctors and to us that Mother was not going to recover. Tests had confirmed what my own eyes had already told me. The neurological evidence for profound brain damage was clear. She was essentially brain-dead.

An old family friend, J. D. Herndon, came by with his wife. I hadn't seen him in many years, but, like many of our visitors, he was someone I remembered well. We told stories, and then, as our visit drew to a close, Brother Herndon said, "Before we go, I'd like to lead you all in a word of prayer."

Oh, how I wished such prayers could heal her. But as the pieties continued to follow their predictable pattern, my irreverence mounted. "Brother Herndon," I said to our old friend. "We've had more preachers in here leading us in a word of prayer than we can shake a stick at. If leading us in a word of prayer would have made any difference in Mother's health, she would have picked up her bed and walked out of this hospital by now."

Brother Herndon looked at me with a twinkle in his eyes. "Jackie, you haven't changed one bit since you were four years old," he told me. I was reassured to know something here was unchanged. We all joined hands and bowed our heads.

The next morning, Daddy and I didn't get to the hospital until ten. Worn out, we first took time to do a load of laundry and have a good breakfast. When we arrived at the hospital, a man we had met the day before was already keeping watch for his loved one. Daddy spoke to each person he encountered in the lounge area, asking after the person they were waiting for and inquiring about whether they belonged to a church in Louisville. Lifelong habits held him in their grip. He could not prevent himself from behaving like a pastor between his visits with his own friends. This man, a Presbyterian waiting for his mother, told us that we had had a visitor earlier. "I can't remember what he said his name was," he said. "But he was an older, bald-headed gentleman, a preacher."

I raised my eyebrows at him and laughed. "Haven't you seen enough of us by now to know that old, bald-headed preacher does not really narrow the field? We're up to our eyeballs in old, bald-headed preachers."

"Jackie, you're terrible," Daddy said. But he was laughing.

Our new friend chuckled, too. "OK, let me see. He had a cane."

"Ah," I said. "Now we're getting somewhere." I looked at my father, and he ticked off the names of two pastors who fit that description.

Mother passed away two days later on October 25. We gave her a beautiful service. The church was filled with music and singing and over three hundred friends and family members. My family sat beside me. Six-year-old Lucy drew a picture on the back of an offering envelope of her Grandmama in heaven with the angels. In the limousine, Lucy marveled at all the unusual events of the day, "We went to church on a Saturday," she pointed out. "Now that's a heck of a note."

October 28, 1995, was a cold, gray day in Louisville, Kentucky. At Cave Hill Cemetery, the trees had already dropped most of their splendid autumn leaves. No flowers bloomed. As they lowered her casket into the cold ground, I looked at the bare, late autumn landscape rapidly turning toward winter. I could not help but remember, just as she had meant me to, the sun- drenched spring day when Mother and I had stood in this exact spot, laughing together about all her nice neighbors. In the leafless, lifeless landscape I was entering, she was still busily reminding me, from beyond the grave, of past and future springs.

17

Broken

In the months that followed, I felt as if my life were shattered. The day after the funeral, Carol and the girls drove back to Chicago. I stayed on to help my father. We couldn't bear to go to church that Sunday morning. Instead, we drove out to Burnheim Forest, a woods Mother had loved, and puffed up and down a steep trail. The trees were bare and indistinguishable to me. Mother would have been able to identify each one by the shape of their leafless skeletons, the texture of their bark. The sun shone improbably in a brazen autumn sky. We were worn out by the time we got back home, not so much from our short hike as from the grueling, heart-wrenching week.

Yet, with typical Taylor efficiency, we set ourselves to cleaning out her closets and drawers almost immediately. Daddy believed we needed to get her things out of the house. He didn't want to live in a museum. As we sorted through her clothes, we found neatly folded squares of Kleenex in every pocket and purse. The embroidered handkerchiefs of her youth had passed out of style, but she continued her lifelong practice of carrying the modern version of the clean folded handkerchief her mother had taught her never to be without. Little sachets of lavender perfumed her bureau drawers. Rows of beautiful pumps, some twenty or even thirty years old, still rested in their original shoe boxes. These were the clothes of a gracious lady from a bygone era.

We were ruthless. We paused from time to time to talk about memories attached to a particular garment, then moved ahead, creating careful piles to give to the church. Only the hats were spared. I claimed them all, the hopelessly out-of-date, the could be good with the right outfit, and the perfect to cover a bald head during chemo.

When I sat down in her maple rocking chair to rest, I fell asleep and dreamed that the house was leaking. I tried to call Mr. Bill, the fellow who keeps my Chicago house in good condition but, although I dialed and dialed, I could not get the telephone to work. Water was pouring down from the ceiling. As I struggled awake, the soundtrack of my dream began to play "This Old House."

> *This old house is getting leaky,*
> *This old house is getting old,*
> *This old house lets in the rain,*
> *And this old house let in the cold,*
> *Ain't got time to fix the shutters,*
> *Ain't got time to fix the doors,*
> *Ain'ta gonna need this house no more.*

More fully awake, I considered my dream. It was too obvious to be interesting. My shelter was gone. The roof was leaking or, more accurately, gushing. I couldn't get through to anyone. Not only that, but the body was a house in the process of decaying, a house that even I, who had thought myself so young, wouldn't be needing all that long.

On Monday night, two days after the funeral, I flew home. It was Halloween, and I wanted to be with the girls. I wanted to drop candy into the maws of the extended bags thrust forward by the dazed and sugar-glutted trick-or-treaters. I wanted to be happy about my children's Halloween excitement, but instead the parade of tiny ghouls and Disney characters across my porch, the whole carnivalesque atmosphere, jarred me. I don't recall Lucy's and Gracie's costumes that night, but I remember feeling more of a liability than an asset. Carol had dressed up as the Grim Reaper. Her costume had been planned for a couple of weeks. She walked into the living room wearing a long black robe and chalk-white face paint. In her hand, she carried a rubber scythe. I stared at her, transfixed. I remember thinking, this is so bizarre it would be funny if I weren't so tired and sad.

For months I felt broken. I worried about Carol and my daughters, who had to put up with the cracked and empty shell of what had once been a vital, vibrant person. I created a small shrine to Mother in a corner of the sunporch. I set out pictures of her, her Bible, a box of Tabu talcum powder, the embroidered black silk purse and black kid gloves she had brought home from Paris, some stones and shells she had loved, a beautiful silk scarf. I added a copy of Roger Tory Peterson's *Field Guide to Birds* and, later on, a bird's nest the girls found. Sometimes I would place fresh flowers there. In a comfortable chair next to this shrine, I would sit and cry at night after I had tucked the girls in bed. Several times Lucy heard me snuffling and came out to give me a hug. "It will be OK," she comforted. "Don't worry." One night Gracie found me in my soggy corner. She circled her arms around me and said, "I know just how you feel." And she did. My little girls were already experienced in mother loss.

Just a year earlier, our cat Louise had died. We buried her in the backyard, and the girls made good-bye cards for her. This had been their first encounter with death. We had lasted only a few days without a cat before we went to the animal shelter and adopted two, a small, orange tabby with an improbably loud purr whom we named Brenda Starr, and Big Boy, a magnificent, giant-sized, black and white cat with long, soft fur. Lucy liked to point out to anyone who would listen that he was the only male in the family. Now, as I sat in my chair and missed my mother, Big Boy would leap into my lap and curl his enormous self against me. Brenda Starr would stand nearby, purring like a small helicopter.

Dream: Daddy is divorcing Mother after fifty-three years of marriage. I beg him to reconsider, but he is adamant. Mother pleads with me to talk some sense into him, but I am powerless to change his mind.

Dream: Mother has wandered off from the house in a state of mental confusion and gotten lost. We can't find her anywhere. We believe her dead. But she isn't. She is living in a nursing home. She wants us to come and get her right away. I am thrilled but also horrified. What will she think when she learns that we have given away all her beautiful clothes? I try to make arrangements to bring her home, but none of my plans works. Sometimes I lose her again; sometimes I can't arrange the transportation. Finally, I bring her home, but when we pull into the driveway Daddy is standing there with his new wife. He has remarried. Mother is furious, but what can we do? We had thought she was dead. The new wife makes awkwardly friendly overtures, but Mother and Daddy look stricken. I awaken to find that even this scenario is not as awful as the reality. She is gone. We will not find her. She is not on her way back to us.

Dream: I am teaching a night class. During the break, I enter the restroom. I collapse onto the floor and lay my head up against the bathroom stall, where I begin to weep in great, loud, wracking sobs. The door of one of the stalls opens, and a confident and crisply groomed, professional-looking woman emerges. Without a glance at me, she marches to the sink, washes and dries her hands, and, stepping over my sobbing body, exits the restroom, oblivious to my desolation. I awaken. Yes, I think, I am both of those women: the one who sits sobbing on the floor of the public bathroom and the one who steps briskly over that crumpled wreck to go on about her work.

I marveled at how I had believed until Mother's death that I was an I, that I was doing things myself. Now, I realized, I had always been a we. I had never done anything without the strong sense that she was watching my back, that win, lose, or draw I was splendid, I was hers, and if it didn't work out as I hoped I could cuddle into one of her big, soft hugs and find comfort.

Now I was the oldest mother in my family. Daddy and Jeannie and her husband came to Chicago for Thanksgiving, and we made dinner for them. I fixed the dinner as Mother would have fixed it, preparing the sage and cornbread stuffing according to her recipe. Somehow, bit by bit, I would have to learn to be a mother without a mother.

Daddy and Jeannie were much pluckier than I. In January, Daddy gave his first dinner party, entertaining three couples. While I was still wishing for someone to bring me covered dishes, he served up a roast, vegetables, and a Jell-O fruit salad, capping the sumptuous meal with a pecan pie he had baked from scratch. As Mother's health had failed, his load of cooking and housework had grown until, by the time of her death, he was doing nearly everything. Doing for himself was not an adjustment.

But he was unbearably lonely. He called often, delighting in my family more than he ever had. But we could not replace the daily companionship he had lost and for which he yearned.

By February, not quite four months after Mother's death, he began to talk of dating. He pulled out the church directory and pointed to photographs of a couple of attractive women.

"What do you think of her?" he asked.

"She looks nice, I guess," Jeannie replied. "Are you looking in the catalogue for your next wife?" He had, after all, found the first while leafing through his high school yearbook.

"I'm so lonely," he said simply. "I loved your mother with all my heart. I never looked at another woman while she lived. I was the best husband I knew how to be. But she's not here anymore, and I need a companion. I don't need someone to cook and clean for me. I can do that. But I need someone to talk to, someone at my side."

Who could argue with this? By March, he was flirting at Wednesday night Prayer Meeting with a pretty widow. She had short blond hair and perfectly manicured fingernails. She also had a twinkle in her eye and a quick rejoinder for every teasing remark he proffered. She never missed church, even singing in the choir. Tenor. A whirlwind courtship ensued. As near as I could tell from his accounts, they went from flirting to dating in about one week and from dating to engagement in the second.

He was like a teenager. He called to tell me how he had kidded her and to ask if it sounded to me like she could be interested. (He was sure she was.) How long, he wondered, before he could ask her out? A day or two later he called to say that they had a date scheduled for Friday night. After he got off the phone, I wondered how long it would take him to get serious and whether he would tell her about me, his wicked lesbian daughter who had gone off to live among the Yankees.

I didn't wonder long. The next morning he called to tell me what a grand time they had. He had come out to her about his lesbian daughter on the very first date. He needed to know where she stood before he got involved. I had to love him for that.

He was extraordinarily proud of her response. So proud, in fact, that he told me three times how she had taken this news of a lesbian daughter in stride. She hadn't batted an eye. "I don't have a problem with that," she told him. "One of my sons had a good friend who turned out to be gay, and one of my friends has a gay son. We could learn a lot from some of those people." Daddy was delighted. "I told her," he recounted and recounted and recounted, "Jackie knows that I don't condone it, and I don't understand it. But she's my daughter, and I love her." Those were the very words he kept repeating to me: "I don't condone it, and I don't understand it. But she's my daughter, and I love her." The first time he told me this story I told him that was nice. And in truth I was relieved that he had chosen someone who, by Southern Baptist lights, was open-minded. The second time I must have mumbled something mildly supportive, although I can only remember my temper rising. By the third time he told me, it was a week after they had begun dating, and he was in Chicago for a short visit. The relationship was growing intense. His excitement about her and pain at the brief separation were palpable. Indeed, they had already begun to talk marriage. As we sat together on my sunporch, he launched once again into praise for her gracious response.

He had come so far. Perhaps it was churlish of me to want more. Perhaps I was harder on him than I needed to be, than was fair. I was still feeling so bereft, and here he was falling in love. Here I sat, twelve years into a lifetime relationship with a beloved I could not marry, while he heard wedding bells after a week of dating. I was a roiling mass of fair and unfair resentments. I was growing to hate this story. Its language of judgment and righteousness set my teeth on edge.

"Every time you tell me this story I'm getting more and more irritated with you," I said. "We need to talk." "OK," he said, unable to imagine what could be wrong.

"It's about this statement you keep making," I said. "You don't condone it, and you don't understand it. Since you're not gay and you're not God, I'm having a hard time figuring out who put you in the judgment seat. I have two choices here. Either God made me gay or God didn't make me. Which would you prefer I choose? I've chosen a God who made me gay over a world with no God." As I spoke, I worried that I was simplifying my own and others' reality by suggesting that all gay people are born that way. In truth, who knows what mix of nature and nurture produces sexual orientation? But of this much I am sure: sexuality is a gift from God. The debate among people of faith should be about what constitutes respectful and life-affirming use of that great gift. Right now, however, I was barreling forward, pressing my argument by pointing out that just as surely as he disagreed with some of my choices I disagreed with some of his (getting engaged after a week of dating, for example, though I left this unuttered). Surely we could respect the core of integrity that ran through both our lives. He was listening quietly, letting me talk myself out, not even trying to interrupt.

"Now, second," I said, numbering my major points as he always did in his sermons, "I want to respond to your saying you don't understand this. When you told me in 1988 that you didn't understand, I let it pass. We were only six years past my coming out. At that point, a loving connection seemed like achievement enough. But we're now eight years farther down the road. You have been in Carol's and my home for twelve years. You have seen our love and commitment. You have seen the way we have stuck with each other through good times and hard times. You have seen the loving home we provide for our two children. What is it about this that you do not understand? The feelings that are calling you and Helen together are the same feelings that brought Carol and me together. Heart calls to heart. What about this is beyond your understanding?"

My father is a good man. He looked me in the eye. "I'm glad you talked to me about this, Jackie," he said bravely. "I think maybe the language I used doesn't accurately reflect where I am at this point in my journey."

He never meant to raise a daughter quite like me. He must have imagined someone less bull-headed and more devout. But he has loved me enough to teach me to speak up for myself and to listen when I do. He has had the grace to love the daughter he got. I suppose you can't ask for much more than that.

During that short visit, his mind was ever on Helen. I was happy to see him so excited and yet pained, too, to watch him fall in love so soon after Mother had died. He grew young in his exuberance. He confided that he and Helen were powerfully attracted to one another but that they had pledged to wait until marriage to be intimate.

"Don't tell me," I replied.

"It won't be easy, but we know we can do it."

"Don't tell me," I insisted.

"Your mother and I loved each other very much, but we pledged that we would wait until we were married, and even though we dated for a year we waited."

"Don't tell me."

"It wasn't easy. But we waited."

"Don't tell me!" I almost shouted, but I was laughing. He could not help himself.

Carol drove him to the airport. He was giddy with delight at heading home to his new girlfriend. "Have fun, Eldred," she said as she let him out of the car.

"But not too much fun," he replied.

She grinned at him. "Have all the fun you want for all I care."

Within three months, he had married Helen.

"Well," my sister said to me on the phone, "you know that old question about if a tree falls in the forest, and there's no one there to hear it, has there been a sound? With Daddy, it's like this. If he has an experience, but there's no one there to tell it to, has he had an experience? Answer: no. He can't survive without an attentive audience."

She had a point. Anyway, they were visibly happy, and life was moving on with or without us. So we gave them our blessing. Helen had four grown sons and five grandchildren. The night before the wedding we all gathered for a meal at the home of one her sons. Daddy was exuberant. He eagerly explained that their courtship was not as brief as it seemed because they had spent so much time together. "Calculated in dog years, maybe," I rejoined. He was enough of a sport to laugh.

And life did move on. Helen was not my mother, and she had the grace not to try to be, but she loved Eldred and brought him a happiness he had not had in a long time. The growing burden of care for my mother had fallen on him far more heavily than I could bear to imagine. He seemed suddenly younger, with a renewed spring in his step. Helen gave him a makeover, teaching him to let his slacks ride a couple of inches lower on his waist, getting him to sometimes forgo ties and white shirts in favor of snappy black turtlenecks and sport coats.

I limped through the circle of a year without my mother and hoped the worst was over. Little by little joy seeped back into my world. Gradually, Mother started holding me up again. Or maybe she was doing so all along, but it took me that long to get to where I could notice it. However it was, I awakened, as if from a long sleep, in the summer of the second year after her death. I realized that, although I felt much better, I missed being adored. Carol loved me dearly, but if she had ever tried to dote on me like my mother did she would have driven me crazy. My children certainly weren't going to fill that void. I missed being Mother's moon and stars. And then, that second summer, I realized there was a small thing I could do about the hole in my life her death had created.

I could get a dog.

To our already full-to-bursting household, I added a nine-month-old Corgi named Bonnie. Big Boy and Brenda Starr hissed and arched their backs for a couple of days and then decided she was family. I fed, walked, and trained her. And she boisterously welcomed me home each day and followed me about with an adoring look that helped heal my broken heart.

With such simple steps, and more and more each day, I returned my care and attention to my life with my chosen family. I had never stopped being with them and doing for them, but the sense of being and doing as a hollow shell receded. I gradually came to inhabit my body again. I remembered to breathe. I closed the shrine and distributed the pictures and mementos of Mother around the house.

"Onward through the fog," Mother often quoted. Now I said the same, walking in the cloudy present toward whatever was coming next.

18

Sailing through the Sky

W hen are we going to visit Peru?" Lucy asked again. She was beginning to sound exasperated. We had been talking about this trip for
years.

It was the spring of 1998. Lucy was nine. I looked at her. She and Gracie were at an age where they loved making trips with their family. They
were poised in that precious interval between early childhood and
puberty, old enough to have a clear sense of the outside world, young
enough to center their lives in their family. It was time, I thought.

"Let's start saving for it today," I replied. "Let's get a jar for a Peru
fund, and whenever we have any extra money, let's throw it into the jar."
Lucy loved this idea. She had a picture book about a girl who helped her
mother save every spare penny until they could afford to replace a chair
destroyed when their apartment burned. Lucy liked it when life imitated
art. She tore down to the basement and returned with a large plastic
pitcher. We sat it on the desk in the kitchen. Right away, she threw in two
dollars saved from her allowance. I emptied my pockets of change. There
was no turning back now.

Carol contacted a travel agency that specialized in creating two-week
group tours to countries of origin for international adoptees and their

families. One of our friends and her adopted Peruvian daughter had made such trip a year earlier, with a group of other adoptive families, and had come home telling good stories about the experience. Carol learned that a Peru trip was scheduled for August 1999. We signed on.

During the next year, if we got any unexpected money or found a way to spend less than we expected, we deposited whatever we had gained into the Peru pitcher. The girls counted our accumulation obsessively, dumping the loose change and dollar bills onto the living room floor, sorting the bills, and stacking the coins into neat towers. After a few months, we opened a bank account. Although the Peru fund ultimately supplied only a fraction of the cost of our trip, it gave the girls a way to participate actively in making our dream a reality. I was surprised to see them deposit not only portions of their allowance but even gift money from grandparents and aunts and uncles.

Although she cheerfully tossed money into the pitcher and thoroughly enjoyed the money-counting sessions, Gracie was much less interested than her sister in thinking about the future. Once, when I was talking with the girls about vacation plans, Gracie stopped me cold. "I don't like future planning," she said, and it was true. She has always had an enormous gift for living in the moment. She had not pressed for this trip, as Lucy had, and she was not altogether sure she wanted to go. Although Gracie is inclined by disposition to take each day pretty much as it comes, she doesn't like to be away from home and her animals for very long.

As we planned our trip, Carol and I worried about whether the expectations the girls had for this vacation could possibly be met. Lucy had been longing to travel back to Peru for at least as long as she could talk. This longing was connected, I was certain, to her desire to find her mother and other family members and in some way reunite with her clan. Such a reunion would probably not be possible on this tightly scheduled trip, particularly since we no longer knew where her mother was or how we might try to reach her. I wondered if we were going to great expense and trouble only to produce a massive disappointment.

I talked to Lucy about the likelihood that we would not be able to uncover any news about her mother, but I was not sure how well she understood this. And in truth I had not entirely dislodged my own fantasies about arranging the perfect reunion for her.

One day, a few months prior to the trip, some friends were visiting. We eagerly described our travel plans. Lucy and I sat together on the couch. I tucked my bare toes under her knee. She rested her hand on my ankle. As we talked about our impending trip, our friend said, "That sounds like a wonderful adventure."

"Yes," I said. "We'll just have to go down there and see what and who we find."

"And what and who we don't find," Lucy added, shooting a meaningful look in my direction. I knew then that she understood the tenuous nature of our dreams at least as well as I did.

Still, we worried about the likely gap between the trip they were expecting and the one we could provide. We had no way of reconnecting with Gracie's family of origin. We were not certain we could find any trace of Lucy's. Given these uncertainties and potential disappointments, we decided we'd better find out what the girls wanted to do in Peru that we could guarantee.

"I want to see a llama," Lucy told us, "and Machu Picchu." Easy enough. Both were inevitable on this particular trip. "But most of all, I want to see the Nazca lines."

"Yes," said Gracie, who had talked much less about the trip than Lucy. "We have to see the Nazca lines."

At first we told them all the reasons we could not. They were not on the tour. Adding this leg to our journey would extend our stay a couple of days and cost even more money. Peru was a big country, and we couldn't hope to see it all in one visit. We would be traveling to Peru again, and next time we would include the Nazca lines. But at Inter-American Magnet School, all third graders learned about the mysterious geometric figures etched into the gravel of the desert plane near the town of Nazca along the southern coast of Peru. Some of these figures form the shape of a spider monkey, a hummingbird, and a condor. Some are just mysterious shapes whose meaning is not known. These giant figures are clearly visible only from the air, yet they are hundreds of years old and have left scientists, anthropologists, and everyone else wondering why and how they were created. The mystery of the lines captured the imaginations of the third graders. The children at Inter-American learned about Maria Reiche, a German mathematician who spent decades in Peru studying the lines. They each made their own three-dimensional model of their favorite Nazca drawing, a project that involved construction paper, glue, and kitty litter. By now we had one of these gritty compositions tucked away in our basement stash of school projects and another drying on the window ledge in Mr. Emmer's third-grade classroom. Lucy had talked about the Nazca lines incessantly when she studied them the year before, and now, as we made the final plans for our trip, Gracie's imagination was fired by the same subject.

At last, Carol and I decided the girls' desire to see the lines was more important than our budget. We pulled out our credit card and added a final leg to the journey.

By the time we boarded the flight from Chicago to Miami, excitement was running at almost lethal levels. Our beautiful new suitcases had been packed tight and carefully tagged with the special labels provided by the travel agency. Our animal friends, Bonnie, Big Boy, and Brenda Starr, had been handed over to the care of friends. We were off.

Gracie worried about air travel. Flying made her stomach feel funny. She sat nervously across the aisle from me. When the takeoff went smoothly, she started to feel more optimistic about being airborne. She and Lucy donned their earphones and began flipping channels on the dials on the consoles between their seats but, perhaps to reassure herself that I was nearby, Gracie tapped my arm every few minutes.

Tap, tap, tap. Tap, tap, tap. I lowered my book. "Will they be serving drinks soon?" I indicated that I thought they would and resumed reading.

Tap, tap, tap. Tap, tap, tap. "Can I get some 7UP?"

"Sure, honey, knock yourself out. You're on vacation."

"Will you go to the bathroom with me?" I would.

"How long until we get to eat? Are we almost there?"

"I don't want the rest of my meal. Can I throw it away?"

Then, "I think that girl two rows in front of us is on our trip. She has tags like ours on her luggage, and her hair is black and her skin is brown, but her parents are not brown." Gracie gestured toward a girl of about eight or nine who was sitting two rows in front of us with her middle-aged parents. I had noticed her, too. The girls were experts at picking out other adopted children. We surveyed the other passengers. It looked as if there were at least two other families who might be part of our group.

In Miami, the little streams of Peruvian adoptee families began to flow together. We introduced ourselves to the families we had seen on the plane. Then, as we began to make our way through the terminal to our connecting flight to Lima, we encountered still more families. They were easy to pick out of a crowd. The children were all between the ages of seven and thirteen. The parents were thirty-five, forty, or even fifty years older. And, as Gracie had put it, all the children had black hair and brown skin, but the parents were not brown.

At the gate, we had an hour and a half wait. Lucy and Gracie whipped out a deck of cards, and soon the children were in the thick of a spirited and noisy game. Clustered around them, the adults talked, as adoptive parents will, about how old our children were when we got them and in what year we had traveled to Peru. We named the village or city where each child was born. We compared the length of time it had taken to complete each adoption.

I was already choked up, and we hadn't even embarked for Peru. Why was this so moving? In part, it was seeing this group of thirteen beautiful Peruvian children together. Although Lucy and Gracie attended a school whose population was about 65 percent Latino, I was not used to seeing them surrounded by so many children who resembled them so strongly. But perhaps even more moving for me was looking at all these other adoptive families and thinking about how we had come to be. We were all in Peru adopting our children at approximately the same time. When we completed our paperwork and sent it to the adoption agency, we received a referral to the next available baby. What if we had sent in our paperwork on a different day? What if Lucy and Gracie had landed in some other family (or families)? The process for assigning the children to families was a random one, and yet it seemed to me (and, I guessed, to all of the parents) that we had received the children meant for us.

I wondered if this trip would cause any of the children to speculate on how they might just as easily have landed in a different family. If they thought about it, would they feel relief that it had worked out as it did or would some of them suspect that a different assignment could have produced a better fit? Biological children sometimes look at their friends' parents and think either "There but for the grace of God . . ." or "Why couldn't I have had those parents?" Surely similar thoughts might occur to our children.

I thought about how different Lucy's and Gracie's lives might be if they had landed with the middle-aged couple from a small town in Wisconsin with the almost grown daughter or with the free spirits from Hawaii who seemed content to let other parents ride herd on their three children (or not) while they relaxed and enjoyed their vacation. I looked at the other children, so familiar to me because of the ways in which they resembled my own and yet so unfamiliar. I looked at my own girls, who I knew right down to the last freckle and cadence. I knew without looking just how each one of their toenails was shaped. I wanted to hug them in relief and celebration that these two girls of ours had found their way to us, right where they belong.

As the trip unfolded, I came to believe that all the children were well matched with their parents. Was this, I wondered again, a story we adoptive parents tell ourselves for comfort or had fate brought us all together according to some grand design? Was God present in the creation of our families? For Carol's and my family, I was certain that our lives were entwined in a particular and predestined pattern, certain that we had been called to parent these two special girls, and equally certain that I needed to believe this was so.

Our tour catered to the needs and interests of our thirteen children. On our first full day in Lima, we visited museums and various sites of interest. We also visited an orphanage, one with personal significance for one of the little girls on our tour. She had lived there until she was nine months old, and ever since she and her family had maintained contact with the orphanage. Now she was welcomed back to her first home with warm hugs and kisses. She wore a shy, lopsided grin as the director enfolded her curly black head against her chest. Our children presented gifts to the orphanage. Then we spent time playing with some of the toddlers and babies who lived there. These little ones ran toward us with their arms outstretched. We lifted them up and sniffed their sweet-smelling heads. We remembered our own babies, the feel and smell of them, babies who had now grown into children scampering around the room and holding babies themselves.

The staff members walked us through the orphanage. It was clean and well-organized, with courtyards and gardens and playgrounds. Children were assigned dormitories by gender and age. The workers seemed to care deeply for the little ones entrusted to them. Yet it was hard to think of children growing up here without families of their own. We walked through a room with twin beds lined up in a row along the wall, much like the beds of the girls in the *Madeline* books. Each was neatly made, with tightly tucked corners. At the top of each bed lay a little doll, each identical and each in precisely the same spot, her little doll head barely denting the center of the pillow. Somehow, that symmetrical row of perfectly positioned dolls spoke not of play and companionship but of institutionalized care, loneliness, and loss.

The children on our tour enjoyed meeting other children who were Peruvian adoptees, and within a few days they had formed a group. The girls even began to dress alike in matching hand-knitted Peruvian caps. Meals were often lavish buffets with deliciously fresh seafood and produce prepared in wonderful sauces. While the parents filled their plates with local delicacies, the children ate french fries and drank Inca colas and longed for the food of their homeland. Much of the time, we traveled by bus. The children rode together in back while the parents gravitated to the front. We had plenty of time to do what parents of children often do together—talk about the joys and challenges of raising our kids. But in this case we had the added commonality of international adoption to talk over.

The parents recalled how difficult our earlier trips to Peru had been, the trips we had made to adopt our children. Peru as a country was doing better than when we had been there nine or ten years earlier. And of course we now had the pleasure of a well-organized trip to beautiful sites, whereas before we had faced the frustrations and challenges of seeing an adoption through while caring for a new baby. But for Carol and me there was an added pleasure in our return. Now we were able to travel as a family rather than masquerading as two single women adopting independently.

The families on our trip began to see how we were all linked by circumstances and yet distinct. Most parents tried to give their children some additional link to their past. In some cases, this meant an actual reunion with a biological mother or other relatives. In others, a visit to an orphanage or the hospital where the child was born was all that was possible. Witnessing the range of experiences was helpful to our family, for it underscored the point that everyone's story was a little bit different and yet connected to the stories of many others.

With the help of our tour leader, Bea, we located the hospital where Gracie was born on the outskirts of Lima. The drive took more than an hour from our hotel in Miraflores. We drove past neighborhood after neighborhood of what are known as *pueblos jóvenes,* or "young towns," a term that belies the grim conditions of these makeshift neighborhoods.

The city of Lima is ringed with hundreds of *pueblos jóvenes,* which spring up as thousands of Indians leave their homes in the Andes and come to the city in search of a better life. The houses they construct have walls made of grass mats. Many have dirt floors. Running water and electricity are not available. The hills on which these neighborhoods perch are bare and brown. Near the top of the hill, the name of the neighborhood is often etched in white letters. Sometimes, higher still, there stands a large cross. One hillside holds a giant statue of Jesus.

At last, we reached the hospital. Gracie had fallen fast asleep in the backseat of the taxi. Slowly she struggled awake and climbed out. She blinked her sleepy eyes at the building before her. Hospital Sergio E. Bernales was painted a pale aqua with accents in a brighter blue. A line of red scallops laced the stucco wall above the arched doorways. We walked up to the wrought-iron gate to find it firmly locked. Visiting hours were over. I wondered if this distant view of Gracie's birthplace would be enough for her. Disappointed, we stood outside the gate and looked up the driveway at the bright blue walls in the distance. We turned to look at the bare brown hills surrounding the hospital and at the neighborhood from which her birth mother came. I thought about her, a young woman in labor, walking up this drive and into the hospital to give birth to our daughter. I wished that unknown woman could see the beautiful, healthy, happy daughter she had borne, could see her now, nine years later, and know that she was well. We took pictures of our family standing outside the gates of the hospital. I wondered what Gracie would make of this small addition to her story. It was too soon to tell. But in less than two years, for a fifth grade assignment, Gracie, asked to create ten clues her classmates could use to identify her, would write these words: "I was born in Lima, Peru, in a blue hospital." The hospital, in all its vivid specificity, now occupied a concrete position in the narrative of Gracie's arrival in the world.

Of Lucy's origins we knew much more. Yet we doubted our ability to find any of her relatives. For years, we had sent letters to her mother, care of Ana Maria, the attorney who had handled the adoption. But we had never heard from her and doubted that any of our letters had made it into Maria Chacpa's hands. We had tried to telephone Ana Maria from the States, but the phone number was no longer in service.

When we arrived in Lima, we learned that Bea had secured Ana Maria's phone number. Ana Maria sounded delighted to hear from us and met us at the hotel bar on our second night in town. Carol and I were both happy to see her again. She had helped us with each of our adoptions. She hugged our daughters and told us that she now had four girls (she had only one baby in 1989). She referred to them as the four Marias, for each one had Maria in her name. I asked Ana Maria if she was still in contact with Esperanza. "Yes," she told me. "I still see her sometimes."

"We would like to try to get in touch with her," I said. "I think Esperanza may be Lucy's aunt."

Ana Maria laughed. "Oh, Esperanza is everybody's aunt." During the adoption, the translator told me that many Peruvians call anyone from their village "aunt" or "cousin." The titles do not necessarily denote biological kinship. But Esperanza was from the same village as Maria Chacpa. She had introduced Maria Chacpa to Ana Maria and had carried the adoption decree back to Huasahuasi and returned with the new birth certificate. Ana Maria agreed to help us make contact. "She doesn't have a phone, but I know where she lives," she told us. "If I can't reach her, I will go to her house."

We were flying out of Lima the next morning, but we would be back in nine days. If by some chance Esperanza could see us during the afternoon of our final day in Lima, we might be able to learn more about Lucy's kin. Ana Maria was our only hope.

We flew to Arequipa. Our guide took us to see the three beautiful volcanic mountains that ring the white city and the lush valley that enjoys three growing seasons. We visited a church with a pair of intricately carved columns made from volcanic stone. He explained that when the conquistadores ordered the Indians to carve columns representing paradise, the Indians carved these representations of the paradise on earth where they already lived. So the Catholic church has columns carved from the beautiful white volcanic stone of Arequipa to reveal the jaguar, various native plants and birds, and the face of an Indian god. This, it seemed to me, was another way to interpret the proclamation of John the Baptist and Jesus that "the Kingdom of Heaven is at hand." The Incan stonecutters were theologians. "Paradise is all around you," their columns proclaimed. "Oh taste and see."

After a couple of days in Arequipa, we flew on to Cuzco. As the bus carried us from the airport to our hotel, we began to notice rainbow flags flying all around the city. At the hotel, we drank coca tea to help us with the altitude and rested in our rooms before meeting our group for lunch. On our way to the town square, we again saw several rainbow flags. "Why do they have rainbow flags all over this town?" Lucy wanted to know. "Are there a lot of gay people in Cuzco?"

"I don't know," I said, "but I'll find out."

We asked the guide. She explained that this was the Quechua flag and also the Cuzco flag. Lucy, Quechua herself, smiled with delight at this answer. "Now I get it," she said. "The rainbow flag is the gay flag, and it's the Quechua flag. You see how everything in our family fits together?" We did see. We bought a giant Quechua flag that we could unfurl from our front porch in celebration of a whole wealth of connections.

Everywhere we traveled, the Peruvians we met welcomed these children who had come to learn about the country of their birth. In the Sacred Valley, we visited a pottery shop where the artist worked with his wife and a large group of employees to make pottery and ceramic art using traditional methods. One large piece hanging in the courtyard depicted a Peruvian woman flying through the air. There was an ethereal beauty to the Sacred Valley that made the idea of a woman in flight seem entirely plausible. In a way, during those magical days of our visit, I felt as if I were in flight myself.

As she always does when she comes to a beautiful place, Carol turned to me and said, "Let's retire here. Let's buy a place in this valley and come back here to live when we retire."

"OK," I said, "let's do."

A realist from our group interrupted this daydream to caution that if we stayed out of the country for more than six months a year we would lose our Medicare benefits. But we were not making real plans. We were just imagining ourselves in this glorious place, immigrants to the country of our children's birth, continually happy and always on vacation.

At Machu Picchu, our Quechua guide told the children, "I think of this beautiful place as my house because my ancestors built it."

"Their ancestors built it, too," one of the mothers reminded her. "These children are all Quechua, just like you. These two," she said, placing her hands on the shoulders of her own daughters, "were born near here, in Cuzco."

After the guide had walked us through some of the breathtaking ruins that comprise this spectacular archaeological site crouched between magnificent peaks at the edge of the jungle, she brought us into a gorgeous open field in the midst of Machu Picchu. She asked the children to form a circle, pulled a bag of coca leaves from her pocket, and gave one to each child. She led a ritual of thanks. The children chorused thanks to their parents for bringing them to Peru and to Machu Picchu for letting them visit. They acknowledged the sacred power of the space and promised to return. They offered their coca leaves up by placing them together in a scarf and leaving them in a corner of the field. "If this were a real Quechua ritual," the guide explained, "it would last for two hours, and at the end we would burn the coca leaves. But we are not allowed to set fires at Machu Picchu now, and I do not think you want me to give you a ritual that lasts two hours." She was right. But the children entered with wide-eyed reverence into her pared-down ritual.

The night before we flew back to Lima, I called Ana Maria. I had tried not to expect much, but now I learned that Esperanza was planning to meet us at our hotel the next day at two o'clock. Esperanza remembered Lucy. "Ay, Maricruz," she said with delight when Ana Maria reached her. We told Lucy she might get to meet someone related to her birth mother, someone who had known her as a baby. She was thrilled. We joined our group for a night of wonderful food and dancing. Live bands and folkloric dancers entertained us while we ate. Our translator, the beautiful Elizabeth, who had been with us throughout our trip, was joined at the restaurant by a handsome young man. He and Elizabeth took to the dance floor, swinging their hips with an ease and freedom that looked to me like a variation on flight. The children laughed and clapped. Then Elizabeth and her gallant companion reached their hands out and led the children onto the floor to join in the revels.

Back in Lima the next day, the children went to visit a school. Lucy and Gracie visited classrooms and talked to the children in both English and Spanish. Lucy was invited to help teach the English portion of the class and was proud to do so. She happily reported to me that her class at Inter-American was much farther along in English than the Lima class. She thought she had been a big help to the Peruvian students.

That afternoon Esperanza and her sister arrived promptly at two. We greeted one another with hugs, like family. The two sisters sat with Lucy and Gracie, touching and hugging and exclaiming over them. With the help of Elizabeth, we learned that Esperanza and her sister were cousins of Maria Chacpa.

Each of them had placed daughters for adoption. With no information about what had become of their children, they longed to know that they were well. They told us about the girls they had surrendered and their worries about how they were doing. It was evident that they hungered for contact with those children and that, for them, this visit offered hope that their girls, too, had found homes where they were happy and well loved.

As they described their own adoption experiences, I began to see how it was that "Esperanza is everybody's aunt." Several women from their family and village had surrendered children for adoption. They told us that Lucy had cousins who had been adopted. For a few minutes, they wondered aloud whether Gracie could be the daughter of a woman they knew. But as we compared details of Gracie's story and the story they recalled it became clear that she was not their friend's daughter.

Both Esperanza and her sister looked like family. Like Maria Chacpa and Lucy, they were short, less than five feet tall, with stocky bodies and long torsos. They had round faces like Lucy's and thick, shiny, black hair. Anyone would be proud to claim kin with these two, they were so kind and welcoming. They hugged both girls, just as you would expect long-lost aunts or cousins to do. Lucy grinned broadly as she sat between them encircled in a warm embrace. On our next visit, they told us, we must plan to stay with them, not in a hotel. Next time they would gather other family members together and see if Lucy's birth mother could come to town. Next time we would have a party. We wondered what they made of our two-mom family, but if they found anything unusual about it they gave no sign.

Lucy's birth mother had married, they told us, and given birth to three more children, two girls and a boy. She lived with her husband in Huasahuasi. They had little money and struggled to take care of their family. Her first son, born before Lucy, did not live with Maria Chacpa but with one of his grandparents. That last piece of information answered a question that had long troubled Lucy: Why had her mother kept her brother and not her? Now we had an answer that suggested her mother had not been able to keep either of the children she bore before she married.

As the adoptive parents participated in these various reunions, we did so with a mix of emotions. Uncertainty about how the visit would go made us anxious. We longed for our children to have good, meaningful, healing reunion experiences. We also wanted to know that in the end we, the parents who cared for them each day, would not be replaced. As the various reunions took place, it became clear that the visits were interesting, important, and valuable for the children, but that most of them, after their initial contact with these unfamiliar kin, grew restless. They visited for a while and then were ready to run off and play with their new friends.

Lucy's response followed this pattern. She enjoyed meeting Esperanza and her sister. She was happy to have some news about her other biological relatives. She participated in the conversation for a while, and then, apparently having heard enough, left the table to play with Gracie and some of the other children from our tour. The meaning the visit had for her would emerge only over time, perhaps years.

Adoption creates whole families out of broken ones. Children who need parents receive parents who want them with their whole hearts, parents who have gone to great lengths to bring these children into their lives. Yet nothing can erase the multiple losses that are woven into the fabric of adoptive families. Lucy loves all of her family: her adoptive family (Mama-Carol, Mama-Jackie, her sister Gracie, her cats Big Boy and Brenda Starr, and her dog Bonnie) and her biological family (Maria Chacpa, Esperanza, two brothers, two sisters, and all the others who are part of her clan). She would never want to choose among them, for she loves us all, all of the time. I know this is true because when I try to admonish Lucy for some rudeness toward her sister by reminding her that Gracie is the only sister she will ever have she immediately asserts that, as a matter of fact, she has two other sisters and two other brothers. Her older brother, she likes to tell me, is practically perfect. He has never teased or aggravated her, not once.

Esperanza and her sister traveled far and arrived early for their visit with us because, even though she is adopted and living on another continent, Lucy is still family to them. They returned to our hotel once more, on our last day in Peru, bringing one of their daughters with them, a little girl a year younger than Gracie dressed in her school uniform. These women hold Lucy and all of us in their hearts, as they hold not only the children they care for every day but also the ones they relinquished.

We can never love one another enough to make these losses disappear. But I have to hope that by making room for all those loving bonds to survive, and even be cherished, we make the losses more bearable.

On our last two days in Peru, we said good-bye to our friends from the tour group and took a bus south. It was time to visit the Nazca Lines. By midmorning, we were checking into a beautiful resort hotel in Ica, Las Dunas. This was the sort of hotel to which the girls give a four-star rating. It had two large swimming pools, one of which featured a large twisting water slide. Llamas and peacocks wandered the beautifully landscaped grounds. There were tennis courts and shuffleboard courts and horseback riding. As far as Lucy and Gracie were concerned, this was the best hotel of the entire trip. We settled into our room and then met our guide, who took us to the nearby airport for our flight over the Nazca lines.

It was a spectacularly clear day. We climbed aboard the tiny eight-passenger plane and took off from the miniature airport. Even before we reached the Nazca lines, the view was spectacular. The ocean stretched out on our right as we flew south, and the mountains rose up on our left.

Below us was the Pan-American Highway. Lucy sat next to one window, and Gracie sat next to another. We sat beside them and, with our heads touching, peered out at the dry dunes below. After about twenty minutes, the pilot told us the lines were coming into view.

At first, all we could see were geometric shapes. Then we reached the part of the Nazca Plain where the most elaborate figures can be found. For about twenty minutes, we flew past the spider monkey, the condor, the hummingbird, the astronaut, and others. Every drawing could be seen with perfect clarity. Lucy and Gracie were wide-eyed with excitement and delight. Lucy grabbed the camera and began snapping pictures, unwilling to trust a moment this important to my limited photographic skills.

Why did the people of the Nazca Plain labor at such cost in time and effort to create these marvelous, giant drawings most clearly visible from the air? How did they even imagine aerial views of their world? Perhaps they were marking the seasons; perhaps they were preparing messages for airborne beings from another planet, celebrating sacred forms of life, knitting together the planets and the stars, or connecting people and animals and the heavens in the larger circle of life.

I could not know. But I knew this. Two little girls, who, for all we knew, might be descended from some of those same artists and laborers, were sailing through the sky, peering down in awe and wonder, weaving together their North and South American worlds in a complex pattern of their own making. Surely creating this family with Carol, living this moment with our precious girls, flying above the Nazca Plain on this perfect day, surely this was calling enough for a lifetime.

Afterword:
The Voice in the Night

Leaving home to find one's self is an old narrative. For me, that narrative tangles with one of leaving the church to find my own spiritual path. Leaving home and leaving the church always felt so much alike that at times it was difficult to tell them apart—the homesickness for a good round of hymn singing as sharp as the hunger for my mama's poke greens. It took years to find a way to make my home in the world, and years more to discover how to tell the stories that would circle back around and gather up what I needed, what was worth keeping, from all that messy mixture of heart and hurt that had gone before.

The call, it turns out, unfolded in my life while I waited. And continues to unfold, as I am able to have the courage to be wholly alive, authentically myself, and actively connected to the world around me. When I quiet the voices of external expectations, when I quiet my own desire for the approval of others, I can begin to attune myself to my own inside voice. It is through this inside voice that God's call comes to me, and that call invites me into a life of celebration and service. Frederick Buechner put it this way.

The kind of work God usually calls you to do is the kind of work
(a) that you most need to do and (b) that the world most needs to
have done. . . . Neither the hair shirt nor the soft berth will do.
The place God calls you to is the place where your deep gladness
and the world's deep hunger meet.

Waiting for the call. It is the necessary task of a girl like me, raised to
believe in a concrete and imperious deity. Pretending not to expect any
divine messages or intervention but with one ear always cocked for the
voice in the night that would call me by name. I waited, and while I waited
I made what I thought were my own plans. And while I waited I found my
way to useful work, to woman loving, to Carol, to Lucy and Gracie, to a
radically welcoming church, to a round, rich world of family and friends.
As I sat with my mother on her hospital bed and loved her entirely, without the least desire to add or take away one thing, my heart found its way
back home.

I tried to work out the problem of how I would relate to the church.
Like many gay Christians, I loved the church I had grown up in. I hated
it, too, for the violence it had done me and others, for making it so
painfully difficult to come home to ourselves. The church has been a
source of both nourishment and injury in my life. Church teachings often
provide the foundation on which people build their discrimination
against and even hatred of gay and lesbian people. That's too polite. An
awful lot of churches spew hatred of gay people, disguising human hatred
as something ordained by God. Many churches refuse to ordain openly
gay clergy or to provide holy union ceremonies for gay couples. More,
they depict love between gay people as perverse and depraved. Pope
John Paul II, outraged by the growing acceptance of gay marriage,
described gay parent adoptions as a source of "violence against children." Unfortunately, such language sets the stage for real violence
against both children and their parents. Rabid denouncements of gay
people and their families are all too common among the evangelical
Christians from whence I come. When I learn that someone is a deeply
committed Christian, I often feel a knot in my stomach, a real sense of
danger, until I have a chance to learn more about how that commitment
shapes his or her attitude toward sexual orientation. Many gay Christians

have solved this problem by severing their connection to organized religion and sometimes to their faith as well.

My father, knowing how the Southern Baptist stance on women and gays had hurt me and longing to persuade me not to write off the whole lot, sent me, sometime in the early 1990s, copies of two sermons. In "Baptists and Women," W. Robert DeFoor of Harrodsburg, Kentucky, took issue with the traditional Baptist teaching that women's roles in the church should be restricted. Paul Duke's "Homosexuality and the Church" looked at recent biblical scholarship on many of the scriptures regularly used to condemn homosexuality and concluded that there is no longer absolute certainty about that condemnation. He preached:

> I dream of a church where people are safe to tell all their secrets.
> I dream of a church where no one has to struggle alone with who
> they are and what they desire. Where those who find themselves
> with homosexual orientation can say so and be answered with
> empathetic love and prayers and support. . . . Where no one has
> to hide and slowly, quietly die of loneliness in the house of God.

I was touched to see Daddy continue the conversation through the words of his fellow pastors. He was telling me he still believes texts are open to interpretation and more: God isn't done with any of us yet, not him, not the church, not me.

In 1998, the church we now belong to, Broadway United Methodist, found itself vitally engaged in the denomination's struggle over sexual orientation issues. Our pastor, Gregory Dell, performed a holy union service for two gay men from our church. A United Methodist from outside our congregation filed charges against Pastor Dell, and a trial ensued. Eventually, he was suspended for a period of twelve months. Throughout the trial and its aftermath, our congregation remained united in our support for the full inclusion and celebration of gay and lesbian Christians in the life of the church. A key moment during the months leading up to the trial came in November when Fred Phelps announced a plan to demonstrate outside our church. Phelps is a Baptist minister from Oklahoma who has achieved notoriety by organizing protests against gays and lesbians (and recently even against the families of American soldiers killed in Iraq, alleging that the U.S. government promotes homosexuality). He and his small band of supporters display signs with slogans such as "God hates fags." Just a month before Phelps's planned protest at our church, he and his ugly band of followers had demonstrated at the funeral of Matthew Shepard, a young man who was taken from a gay bar, beaten to a pulp, and left to die hanging on a fence in Wyoming. Our church did not want to do anything to give energy to Phelps's demonstration, but, coming as it would on the heels of the Matt Shepard funeral, his presence, we believed, required some sort of response. Calling on people from the Lakeview neighborhood, where the church is located, and beyond, the church invited folks to join a counterdemonstration, the formation of a circle of love that would surround the church on the day of the demonstration.

I was out of town that day, attending a professional meeting in New York City. Carol, Lucy, and Gracie made their way to the church, parking several blocks away because the crowds made access to the parking lot impossible. That night I called home to find out what had happened. Carol told me that the circle of love had included between fifteen hundred and two thousand people from the neighborhood, from around Chicago, and from hundreds of miles beyond. The circle of love was coalition at its best, crossing boundaries of geography, religion, race, and sexual orientation to bring together a diverse throng with a shared passion for justice. Hundreds of police officers were on hand to keep the crowd safe. Fred Phelps was there, as well, with a small band of demonstrators carrying their viciously hateful signs. But his group of fifteen or so was outnumbered more than a hundred to one. Inside the circle of love, the church was packed, and the service that took place that morning was marked by a great spirit of love and unity.

Lucy grabbed the phone to give me her version of events. "Mama-Jackie," she said excitedly, "it was great. The crowd was huge, but most of them were for us. The love side was so much bigger than the hate side." That's how we want it, I thought. We want a world where the love side vastly outnumbers the hate side, where circles of love surround and protect all we hold dear, where a love of justice makes neighbors and family of us all.

Acknowledgments

Although the writing of a memoir might appear to be a solitary activity, I could not have completed *Waiting for the Call* without the help of many writers, friends, and family members. My first thanks go to my original writing group, Eileen Cherry, Malcolm Dino, and Reginald Gibbons, who encouraged, fed, and challenged me through the creation of the book's first draft. Those great conversations (over great meals) made a better writer of me while giving me faith in the project and my ability to see it through.

Many friends read and commented on drafts. I would like to thank Cornelia Spelman, Nicole Hollander, Elvia Arriola, Anna Vaughn Clissold, Midge Wilson, Elizabeth C. Fine, Lynn C. Miller, Gregory Dell, Eileen Seifert, Janis Kearney, Liam Heneghan, Michele Morano, Darsie Bowden, Ann O'Bryan, Kathleen Browne, and Ginger Senter. I am indebted to David Csontos for his early faith in the book and for his guidance regarding both what needed cutting and what was missing.

My editor, LeAnn Fields, has been a terrific champion. She understood and helped me to see where the heart of the story was. I'm deeply grateful to her, to the external reviewers, and to her colleagues at the University of Michigan Press who have worked to make *Waiting for the Call* a reality.

ACKNOWLEDGMENTS

A special thanks goes to my church family at Broadway United Methodist, who over the past ten years have contributed mightily to my ability to imagine a truly inclusive faith community. Thanks also to those Broadway folks who have helped me get the word out about this book, especially Greg, Cathy Knight, and Jim Bennett.

Small portions of previous essays appear, in substantially revised form, in several different chapters in this book. Those essays are "On Being an Exemplary Lesbian: My Life as a Role Model," first published in *Text and Performance Quarterly* and reprinted in the volume I coedited with Lynn C. Miller and M. Heather Carver, *Voices Made Flesh: Performing Women's Autobiography* (University of Wisconsin Press, 2003), and "Performing Commitment," in *Intercultural Communication in Contexts,* Judith N. Martin and Thomas K. Nakayama, eds. (Mayfield, 1997).

Readers of this book will quickly learn that I have the most wonderful family. Even before I began writing this book, I was always telling stories on them. While I have worked hard to make this account as accurate as possible, some of them might want me to remind the reader that this is my version of these events. Each of them would tell it somewhat differently. My father, Eldred M. Taylor, and my sister, Jeannie Taylor, believed in this project and helped me remember details I had forgotten. Their love and support, not just during the writing of this book but throughout my life, are a great gift. Most of all, I thank Carol, my life partner, and our two daughters, Lucy and Gracie, for the rich joys of the life we have created together. I'm truly blessed to count them as family.

Text design by Jillian Downey
Typesetting by Delmastype, Ann Arbor, Michigan
Text and display font: Monotype Bulmer

The font Bulmer was orginally designed in 1792 by William Martin,
and Monotype Bulmer was created for American Type Founders in
1928 by Morris Fuller Benton.

—Courtesy www.adobe.com